Leslie Kenton

LOVE AFFAIR

St. Martin's Press ♨ New York

The author would like to thank the following for permission to use copyright material: OUP Oxford for material from *The Oxford Companion to the Mind* edited by Richard L. Gregory (second edition 2004). The extract from 'The Stan Hardly Anyone Knew' by Noel Wedder appears on www.home.comcast.net/~nwedder/another_view_of_stan2.html. The poem 'Please Call Me by My True Names' which appears in *Call Me by My True Names: The Collected Poems of Thich Nhat Hanh* published by Parallax Press, 1999.

www.stmartins.com

Library of Congress Cataloging-in-Publication Data

Kenton, Leslie.
    Love affair / Leslie Kenton.—1st U.S. ed.
        p. cm.
    ISBN 978-0-312-65908-0
    1. Kenton, Leslie—Childhood and youth.   2. Incest victims—Great Britain—Biography.   3. Jazz musicians—United States—Family relationships.
4. Alternative medicine specialists—Great Britain—Biography.   5. Kenton, Stan   I. Title.
    RC560.I53K46 2011
    616.85'83690651—dc22

                                                                    2010037532

First published in Great Britain by Vermilion, an imprint of Ebury Publishing, a Random House Group Company

First U.S. Edition: January 2011

10   9   8   7   6   5   4   3   2   1

For Stanley
with all my love

CONTENTS

PART THREE: GRACE

PREFACE

Thousands of feet of 8mm film beckon to me from their dusty containers. It is time for me to explore the celluloid images they contain of two lives lived more than half a century ago. I know I need to pay attention to them but I am uneasy – not sure what to expect. I thread the projector and turn it on: a man is holding a small child against his bare chest. Uncertain what to do with his package, he seems both entranced by and frightened of it. I fast-forward five years or more the way film so easily lets you do. Now the man wrinkles his nose at the child, then grabs at her body as though reaching for a tempting morsel to eat. The girl looks up, pulls away, sticks her tongue out at him. He buries his knuckles in her sides tickling her. She squirms. They laugh.

Fast-forward again . . . now I am watching a birthday party in a garden. The girl is wearing a pink floral dress and her first pair of white high heels. I can tell this since she moves as awkwardly as a foal trying to plant its feet upon the ground without falling. He circles her, smiling. Almost predatory, he grabs hold of her waist, draws her to him and kisses her. She smiles what looks like an embarrassed smile then moves away.

Spellbound, I watch as they circle each other. Like strands of DNA trapped in the force field of a double helix, the circling becomes almost balletic. One moment they laugh. Then, a turn of a head, a shift in a body, and their playfulness is replaced by something darker. I sit viewing all this in an abstracted way, rewinding the movie again and again, vaguely aware of a fascination in me tinged with both fear and excitement. Suddenly, the spell is broken. What I thought I could watch from a safe distance – records of decades of my life with my father – is no longer *them* but *us*, no longer *then*, but *now*.

From such beginnings this book was born. I had little idea that day where the writing of it would take me. Often we think we have 'handled' challenges in our life. Then we find ourselves doing the same stupid things over and over again. I certainly have. And wonder why. Why does one or another part of our life never seem to come right? Why do we feel helpless to change that?

Or maybe we have come to a place of relative comfort, as I thought I had. We have wonderful friends and loving family, and many blessings to celebrate. Without ever articulating it – even to myself – I had come to feel that, like a magic carpet on which I could ride, the good life I had created would continue to keep me safe for ever. Then something unexpected occurs – maybe somebody dies or flashes of long-forgotten memories come to the surface, or perhaps we get sick or badly injured. Suddenly the magic carpet is ripped out from under us. We find ourselves tumbling through the sky and we wonder, with a strange detachment, if it is going to kill us.

In my case, it was not just revisiting lost memories that brought such things to the surface when I began to write *Love Affair*. Something mysterious within me had awakened. I could not name it but it seemed to be present with me day and night. An unseen threat? A benevolent guide? A dark shadow from my past? I didn't know.

When my work on this book began, I did not realise I had access to masses of research materials, inherited on the deaths of my father, my mother, their parents and our ancestors before them. I had never looked at most of them: diaries, medical records, itineraries, thousands of photographs, dozens of reels of 8mm and 16mm film documenting my family's lives and revealing much about my parents and their ancestors – especially on my father's side. Some had only come into my hands two years before when, as a consequence of a stepfather's death, my mother's private papers, personal notes, books and journals were sent to me by his lawyers.

Letters, many yellow at the edges, had been dutifully stuffed back into envelopes. Some written long before I was born told of frustration, love, excitement and despair in the lives of those who wrote them. They were tied with string or held together by rubber bands long past their use-by date. When I tried to slide them off, the rubber bands disintegrated in my hands.

The papers, including the letters, were often so descriptive that, together with my father's itineraries, and the reports of dozens of people whom I interviewed for the book, the task of pinpointing when and where various events took place turned out to be easier than I had anticipated. I began by reading and dating them according to the postmark.

Going through all these materials took me back more than a century, plunging me into another time, another world. As I read, vivid memories began to surface – smells and sounds, fragments of events and places. Slowly I began to pull them together. I felt like I was trying to mend a broken mirror or staring at the jumbled pieces of a giant jigsaw puzzle.

Gradually, I began to gaze into that jigsaw puzzle, then to live in it. As this happened, my whole life was turned upside down. I had looked on the task of writing this book as a mechanical process of gathering together intricate and demanding information, creating a certain order out of it all, and producing a narrative of events about what had happened to me and my family. The more I came to live in this broken-mirror world, the more I came face to face with the shattered depths of my own life and the lives of others who make up this story – my parents, their parents before them and back and back. Intricate patterns emerged – variations on bloodline themes, as one generation gave birth to the next. They were unmistakable.

If I have learned only one thing from the years between my birth and my father's death it is this: we are each of us perpetrator and victim, the rapist and the raped, the torturer and the tortured. For us to become who, at the core of our being, we truly are, we must be willing to dive deep into our own darkness and illuminate it. Darkness longs for light to bring it comfort. Light is drawn to darkness to deepen its compassion and reveal its value.

It is my prayer that the writing about what follows will bring comfort and peace to all who participated in its making.

PART ONE

INNOCENCE

TWO BIRTHS

WHAT FOLLOWS IS a true tale of innocence, blood and grace. It begins with two births and ends with a death. It tells of the man who was my father and of the daughter who loved him. It journeys into the darkness of isolation and unknowing that, sooner or later, each of us is called on to enter – a borderland of being, where known rules and structures no longer apply. When I began to write, I believed this story was personal to me. Now, as I near the end of my work, I see that it is a tale belonging to all of us and to these dark times in which we live.

Each of us enters the world as an innocent. We arrive on earth, take pot luck, and hope to survive – maybe even to thrive. For some, my parents among them, innocence lasts way beyond childhood. Timid yet headstrong, passionate yet terrified of life, my mother was still adolescent when she gave birth to me at the age of twenty-six. The letters she wrote are filled with young girl preoccupations: clothes she wants to buy, parties she is going to, how drunk she plans to get. My father was as innocent as she. Smart yet naïve, gifted but with little belief in himself, he was an awkward 'country boy' driven by a powerful need to make his mark on the world and a terrible fear he might never manage it.

Fate, choice, providence – who knows what – managed to turn the three of us into a family. At times each of us was singular, as isolated from each other as three animals of different species. At others, together and crazy, we swam with sharks, slept in the back of cars (or forgot to sleep at all), smuggled whisky into dry states, drowned in seas of screaming brass and blundered our way across the Americas year after year – from the insanity of Hollywood to the sultry streets of New Orleans and snow-covered peaks of the Andes.

I, Leslie, was born at the Queen of Angels Hospital in Los Angeles – a Catholic edifice of vast proportions where Dr Alfonso McCarthy, head of obstetrics, reigned supreme. On a warm June day in 1941, Dr McCarthy stood by, holding my mother's hand through an agonising, endless, gas-filled labour.

My mother's name is Violet. She curses so loud that incense-laden, black-robed priests, floating down corridors to chant last rites for the dying, are stopped in their tracks by her shrieks and her profanity. 'Stanley, remind me never to do this again!' my mother will say to my father for years to come.

But my father is nowhere near the Queen of Angels Hospital while his wife of six years struggles to bring me into the world. She has been left to sweat it out alone in a dreary little room, until finally I emerge, scarred and bruised by the metal forceps used to get me out. I am not a pretty sight; at least according to my paternal grandmother, Stella. When she sees me a few hours later, Stella takes one look at me and declares, 'This child cannot possibly be a Kenton. She is far too ugly.'

The phone call comes from the hospital in the late afternoon of 24 June. My father, Stanley Kenton, a six-foot-four, lanky piano player with size 13½ AAA feet and ambitions to match, is rehearsing for the night's performance in the Rendezvous Ballroom in Balboa, California: my birth has taken place the same month and year that my father has pawned everything he owns (and it isn't much) to start his own jazz band. 'The Stanley Kenton Orchestra' consists of fifteen men and its birthplace is the Rendezvous. At this time, my father has no track record for success. Nor does he see himself as a leader. Shy and self-deprecating, he had tried hard to find someone else to front the band. When that failed, stuck with the job, he got on with it himself.

'Mr Kenton, congratulations, you have a strong, healthy daughter,' says Dr McCarthy.

Stanley tells no one at first. No cigars are handed out. No celebration takes place. After the job that night, he and two friends – a woman named Audree Coke and her fiancé, Jimmy Lyons – wander over to a nearby bar, the Bamboo Room. There, huddled over drinks and empty glasses, he confides, 'Violet has given birth to a baby girl.'

Back at the Queen of Angels, the hospital staff take me from my mother, place me in a glass cage and stick a bottle in my mouth. They say this will give her a chance to rest and regain her figure after the messy business she has been through. My mother never deals well with messiness. It does not belong in her world.

While there was general agreement that my own birth was best forgotten, the other Kenton issue – the birth of the band – was greeted with great celebration. Even so, it plunged my father into a morass of anxiety. 'How am I going to pay these guys? Oh my God, have I done the right thing?' And, 'Jesus Christ, why is Violet in that hospital instead of here with me when I need her?'

That first summer my father worked like a man possessed. Each night when the job was finished, the guys in the band would head for the Bamboo Room to jam or wind down: Chico Alverez, Red Doris, Howard Rumsey, Jack Ordean, Marvin George and the rest. Stanley remained on the bandstand. Alone in the now empty ballroom, hunched over the piano, every night he composed and arranged the music he wanted to play the next night. Two or three hours later, when his musicians passed by again on their way home, he would still be sitting there, playing chords and scribbling on sheets of paper.

The Kenton sound was like nothing anybody had heard before. Kids got high on it. As for Stanley himself – he mesmerised them. All his life – even towards the end when he was ill, incontinent and too weak to move centre stage to conduct – my father's presence on a bandstand was something wondrous to behold.

I can see him now as he strides centre stage, spreads his arms like a commanding angel, pounding the floor with his right heel so hard that the whole ballroom shakes. This signals the downbeat. Jazz reviewer Del Bodey once wrote: 'What Toscanini does with his head in conducting, Kenton does with his whole body.'

As the first strains of my father's theme song, 'Artistry in Rhythm', burst forth, mouths would drop open. People stop breathing. Screaming brass, drum rolls, offbeat syncopation. They give way to lush piano sounds, changing tempos, changing time – always surprising, yet somehow forever the same. As a young child, I was to spend most of my life on the road with the band. I would hear 'Artistry in Rhythm' three or four times each night. Over the years Stanley orchestrated more than a hundred permutations of it. Each time I heard it, the hairs on my arms rose to attention. Chills ran through my body. They still do.

My parents loved to tell stories. While I was growing up they told me endless tales – about my birth, about our ancestors, about how they met, who said what to whom – about what Stanley did, what Violet did, what I had done. Many of their stories were repeated so often that they became etched deep into my memory bank. Sometimes when I close my eyes, images dance out of the darkness as though they portray events in my own life. Like the way my parents met.

A shining, scrubbed, wholesome blonde, my mother had not been an easy catch for my father. He first spotted her in 1934 at the Rendezvous Ballroom where he was playing piano for the Everett Hoaglund band. She liked music. She loved dancing.

'When she moved,' my father always said, 'she stood out on the dance floor like a gem in a swirl of pebbles. I was far too shy to go near her. So I watched, I hoped and I waited.'

One evening, this man-who-would-one-day-be-my-father trotted home to his mother, Stella, and announced, 'I've just seen the girl I'm gonna marry.'

'Oh, really?'

'Yeah.'

'Who is she?'

'I don't know yet. But I'm gonna find out.'

Weeks passed. Every time Violet showed up at the ballroom, he watched her from afar. She hardly noticed the gangly piano player who had already made up his mind she would spend the rest of her life with him. Every Saturday night she showed up on the arm of a different man. There was never a shortage. To her they were all the same: OK so long as they danced well. If one of them tried to get serious about her, she just moved on to the next in line.

One night, after hours on the dance floor, my mother's suitor-of-the-moment drove to the top of a mountain, parked his car overlooking the romantic lights of Los Angeles and swore eternal love for her. Then he asked her to marry him.

'No,' she said.

'Why not?'

'I don't love you.'

He pleaded. To no avail. Hurling himself from the car in tears, the young man staggered towards the edge of the cliff. 'If you won't marry me, I'll kill myself!' he shouted.

'Jump,' was her reply. Needless to say, he didn't.

I remember when this story first came alive for me. I was sixteen and beginning to find my own way into the dating scene. I was so impressed by the way my mother had handled the guy's blackmailing melodrama. If it had been me, I would have promised him anything just to get us down off that mountain. Then I would have run away as fast as I could. Not my mother. She could be sharp as a stiletto – a woman who brooked no nonsense.

After weeks of my father watching Violet from afar, one night their eyes met. By all accounts – and there are many of this event – it took place just like it does in the movies, but almost never in real life.

He is playing piano. She is dancing with the latest beau. Suddenly she stops and stares up at him. His fingers switch to automatic pilot on the keyboard. Everyone around them disappears. Alone in this huge room, woman and piano player meet right here, right now. This is it.

Leaving the piano, Stanley jumps off the bandstand and asks her to dance. She accepts. But he has forgotten something. Since, like most musicians, he has spent most of his life on a bandstand, he has never learned how to dance. Together they stumble around the floor for five minutes. Embarrassed, he suggests she might like to 'sit this one out'. She is quick to agree. He buys her a Coke. They talk.

He tells her how he dreams of doing 'something great'. An inveterate dreamer herself, she drinks in his words. 'His innocence and awkward charm disarmed me,' she always said. 'But there was something else too. Some kind of energy that flowed from him. He was radiant – like a beacon of light.'

As far as he was concerned, she was the most wonderful creature he had ever met. It was not just her looks that grabbed him either. In her he sensed something he had not encountered before. He never could describe it, but whatever it was, he wanted more of it.

While courting my mother, my father did everything he could to spend as much time as possible with her. He wanted to enchant her. He played songs he thought she might like. He got to know her favourites. High on the list was 'Sophisticated Lady'. He always let her know whenever he was going to play it so she would know it was just for her. He searched her out at every intermission. He asked if he could drive her home after the job. Sometimes she said yes.

That night in 1934 when they first spoke marked the beginning of a lifetime of animated conversations between them; eventually between all three of us. Stanley and Violet talked in the car, in the shower, at meals, from early morning to late at night.

My father often spoke about his work, his dreams, the hassles he was forever getting into with managers, promoters and musicians. When I was older, he would invite me into his inner world, the secret repository of all the energies that fuelled his ambitions. Sometimes he would speak with passion and determination. Others, his words would be dipped in sadness, like when he spoke of his longing to compose 'great music' – music that would take audiences to places in the Universe they didn't know existed.

Most often my mother talked about what was beautiful. She loved paintings, especially the works of Rembrandt. All her life she wanted to go to Berlin so she could see, first hand, *The Man with the Golden Helmet*. She never did. She too spoke of her longings, but they were different from Stanley's. She ached to live in a magnificent house and to wear fabulous clothes. She wanted to visit Paris and Rome and Rio.

A lot of Violet's words were designed to encourage Stanley, to bolster his confidence, to help him solve his problems. Again and again, she urged him to hold on to his dreams. 'One day,' she said, 'they *will* come true.' She was sure of it.

My mother's belief in her husband, coupled with his own all-encompassing commitment to fulfilling his dreams, made them a formidable pair. Come hell or high water, at the time of my birth they were riding the rising wave of creative optimism they sensed all around them. The excitement was palpable. Stokowski and Disney had brought *Fantasia* to birth. CBS had demonstrated the miracle of colour TV and begun experimental broadcasts from the top of the Chrysler Building in New York. A search for 'Rosebud' was on, to wild acclaim, as Orson Welles made his Hollywood debut with *Citizen Kane*. Meanwhile, 400,000 coal miners in Harlan County, Pennsylvania, ended a protracted strike for a $1 pay raise, elated that they would be earning $7 a week from now on – before taxes of course. These were *hopeful* times.

When my parents first met, my mother was living in a small apartment with her lifelong friend Nona La Force and Nona's sister Rae. Violet and Nona had known each other since high school when they shook pompoms and cheered together at ball games. Like most young women in the 1930s, they went dancing every chance they got. Their favourite dancing spots were the Rendezvous in Balboa, where my mother met my father, and the Biltmore Bowl – an extravagant dance hall in Los Angeles' Biltmore Hotel, where the Academy Awards were held each year. The Biltmore held tea dances every Sunday afternoon. Violet, Nona and Rae seldom missed one. Saturday afternoons they usually spent at the Coconut Grove discussing men, clothes and parties, always on the lookout for fun wherever it might present itself.

My mother was devoted to glamour. This was not so much out of vanity as from a frightening belief – at least it frightens me – that a woman's worth is determined by physical beauty alone. Yet Violet had the potential to be far more than beautiful. Her vibrant, unstable spirit came packaged with some amazing talents: like the gift of making beautiful everything she laid her hand to. And her ability to see right inside people and know what was real and what was bullshit. In her late twenties, she shimmered with a passion for just being alive. It was as infectious as her laugh.

Given her devotion to the high life, it may seem curious that she had been briefly married to a truck driver; a marriage Nona disapproved of and which was swiftly annulled. When Stanley came along, following Violet's long line of what Nona and Rae looked on as 'boring young men', they celebrated his presence: 'He was interesting, awkward and shy,' says Rae, now in her nineties. 'He was easily the most charming man any of us had ever met. They looked great together as a couple.' And looks mattered a lot.

At the time, my father was no more than a hired musician in somebody else's band. But he was smart so his responsibilities had already grown far beyond piano playing. Now he wanted to get married.

Violet was not so sure. Then, on the morning of 25 July 1935, with no word of warning, she woke up and went out to find a minister. She and Stanley were married in the late afternoon, and Stanley went to work as usual in the evening. Neither her family nor his showed the least interest in the event. No gifts were forthcoming – neither pots and pans nor money to wish them well. The two of them were on their own.

That night, when Stanley returned from work, he told his wife of several hours that he had just lost his job. It was the middle of the Great Depression. They set up house in a one-room apartment in Hollywood, for which they paid $25 a month. It had a pull-down Murphy bed and little else. There they struggled to survive on a mere 25 cents a day for food. Stanley hustled work with studios and at the Musicians' Union.

'We ate nothing but Boston Baked Beans,' my mother always said. (I have always assumed that is how she learned to cook the best baked beans I've ever tasted.) 'We ate them and ate them until we got so sick of them we couldn't swallow another mouthful.'

Stanley's mother, Stella, continually interfered in their lives. She would arrive uninvited in the early morning, to find them still in bed. When she discovered they slept in the nude, she was horrified. When she learned they took two showers a day, she raised hell. 'That's dangerous,' she warned. As for their sleeping with the windows open, together with all those unnecessary showers, it was bound to make her son catch his death of cold.

On one of Stella's endless surprise visits, she took Stanley on her lap, fastened his arms around her neck, and told my mother, 'Violet, you are taking my baby boy away from me.'

Stella was superstitious. She used to tell Stanley, 'You gotta protect yourself from misfortune. It lurks at every bend in the road.' 'Don't wear clothing to a funeral then wear it again,' she would say, 'else you'll bring misery upon yourself.' And never mention a disease. It might make you catch it . . .

Stella tried her best to teach Violet what was necessary for her son's protection. I don't think my mother even understood what she was on about. To Violet, life was simple: you have a dream? Make sure it's a *beautiful* dream, then follow it with all your might. Sooner or later it'll happen. She had no proof of this, of course, but she cared little for 'proof'. My mother was never a woman to be dissuaded from her beliefs by mere facts.

She had been surprised to discover how many of Stella's weird notions had been passed on to Stanley. Some of her superstitions, such as 'to milk a cow being sent to market brings bad luck', meant nothing to him, since he had not been brought up on a ranch as Stella had. Others, which Violet found equally ridiculous, Stanley paid attention to: 'step on a crack, break your mother's back', was one. Or 'A yawn is a sign that danger is near' and even 'a horseshoe hung in the bedroom keeps nightmares away'.

When it came to hanging horseshoes on the wall of their one-room flat, Violet put her foot down. Nonetheless, my father performed daily rituals designed to keep misfortune at bay. Shoes had to face in a specific direction before he went to sleep. He ate the vegetables on his plate before touching his meat.

'Stanley was always seized by strange fears,' my mother said. 'Out of the blue, he would announce he'd been cursed so he would never do the things he wanted to do. He'd become overwhelmed by guilt for no reason. "I've got the guilts," he would say. "About what?" I'd say. "I don't know, I just feel it." Each time he left the apartment, he'd have to check three or four times to make sure he'd locked the door.'

While I was growing up, my parents frequently disagreed with each other. They were always highly vocal about it. But my father always treated my mother with kindness and respect even when, in the midst of one of her not infrequent hysterical outbursts, her actions were unpredictable and outrageous: climbing artificial palm trees in cocktail bars, preaching uninvited sermons or showering voluminous praise on strangers.

My mother was an enigma – not just to me, not just to Stanley, but to everyone who got close to her. To those who did not know her well, she could appear haughty or cold. A few of the guys in the band believed she thought herself superior to them. It's true that she never turned on the 'ordinary guy' personality that so endeared Stanley to people. She was a woman who did not make close friends easily but the few she chose to befriend remained loyal to her all their lives. Even they could never fathom her. She found it hard to share with others what was going on inside her. I think this was mostly because much of the time she didn't know herself. At times she could seem a woman of great strength. Forceful in her opinions, she did not seem to care if they caused offence. Then, without warning, she would visibly shrink from an encounter with anything or anyone for no apparent reason.

Like my mother's behaviour, her feelings were unpredictable; not so much a response to what was happening around her, but the result of something going on deep inside her. Like a slumbering volcano, they could rise unbidden from somewhere so deep neither she nor any of us understood what was going on. She would leap into a rage with little or no provocation. She would shout at a saleswoman who didn't bring her what she had asked for, or spit fire at a policeman for accusing her of going through a red light. So intense were some of these outbursts that the poor offending policeman might end up apologising to her for having interfered with her journey. Just as unpredictably, her rage could turn to laughter or to tears.

I think my father worshipped the beauty of my mother's spirit. The letters he wrote her – many of which passed on to me at her death – are full of fumbling gentleness and sincere adoration. During the fifteen years of their marriage I never saw him treat her harshly. He looked on her as his *light*, his *compass*, his *home*, and he told her so.

'Stanley was the most tender person I have ever known,' my mother insisted. Years after they were divorced, she was shocked to learn that he had been violent to his second wife, Ann. This was not the Stanley she knew.

What surprised Violet most about Stanley was his lack of belief in himself. She never realised the extent of this until after they were married. His talent as a musician, composer and arranger was blatantly obvious. So was his innate vitality, his passion and his drive to succeed. 'Stanley was not only gifted; he was willing to withstand whatever difficulties presented themselves – including sleepless nights, illness and poverty – to make success happen,' she said. 'Yet, no matter how well he played piano, no matter how skilfully he composed, it was *never* good enough to satisfy him.'

Perhaps this is why he leaned so heavily on my mother, asking her to supply the faith in him which he could not find in himself.

Violet had many gifts of her own. Perhaps the greatest – or maybe it was only the one she made best use of – was her ability to recognise talent and draw it forth from anyone. When it came to helping Stanley, she marshalled all her love, imagination, practicality and devotion in the service of turning his dreams into realities.

And such dreams they were. Forget all those castles in the air: together they would build concert halls. He would lead the most outstanding jazz band of the century. It wouldn't only play in ballrooms, it would play Carnegie Hall and celebrated concert halls throughout Europe and America. He would write a new kind of music: music that would integrate the vitality of American jazz with twentieth-century classical. He loved Stravinsky, Ibert, Respighi, Bartok, Debussy, Ravel. He wanted to do what they had done early in the twentieth century, but for *now*. My mother not only dreamed his dreams, she held them in her heart, and took practical steps to make them happen. Money? They had none. She went out and bought a calendar bank which you had to slip a quarter into each morning to make the date change. They would soon be on their way. She knew it.

Violet was Stanley's impresario, his caretaker and his protector. She knew how to handle his 'night events'. Both before and after I was born, my father would wake from a dream, shouting and thrashing about. She always straddled him, pinning his wrists to the bed until he calmed down. 'Stanley, it's all right. Everything is all right,' I used to hear her say. She never knew what caused these night terrors and they frightened her. 'I lay awake at night, afraid he might harm himself,' she said. 'Sometimes I was scared he would die. He was always so frightened that he would never amount to a hill of beans. I knew he would. We just had to keep going.'

And keep going they did. After all, they had each other and they shared the same dream. She scraped by while he looked for work.

After a couple of false starts, Stanley received the offer of a piano-playing job that seemed to answer all their prayers. Since the 1920s, Gus Arnheim had led a polished dance band. It had appeared at the Los Angeles Coconut Grove with well known singers like Bing Crosby. Now, in 1936, Arnheim wanted to get into jazz and he needed Stanley to help him. This was not only because Stanley was a skilled musician; Arnheim knew that he could draw on his knowledge of jazz, his connections with other jazz musicians and his expertise in arranging.

The Arnheim job meant, for the first time, that my parents would be going out on the road together, away from what Violet called 'cow country'. They would be moving into the big time – Chicago, St Louis, New York – dream cities they had only heard about. Fascinated by the scent of freedom, my parents followed it wherever it took them. They loved being on the road, from endless diners where they ate 'home-cooked' meals, to tacky tourist attractions in the middle of nowhere: 'Meet Paul Bunyan and his Big Ox Babe'. When at last they arrived in New York, they climbed the Statue of Liberty, racing to see who could get up her right arm first. They sailed to the top of the Empire State Building on the world's fastest elevator. They took the Staten Island ferry, planning their future while the wind tossed their hair. They renewed their vows to each other during that first trip East and refreshed their dreams.

Being on the road with Arnheim was by no means one long holiday. They had their first taste of what it feels like when, after weeks of one-nighters, you're so worn out you don't even know what's going on.

One morning in a hotel room in the Midwest, Stanley awakened crumpled up in pain. Violet told me she rang the room clerk: 'We need a house doctor. NOW!'

Fifteen minutes later a man arrived. He looked like a dwarf who'd spent his life under a giant toadstool. He poked around in Stanley's stomach, then announced, 'Mr Kenton, you have a mild case of appendicitis.'

'A *mild* case of appendicitis?' my mother shrieked. 'That means surgery, doesn't it?'

'Not necessarily,' the doctor told her, wiping sleep from his eyes and lowering the pitch of his voice so it sounded as reassuring as he could manage. 'I will leave you a bottle of medicine, Mr Kenton,' he said. Then, turning to her: 'Make sure he takes one tablespoon of this followed by a glass of water every four hours.'

By evening Stanley's pain had eased off enough that he was able to go to work, even though he still felt pretty sick. After the job that night, he went straight back to the hotel, climbed into bed and fell asleep. Two hours later, Violet woke up to the sound of him retching in the bathroom. She rushed to his side.

There he stood, stark naked, a bottle in one hand and a tablespoon stolen from the hotel coffee shop in the other. 'Urgh,' he said, a shudder passing over his body. 'This stuff is disgusting!'

She looked up to find the bottle of medicine, still standing unopened on the glass shelf above the washbasin. 'My God, Stanley, what have you swallowed?' she screamed, snatching the bottle from his hand.

He had been gulping down the white shoe polish she used to clean her two-toned spectator shoes. The two of them collapsed in laughter on the bathroom floor. 'We laughed so loud that the house detective came pounding on the door, threatening to throw us into the street if we didn't shut up,' said my father.

'This made us laugh even more,' my mother said. Twenty-four hours later, the bottle of medicine had disappeared and the pain with it.

Stanley stayed with Arnheim for a year. By all accounts it was a wonderful experience. By the time the band broke up in Los Angeles, my mother's belief in my father's future, coupled with the closeness that had developed between them, had brought Stanley to a place where even he was starting to believe he might be able to write the music of his dreams and convince people to listen to it.

'We decided to live on a little money we'd put away, plus whatever we could scrape together by playing the odd studio job,' my father explained. 'That way I'd be able to forget the idea of finding another job and look for a good teacher of composition.'

He found it in Charles Dalmores. 'Dalmores spoke eleven languages, was a virtuoso on French horn, piano and cello, and knew more than anyone I ever met about harmony and counterpoint,' said Stanley. Seventy years old, Dalmores became a father figure to him – someone he could worship and emulate. Thirty years later, whenever Stanley spoke of the months he spent studying with Dalmores, his eyes filled with tears and he would have to clear his throat.

In the next couple of years my father made good use of everything he learned from his mentor. In 1939, he began to compose. He worked on freelance film scoring and played for various bands. But by the autumn of 1940, he had become disenchanted with the cynicism of the Hollywood music scene. He hated what he described as the dog-eat-dog commercialism. 'The musicians I worked with didn't give a damn about music,' he said. 'What the hell, I figured. I guess there is nothing left for me to do except start my own band.'

'Do it,' Violet insisted. 'Do it now.'

He quit his job and began to write. Living on savings plus $18 a week unemployment, they had to go back to eating baked beans. They didn't care. Their excitement about the new band mounted by the day.

Then the bomb dropped. One morning, at the end of September in

1940, my father confessed that he had fallen in love with one of the 'most beautiful girls in the world' at Earl Carroll's on Sunset Boulevard, the Ziegfeld Follies of the West Coast, where my father had found work as a pianist and assistant conductor.

'I don't know what to do,' he said. The woman was almost six feet tall and dark haired – completely stunning. (My father showed me a photograph of her when I was ten years old.)

Ironically, he chose to confess his infidelity the very same day that Violet had her own announcement to make: 'Stanley, I'm pregnant.'

Years later, my mother confided, 'He wanted me to have an abortion. There was no way I was going to do that. I said to him, "You go your own way. Do whatever you want. I'm going to have this child."'

In the end Stanley did not go his own way. He turned his back for ever on the dark beauty. He and Violet moved back to Los Angeles, reaffirming their commitment to each other and to 'success' on three fronts: marriage, band and baby.

'It felt like we were starting all over again,' he said. 'We decided to go for broke and make it happen.'

2

SURROGATE RULE

O<small>N</small> 3 J<small>ULY</small> 1941, my father paid $105.45 to the Queen of Angels Hospital to release my mother and me from hospital. He had already been forced to plead for an extra $40 from the Musicians' Union just to get Violet into hospital. This had humiliated him. 'It was awful,' he always said. 'I had to stand in front of the Board and confess I had no money – just so you could get born, Leslie. I felt so ashamed.'

He took us home to Lakewood Boulevard in Long Beach, California where for many months he and Violet had been living in a converted garage attached to the house owned by my maternal grandmother, Mom. Mom's name was originally Hazlett Crittenden, but early on she changed it to Yvonne. 'Sounds more exciting, don't you think?' she asked. In fact, it didn't matter much what her name was, since just about everybody called her 'Mom' anyway – family, friends, acquaintances, employers, even many of the guys in Stanley's band.

At Lakewood Boulevard, my mother and father handed me over. 'Here,' they said to Mom. 'You bring her up.'

This was not, perhaps, surprising since Mom did just about every-thing better than anyone else. She was smart, capable and tough as nails. In short, she would do whatever was necessary to ensure survival. Perhaps my grandmother's greatest gift was her will. Her very existence was predicated on its use and she could never compre-hend the 'messiness' of most people's lives. 'What's wrong with them?' she used to say. 'Do they have no backbone?' To her, life was straightforward: you take on a project – raising a child, building a house, building an empire. You focus your will and, like a dog with a rag in its mouth, you don't let go until it's done.

My mother, on the other hand, worshipped Beauty and served it the whole of her life. Despite her vitality and passion, in many ways Violet was a timid creature. Much of her timidity, I believe, came from her having been Mom's only surviving child. Like the flower after which she had been named, the ethereal Violet shrank, often visibly, in the presence of her mother. So inept did she feel in Mom's forceful presence that she believed she was incapable of doing anything successfully – especially looking after a baby.

Moreover, giving birth had plunged my mother into a depression which was to last almost two years. Recurring memories of 'the horrors of childbirth' were to haunt her for twenty years afterwards. She had not been prepared for all that blood, the pain, the slather – the rawness of pushing this thing into the world out of the most private part of her body. She believed that the trauma had left permanent scars on her psyche as well as the odd stretch mark on her belly. She was haunted by a sense that birth had marred her for ever.

The truth was that getting back her waistline did not take long, for during her pregnancy Violet had done everything humanly possible to maintain her slim, sinuous figure intact. I have seen photos of her taken two weeks before I arrived. You could not tell she was pregnant. In fact, family legend has it that men asked her to dance right up to the moment of her confinement. Few guessed she was married, let alone about to give birth. 'Smoke much, eat little and look as thin as possible' was her motto. At the height of her beauty, the last thing she ever dreamed of doing was nursing a baby. It might damage her breasts.

And so Mom stood there, ready and waiting in the wings, more than happy to take over the job of raising me. Mom was well aware that taking on the role of my caretaker placed her at the centre of family power, and made her indispensable. It was just where she wanted to be. Some atavistic sense told her that Stanley was a man to watch. 'Get close to him and stay there,' it said. 'One day he will be useful to you.'

She fed me on lashings of cow's milk and globs of sugar regular as clockwork – even when she had to wake me up to do it. What she never managed to do was to feed me when I was actually hungry. She was out to teach me, beyond all reasonable doubt, that no matter how strong my needs, or how vehement my temper, hers were stronger. Since I inherited some of her will (they say genetic characteristics often skip a generation) Mom and I were often at loggerheads, even when I was an infant.

Mom's third husband, Arthur Kilpatrick – whom we called 'Pat' – went out each morning at 5 a.m. to earn a living at a local refinery. An Irish Orangeman, Pat hated Democrats and Catholics (whom he called 'cat-lickers'), but he was otherwise generous and good-natured. Before leaving work each evening, he would fill up Stanley's gas tank so my father could drive to Balboa that night to play the job.

Pat had led a frugal life before he married Mom and I suspect that his piggy bank had been the lure for Mom. He had not only survived the Great Depression intact; he had managed to save enough money, week by week, to pay off the mortgage on their large home and put away a sizeable nest egg. Their house on Lakewood Boulevard was quite a splendid affair for the time. Covered in white stucco, it looked like an ornately iced cake. Mom liked to bet on a sure thing, and this large house, complete with three duplex rentals attached, looked a comfortable place to install herself. Mom liked comfort.

No doubt she needed it. When she was six years old, her mother had died while giving birth to a baby sister named Hermie. Her father was a travelling man who worked for the Canadian Railway. As soon as the last shovel of soil covered his wife's grave, George Crittenden delivered both his daughters to the door of a nearby convent. There the two girls remained to be raised by nuns. Mom lived in the nunnery for eight years. Hermie was there far longer.

They were fed little and infrequently. When either of them wet the bed, the nuns locked them in a cupboard for three days. The Holy Sisters gave the girls strict instructions on how to behave 'like a lady', informing them of the joys of heaven and the wages of hell. 'You gotta resist Satan's seductive ways every day of your life,' the Mother Superior said. Suspecting she was never likely to qualify for entrance into heaven, Mom looked around for a way out from this place that closely resembled the hell she had been warned about.

Despite meagre meals and years of bashing by her holy guardians, by the age of fourteen Mom had turned into a stunning child-woman: five foot two, with alabaster skin, china blue eyes and coal black hair, she was blossoming into a real beauty. Having grown up under the control of the Holy Sisters, she was nobody's fool. Sensing how valuable beauty can be, Mom decided it was time to put hers to good use. The only way she could see out of the prison in which her father had incarcerated her was to get married.

I'm not sure just how she managed to attract courtship from a convent, but I do know she was shrewd, high-spirited and inventive. Having had to wrestle for eight years with her wild nature, perhaps her pious guardians may even have encouraged the romance, more than happy to see the back of her. So less than a year after deciding she was going to leave the nunnery, she had found herself a suitable man. His name was Warren Rice. When she married Mr Rice, he was in his thirties. The marriage lasted six months.

Divorced by the age of fifteen and a half, on the cusp of the twentieth century, Mom had few alternatives open to her. Her guts, beauty and brains were all very well, but she had no education. Prostitution didn't appeal so she opted for nursing. With the little money she had gleaned from the marriage, she got trained and went to work in a hospital – first as a general nurse, then as a ward sister and finally as a theatre nurse.

In her late teens, she fell in love for the first time. His name was Roy Peters. He was a carpenter who had been admitted to hospital after suffering a life-threatening fall from a ladder. Two or three generations earlier, Roy's family had emigrated from Sweden to America, changing their name from Peterson to Peters. Some of his ancestors married Native American women in Washington State. (Mom always claimed this was the reason both my mother and I were blessed with high cheekbones.)

Tall, lean, blond and handsome, Roy was critically ill. The hospital doctors had no idea what to do for him. Despite the adoring attention Mom showered on him as his self-appointed caregiver, he refused to get better. By then she had a couple of years' experience in the operating theatre under her belt. A highly intuitive woman, Mom 'knew' Roy's fall had done severe damage to one or more of his internal organs. She suspected he had an abscess on one of his kidneys, that the kidney was infected and that this was what was killing him. She went to the chief surgeon, shared her insight and suggested he operate. The gentleman was not amused. He informed her he had no interest in the opinion of an upstart nurse, not yet twenty. She tried another doctor, and another. None of them would listen.

Fearful that this delicious young man would die if she didn't do something fast, she hatched a plan. She stole essential items from the hospital: rubber gloves, scalpels, ether, iodine, gauze, cotton, sutures, needles and morphine. Stuffing them beneath her navy blue nurse's cape, in the dark of the night she lifted Roy single-handedly into a wheelchair, stole him from his room and transported him to the boarding house where she lived.

There, she had made a bed for him, having covered every surface of the tiny room with boiled sheets. Whenever Mom spoke about that night to me – even fifty years afterwards – her eyes would become bright and clear and her face would take on the sprightly glow of a young girl.

I can see her now as she eases her patient into bed. Pulling on rubber gloves and pouring ether on to gauze, she smiles a tender smile. Lying through her teeth, she tells Roy, 'Everything's going to be fine. You'll just sleep for a little while.' She puts the wet gauze over his face. She tries her best to keep her hand from shaking.

If anyone found out what Mom was doing, she would not only lose her job, she would go to jail. If Roy died, she would be up for murder. Worse than both these consequences, if she failed she would lose him. 'I kept telling myself I mustn't let him go,' she said.

Now Roy sinks into a drugged slumber. She props him up with two pillows. Taking care not to overdose him, and making sure he can breathe as he lies on his belly, she paints his back with iodine. Sweat from her brow drips on to his naked back. She picks up a scalpel and cuts into his flesh. Sure enough, there it is: an abscess on the left kidney, just like she had said there would be. Painstakingly, she scrapes away the necrotic material, cleanses the wound and stitches him up. When he moves or groans, which happens every few minutes, she has to stop her work to administer more ether.

The job done, she washes her hands and says her prayers. Praying is the one practice the nuns have taught her for which she is grateful. By now she has rejected their God and their Church. She remains unsure about the heaven and hell stuff; she has decided to worry about that later. But Mom believes in prayer. If ever she has had need of her prayers being answered, it is now. There at the side of her pull-down bed, with Roy still drunk on vapours and breathing softly, my grandmother kneels, imploring the powers that be to make him better. And she prays that the nefarious act she has just committed will remain secret.

Before daybreak, she has returned her patient to hospital and deposited him in his bed. 'I shot him full of morphine, drank three cups of coffee and got ready for the day's work,' she said.

Inevitably, Roy's scars were discovered. But the doctors chose to turn a blind eye to them. Not a word was ever said to my grandmother. Presumably they were relieved to have been let off the hook. Had the patient died, one of them would have had to take the blame for it. Now he was getting well.

Mom married Roy while he was still in a hospital bed. Exactly a year later, she gave birth to my mother – Violet.

Apparently Roy (whom I never knew, as he died a week before I was born) was an intense man. Mom said, 'He could take pieces of nothing and turn them into something great.' He had an acerbic, rakish wit that challenged her sharp intellect. This pleased her. So did his sensuality – something Mom had not encountered before – and his boyishness which, she claimed, he never lost.

I suppose when someone saves your life you never quite see them through ordinary eyes. My mother said her father always looked upon Mom as a saviour – his very own Florence Nightingale. Violet believed he was deeply grateful to Mom and may, at first, have mistaken this gratitude for love. However, in time he did grow to love her.

After the birth of their child, Mom began to lose interest in her life at home with Roy and in her nursing career. She decided to get herself a job and to leave Roy to look after their daughter. She worked out that if she was going to find employment that could support her husband, Violet and herself, she had better make lots of money. This was back in 1915, when electric cookers were first beginning to appear on the market. Mom, who never had enough food growing up in a convent, had a passion for cooking and eating. She went to the electricity company and persuaded them to hire her to travel throughout the United States demonstrating how to cook with their newfangled devices.

At that time, a self-respecting middle-class man was earning $25 a week; a woman less than half of that. Within six weeks, Mom was bringing home $250 a week plus expenses. Her expenses included a huge wardrobe with big hats, jewellery – costume, of course – travel, the best hotels, food, drinks and a visit home every six weeks. She took on the role of celebrated glamour girl on the move and played it with great bravado all over America.

As long as she lived, which was well into her nineties, Mom insisted that Roy was the only man she ever loved. I think she believed she was telling the truth. Nevertheless, as Roy became aware that his vitality would never fully return after his life-threatening illness, things began to fall apart. Faced with Mom and Violet's innate exuberance and life energy, he turned inward and grew bitter. He became insanely jealous of other men. Eventually the marriage ended in divorce, freeing my grandmother to go her own way.

In the years to come, my maternal grandmother would do many surprising – often outrageous – things. She became cook to Hollywood stars such as Joan Crawford, June Allison and Dick Powell. Each time she changed jobs, she would enter a new palatial Hollywood home and, within six weeks, have taken over the running of the household – usually firing most of the staff. She ran everybody's life for them far more efficiently than they could run it themselves.

She regularly gave 'sound advice' to the celebrities with whom she hobnobbed. Ava Gardner, then married to Frank Sinatra, lived next door to one grand Hollywood home which Mom ran. Every morning Ava watered the lawn stark naked while consulting Mom about such things as how to handle her husband's infidelities. She would also ask Mom to tell her what the future held.

Mom was gifted with a natural clairvoyance. Again and again – usually at the breakfast table – she would make a statement such as, 'Laura came to me last night and told me she is passing over.' Later that day or the next, the telephone would ring or a telegram would arrive announcing the death of the person who had 'visited' Mom in the night. Mom was fascinated by the esoteric and read extensively about it. She hung out with as many 'gurus' as she could find – the genuine, the self-appointed and the outright phonies – always in plentiful supply in Hollywood, both then and now.

Given Mom's competence and her will to rule, it was perhaps not surprising that my mother, who believed herself incapable of raising a child, and my father, who at that time had little interest in the whole affair, left me in her care. Thus did I become one of Mom's subjects in the kingdom over which she exercised her not-so-benevolent style of despotism.

My grandmother boasted that she had me toilet-trained by the time I was six months old. It is a claim which has been verified by others who lived at Lakewood during the first years of my life, despite the fact that training a child so young is virtually impossible. One thing is certain: it was not through gentle coaxing that she achieved her ends. How any woman could 'teach' a one-year-old to eat like a grown-up I shudder to think. And yet she made sure I had the table manners of a queen by my first birthday, that I never sucked my thumb or fingers, and that I said 'please' and 'thank you' as soon as I was old enough to speak.

My mother has said again and again that she disapproved of a lot of what happened to me in Mom's house, but she had nowhere to turn to for support. Her mother was far too powerful a figure to stand up against on her own. As for Stanley – Violet knew that he needed her to look after him. He relied on her for everything, including nurturing his self-esteem, which, given his lack of self-confidence and their money problems, was frequently at a low ebb. Even if she had been capable of looking after a baby, she could never have taken on both roles: wife to my father and mother to me. Instead of confronting Mom, she would retreat into the garage where she and Stanley lived. There, alone, she would cry.

'Sometimes I could hear you screaming,' my mother once confessed. 'I would say, "Mom, Leslie's crying," but she would pay no attention and it never made any difference.

'"Leave it to me, Violet," she'd reply. "We don't want to spoil her, do we?"

'"She seems hungry," I'd say.

'"Nonsense, she was fed four hours ago. She'll get fed when I'm ready to feed her. She needs to learn to wait."

'Or I would ask, "Was that the baby crying I heard last night?"

'"Just leave well enough alone," Mom would say. "Let me handle things."'

I don't think Mom ever beat me up – at least as far as I remember. But I do know she hit me often, always, as she used to say, 'for your own good, Leslie'. This happened when I did not follow her wishes to the letter. Her child-rearing protocols taught me something not terribly helpful – something I remained totally unconscious of for scores of years before I realised what I was doing. I learned that the appropriate relationship to my body was to punish it. I have observed that this happens to people who have been raised the way Mom raised me from an early age. Eventually, unconscious of what we are doing, each of us takes over the role of self-punisher. We become scathing judges of our own lives. Yet we seldom realise we are doing this, so we never question if there might be a more humane way to live. Some become anorexic or bulimic. Others forget to sleep or to eat. We may rip flesh from our feet as I once did, or cut gashes in our arms, chew our nails to the bone, or drive ourselves so hard we become ill. No matter how extreme such behaviour appears from the outside, because it was learned unconsciously when we were kids, it is the only behaviour we know.

I discovered early on that getting sick was the most effective way to elicit my grandmother's kindness. Being a skilled nurse, Mom pulled out all the stops. She fed me milk toast with masses of white sugar, tucked me into a fresh bed covered with eiderdowns and tended my every need. When I was only three or four, I wondered if she did all this for me because when I got ill she was scared I was going to die.

I was highly strung by nature. As I was growing up, many people likened me to an over-bred racehorse. I even had – still have, for that matter – a thoroughbred's physical characteristics: tiny wrists and ankles, broad shoulders and a muscular body. And like a racehorse, I was highly reactive to anything going on in my environment. Everything I saw or heard interested me – dogs and flowers and insects and ribbons, rainbows and melodies. Sometimes when I woke up crying in the night, Mom would sit me up at the piano. I would sit there hitting the keys and laughing for an hour at a time.

As a young child, I had unusual powers of concentration. More than anything in the world, I hated to be interrupted. Aunt Mary (who was not my aunt at all, but one of Mom and Pat's tenants in the complex at Lakewood) insisted she had never seen anyone who focused as intently as I did when I was left alone to do my own thing. But if anyone interrupted my concentration, which Mom did several times an hour to stop me sucking my thumb or pulling at my dress, there was hell to pay. According to my father, I would ignore interference as long as I could, then turn into a wild animal. 'You were like a bear with its foot in a snare. You would snap and growl at anyone or anything that came near you,' he said.

Mom dealt with what she called 'Leslie's tantrums' by whacking my bottom. 'You would crawl under the bed, smash your fists and bang your head against the floor,' Mom said. 'But sooner or later, you would come out and go happily about your business.'

Once during the first year of my life, while Violet and Stanley were still living in the garage, my mother came upon a scene that disturbed her greatly: 'I opened the door to Mom's bedroom and found her nursing you at her breast.'

Mom was embarrassed. 'She tried to hide it by getting angry with me for disturbing her. This had been going on for some time, I think. It scared me. I hated that you were being used to satisfy Mom's illicit needs,' my mother explained. 'Later, when Stanley got home from Balboa, I told him what I saw. But he was so taken up with his own worries about the band, I don't think he even heard me. The next afternoon I tried to talk to Pat about it. He only fell asleep in his chair with his cat, Lucky, lying in his lap and a burning cigar in his mouth. I have worried for years that what Mom did with you before you were two or three years old may have done you real harm. But if ever I tried to speak to her about my concerns, she always said, "Don't be silly. Leslie is far too young to remember anything."'

3

GROWING PAINS

THE DAY IN 1940 that my father walked into Earl Carroll's theater to announce he was quitting, the manager laughed at him. 'You're out of your mind,' he said. 'You'll *never* start your own band. Let me give it to you straight, Stanley. You don't have what it takes. Tell you what – I'll find myself a substitute piano player for a year; then, after you fall on your face, you can have your old job back.'

My father drew himself up to his full height, took a deep breath and said, in as firm a voice as he could muster, 'Yeah, well, I gotta do it.' On 25 November 1941 – just over a year later – not only did Stanley have his own band, it would be playing right across the street from Earl Carroll's in the Hollywood Palladium, one of the most prestigious ballrooms in the world.

The Palladium's clientele had class. Glenn Miller, Artie Shaw and Harry James loved playing there. Bandleader Les Brown said, 'It was like New Year's Eve every night.' Now, the virtually unknown Stanley Kenton had joined this rank of luminaries. Each night the band played there, his music was broadcast coast to coast. My mother and father couldn't believe their good fortune. Thanks to the acclaim Stanley and his new band had received during their first summer at the Rendezvous, the crowds they drew at the Palladium broke all the records. It just couldn't get better . . . and it didn't.

On 6 December 1941, my father got home, crawled into bed and was just drifting off when my mother woke him. 'Stanley, Stanley,' she said, shaking him. (He was not easy to rouse.) 'Listen to me. It's terrible. The Japanese have just bombed Pearl Harbor.'

He sat straight up in bed, unable to believe what he was hearing. Along with everyone in America, my parents spent the next eighteen hours glued to the radio. By the time he arrived at the Palladium that night, Los Angeles had turned into a town where every window was blacked out. Makeshift blackout curtains even hung in the Palladium. The whole of the following week, the band played without lights. What surprised everyone was how many people turned up anyway. So impassioned with the new music were Stanley and his men that their enthusiasm had become contagious.

Two days later, Congress declared war on the Third Reich. When people become terrified, their fear seeks an outlet. The Kenton music went a long way towards providing it. Americans sat by their radios from early morning until shutdown. Every night, as the whole of the United States waited for news of the war, they heard the Kenton Band. This catapulted my father's music into nationwide recognition, opening up the possibility of a cross-country tour. The band needed a manager to organise such a major event. They need not have worried: being a consummate opportunist, the ideal manager soon found them. His name was Carlos Gastel.

Gastel had a genius for promoting talent. Eventually he would number Peggy Lee, Nat King Cole, Mel Tormé and June Christy among his stable of celebrities, as well as his first big name, Stan Kenton. He claimed he could make anyone a star.

At his very first meeting with Stan, at a drive-in restaurant in Hollywood, Carlos pronounced, 'It's time for us to head East.'

'East?' Stanley said.

'Yeah, you gotta go where the action is. We'll book a lot of one-nighters on the way to get us there. Then we'll hit the big time.'

'Big time?' my mother said.

'You know, Roseland, Frank Dailey's Meadowbrook in New Jersey. The Panther Room at Hotel Sherman in Chicago – that kinda place.'

My parents looked at each other, wondering if this guy was for real. They never quite made up their minds. But they decided to give him a try. Then and there, Carlos drew up a 'contract' on a paper napkin. All three of them signed it.

'Look,' Carlos said, as soon as he had stuffed the signed napkin into his shirt pocket, '"Stanley Kenton Orchestra" – it don't sound right. Not friendly enough. Let's make it "Stan Kenton Orchestra". Easier to remember – fits better on the Palladium marquee.'

Thus did 'Stanley Kenton' become 'Stan Kenton'. But for all his life the 'Stan Kenton' name would be used for public consumption only. Friends and family, as well as those musicians closest to him, called him Stanley. When the phone rang at home and somebody wanted to speak to 'Stan', I would ask, 'Who's calling, please?' If the voice answered, 'A close friend,' I would know the guy was lying.

The contract signed, Carlos was soon driving around in a white Cadillac convertible, hatching ingenious schemes to whip up publicity for his new client. Through his campaigns, he managed to create a buzz of anticipation around the band's first cross country tour, which began one cold January night in 1942.

Violet, Stanley, musicians, wives, some of their children and one kitten wrapped in a blanket climbed aboard a primitive bus my father hired and set off to make their fortune. Stanley needed his wife with him. He figured his musicians would feel the same about their wives. Children? Why not? Pets? Well, he guessed they could manage that.

Neither small enough to be classified as a kitten, nor large enough to be considered a 'child', I was left behind with Mom.

The tour was not a great success. Although the dates they played on the way East were well received, the Stan Kenton Orchestra's run at the prestigious Roseland Ballroom in New York was a disaster. The crowd, expecting traditional dance music, didn't know what to make of Stanley's innovative new sound. Instead of the eight-week stint for which they were booked, the band played for only ten painful nights before moving on.

The months that followed were tough, but slowly the band began to achieve a little commercial success. My father was desperate to have his music taken seriously. It made him furious when – not infrequently – it was hardly noticed at all. Occasionally, his frustration led him to compose some of the best music he ever wrote, like 'Concerto to End all Concertos'. Lyrical and powerful, with its own kind of magic, its name stands as a testament to the defiance that fuelled both his life and his early writing.

With characteristic magic, Carlos secured a six-week engagement at Frank Dailey's Meadowbrook in Cedar Grove, New Jersey. An hour from New York City by train, the Meadowbrook was way out in the country. Band members lived in a guesthouse nearby. My mother chose to stay in a Manhattan boarding-house, while my father commuted to work each night by train. Three or four times a week, she would come out to the Meadowbrook in the afternoon and remain with him until the job finished. By then she had had her fill of the road – the bad food, the waiting, the loneliness. When she was unhappy, so was Stanley. He turned to his band boy Ed Gabel – 'Gabe' – for help. 'Here's fifty dollars,' he said. 'Go into town. Take Violet out for the evening. Show her a good time. Just make sure she's back by one a.m. when we wrap for the night.' Gabe did this again and again. Together he and Violet went to see Count Basie and Duke Ellington. They took in the show at the Stork Club. They went to Broadway plays and movies. They ate late suppers at Lindy's or Toots Shor's. The distractions helped but tough months on the road had taken their toll. Stanley was consumed by his work. Violet had no life apart from encouraging him, supporting him, caring for him, and waiting for him to come back night after night.

It was around this time that Mom scheduled our first trip East. Finally there was enough money to pay for it. Mom loved travel and all the paraphernalia that went with it. Every time we went East to see my parents, she would dress me in a blue sailor dress with white piping. As I got bigger, so did the dresses. She would pack me up, along with a huge suitcase, three hatboxes, her alligator skin cosmetic case and a stylish – if somewhat mouldy – fox fur. We would climb into Pat's little blue Dodge car complete with rumble seat – great for the hatboxes – and set off, foxtails flying, for Los Angeles' Union Station. There, with the help of two redcaps, we'd board the Union Pacific Railway's state-of-the-art train bound for New York, via Chicago.

Every trip Mom and I made together was always full of food, at all hours of the day and night. She introduced me to the buffet car delicacies as soon as I had my first teeth, which was late. (They all worried that I would never have any teeth at all since they were so slow arriving.) When we travelled or when we ate in a restaurant, she would order a sticky dessert for herself and an éclair for me. When the éclair arrived, she would place it in front of me, cut off a tip for me to eat, then plop the rest of it on her own plate and proceed to devour it. Thanks to Mom's insatiable appetite, I was never allowed to eat the whole of one of these cream-and-custard-filled wonders until I turned eight.

A home movie tells the story of our first arrival at Grand Central: I am ten months old. Mom carries me in her left arm. (Children, she insists, are much calmer if you carry them on your left side so they can hear your heartbeat.) Her alligator vanity case and pocketbook hang from her right arm. Behind us a tall black man wheels her belongings through the crowd.

My mother is there to greet us. She has tears in her eyes when she reaches out to take me into her arms. I am unsure about this stranger. My lip trembles. I start to scream. Quickly she hands me back to Mom, pays the redcap, and steers us to a taxi.

For me, each trip Mom and I made to visit my parents was like leaving a planet where I knew the rules and being beamed down on another where no rules applied. Violet and Stanley were so different from Mom. They were tall and beautiful. They laughed a lot – at least when they were not sleeping. They talked to each other all the time and they told me stories, especially when Mom would disappear for an hour or two to shop, cook or explore the city. They didn't pull my fingers out of my mouth when I chewed on them, the way Mom did. Nor did they seem to care if I got my hands dirty.

My mother tells me that during the first five or six years of my life she was scared to be left alone with me for long. 'I didn't know what to do when you cried,' she said. On one of our trips Violet and Stanley sat and stared at me as though they were trying to figure out what this tow-headed short-legged creature was all about. 'You never stayed still for more than thirty seconds,' my mother said. 'I never knew what you were going to do next.'

I loved Central Park. Little boats in the big round fountain. I captured one and laughed until a horrible man with two children bigger than me pulled it out of my hands. Dogs, birds and people were everywhere. Every chance I got, I would wander away. If Violet and Stanley were with me, they followed. When I'd see them following, I would start to run. I was not great at this running business so I never got away. But I tried hard.

For Mom, New York was movie heaven. Not only did my grandmother initiate me into the splendours of gooey foods, she hooked me on movies. She herself was addicted to motion pictures. At home in Long Beach, we went to the movie theatre two, three, four times a week from the time I was two weeks old. While my parents slept through the mornings, we hit the streets in search of the best Hollywood had to offer, sneaking off to take in a double bill with nobody the wiser. I am sure the movies we saw together penetrated my consciousness and influenced my life. When *film noir* is your weekly fare long before you are able to figure out who murdered who and why, it must help mould your view of reality. So huge a part did movies play in my upbringing that it was not until I was thirty-five that I realised there was life outside the movies. By the time I was forty, I had decided that life could never match up to the magic of stories told on the big screen.

When I was an infant Mom would arrive at the cinema with a bottle of sterilised formula and two wet washcloths – one for my mouth and the other for my bottom – plus diapers stuffed into a Bullocks Wilshire shopping bag. (She also made a packed lunch for herself, of course.) Before I could walk or talk, I had sat through – more likely *slept* through – *The Maltese Falcon*, *The Little Foxes*, *Suspicion*, *Dumbo* and scores of lesser films. The first movie I consciously remember was *Bambi*. I think we saw it on our second or third trip East.

I hated the stupid rabbit with its huge feet. But Bambi and Bambi's mother – oh, the mother. The bad hunter shoots her. I don't want her to die. Bambi's mother is beautiful like Violet. Bambi's mother is sweet like Violet too. Mom says Violet is my mother 'in name only', whatever that means. Her voice is lovely. Just like my mother-in-name-only.

When Mom and I leave the theatre after the movie finishes, I say over and over, 'I don't like fire, don't like fire, don't like fire'. Back to the boarding-house, I carry on repeating, 'Fire . . . No, no.'

Violet and Stanley are sitting at the table, drinking coffee. 'What's she saying?' Violet asks.

'Nothing,' says Mom. 'That's enough, Leslie,' says Mom. 'Stop it. Now.'

I go silent. I know enough to keep my mouth shut when Mom speaks in that voice. She has trained me well.

'It's all right,' Stanley says. 'Let her talk.'

'Yes, she needs to *express* herself,' says my mother.

Mom makes that clicking sound with her tongue, which means nobody better mess with her. I know it well. It usually comes before a slap. I stay silent. My mother looks at me and smiles. Maybe there is something to this motherhood business after all?

Mom must have seen the look that passed between us. On her way to the kitchen, she turns round. 'Raising a child would be a foolish thing for you to try, Violet,' she says. 'You know nothing about it. You know you don't have a knack for these things.'

My father is silent.

*

When I was born somebody gave my mother one of those record books called 'Baby's Own Story Year by Year'. I opened it a few months ago while researching my family's past. A pair of tiny pale pink socks had been pressed between the pages. They fell to the floor.

In this book my mother had written my name in ink. 'Leslie Brooke Kenton, born at 2:25 in the afternoon of June 24, 1941.' She recorded that I weighed 6 pounds 8 ounces and that I had blue eyes, blond hair, small ears, large hands and feet, and long fingers. There was an 'instrument mark on left cheek which disappeared in one day', she wrote. Then, 'body perfect, no redness'. In pencil she has added, 'Showed signs of temper at two days old.'

The rest of the entries in the book are written in Mom's hand. She has dutifully recorded the events she thought mattered most and the age at which they took place. It reads, 'Grasped objects firmly at four months. First said, "Mama" at eight months.' Under 'other first words', Mom wrote, '"Danye", meaning "Stanley".'

From the worn pages of this book, I learned that I sat up alone at four months, never crawled, stood alone at eight months, walked steadily and talked in sentences at ten and a half months and climbed stairs at a year old.

One of the last entries made in the book says, 'Leslie took a trip with me to New York at the age of ten months. We flew back home to Lakewood by plane in 1942.' That trip was the first. Our other trips went unrecorded in 'Baby's Own Story'.

There is a home movie of my first birthday, shot in New York City. Dressed to the nines, my mother looks like a *Vogue* model. Stanley is lean, gaunt and distracted. Suddenly he smiles, and the screen lights up with the radiance of a Christmas tree.

Mom has baked me a chocolate cake. My eyes glow as she places the cake in front of me, with its single yellow candle burning. I clap my hands and laugh. When I reach out to touch it, she slaps me.

4

BACK TO THE SOURCE

Less than three weeks after Mom and I left New York for Lakewood after that first trip East, Violet followed us home. She was exhausted and disillusioned by the consequences of the dreams she and Stanley had worked for more than seven years to bring into being. She would speak to me about this often throughout her life.

This was the first time since their marriage that she chose to leave my father on his own. The band was playing in Detroit. On 20 September 1942, she boarded a train for Los Angeles. It was the first of many separations between my parents, which would become increasingly painful for them both in the years to come.

Violet was continually torn between her love for Stanley, as well as his need for her, on the one hand and her desire to have a home and create a family on the other. 'I kept asking myself is there any purpose to my life beyond giving everything I have to Stanley's career,' she said. She didn't know. She had been focused on his needs for so long, and surrendering her own light to help his burn brighter, that in time, she said, 'I began to ask if I even existed.' Then there was her child. The more time she spent with me – usually in the presence of Mom, of course – the greater her fear that she would never be a competent mother. 'But,' she said, 'I was dying to try.'

Left alone with his band and his music, Stanley's rage to be heard propelled him forward. Nothing was going to stop him. He lost many of his best musicians – to the draft, to drugs, to ultimatums, to discontented wives – but he felt sure the band was gaining commercial success in theatres, clubs and dance halls. He could see critical acceptance was growing. But it wasn't enough. 'I wanted – needed – Violet by my side,' he said. He turned to one-night stands with other women. That didn't work. 'I needed my wife,' he declared.

April 2, 1943: my mother is staying with Mom and me at Lakewood. Stanley is playing the Tune Town Ballroom in St Louis, Missouri. By now he has been separated from her for several months. He calls every chance he gets. This is not an easy task given the difficulty of calling cross-country, the time differences and the expense – but it's necessary. 'Half of my life disappears when she goes back to California,' he tells his friends.

Phone calls are the only way they can connect now. Each call lasts twenty minutes. That is, provided a snowstorm in Kansas doesn't disconnect them or some rookie long-distance operator doesn't pull the wrong plug. Fifteen or twenty minutes is all Stanley can afford. Obsessed with a desire to bask in Violet's love – always in need of her encouragement – each time he calls, he pours forth a litany of anxieties and complaints, about work, guys in the band who have let him down, Carlos Gastel's bad bookings. She always listens in silence.

'I used to wait by the telephone for days in between phone calls, hoping to hear from him again,' my mother said. 'I wanted to know he was all right. I wanted to tell him how worried I was about Mom's rough behaviour towards you, and about her possessiveness.' It seemed to my mother that Mom wanted to own me. She wanted to tell Stanley how left out she felt when she saw Mom and me together, doing things that excluded her: 'I wanted to tell him about your tea parties in the sandpit, about how beautiful you were becoming, about how much I wanted to buy a home for the three of us and to stop living in Mom's garage.'

Every time she tried to involve Stanley in her everyday life or to talk to him about me, he paid no attention. 'When I tried to speak about these things I felt he was just waiting for an opportunity to get back to his own worries,' she explained. 'He kept losing men to the draft.

He was scared he would get drafted. He had worries about transporting the band on the next leg of the tour.'

During their telephone calls my mother began to feel that there was nothing she could say about her own thoughts that would be of any interest to him. The words she had wanted to say would get stuck in her throat, lost in confusion, washed away in tears.

One day she gave him an ultimatum: 'I've got to get out of here, Stanley. I can't live with these separations. You always force me to choose between life with you on the road and sleeping in Mom and Pat's garage so I can be near Leslie. Our daughter hardly knows me. You don't know her at all! She's growing into a little girl. She belongs more to Mom and Pat than she does to us. I hate it.'

'I hear you, Violet. I do,' he assured her. 'We'll find a way to work it out.'

'You promise?'

'I promise.'

Recalling their conversation, my father told me, 'For the first time, I listened to what Violet was saying. I could feel the desperation in her words. I was afraid I could lose her.' He always said that the next three months were agony for him. For the first time since 1935, when they were married, he was truly frightened. What if he lost this woman? Everything he had worked so hard for could come unravelled. Why was all this happening now, when things were just beginning to take off?

By the time Stanley left St Louis for the next job in Champaign, Illinois, that spring, his fears, compulsions and fugues had surfaced in force. He no longer had any doubt about how desperately he needed Violet, and 'Not just to keep the wolves at bay, either,' he said. 'I felt if I were to lose her, everything we'd worked so hard for would turn to dust.' It was time to end the frustrating phone calls. Time to go home.

His decision made, at last his train pulls into Los Angeles' Union. It is 8.30 in the evening. The sky is clear. The air is balmy. There's a new moon – a time for new beginnings. Violet is waiting for him.

Stanley sheds his baggage. Let somebody else take his stuff to the Highlander Hotel in Hollywood where he and Violet have been booked. It is within walking distance of the Palladium where Carlos has secured a six-week booking for the band. The job doesn't start for a few days. This is tonight. To hell with tomorrow.

'Felipe's?' Stanley says.

Violet laughs.

Throwing his coat over his shoulder, he grabs her hand. They dash out of Union Station, running along the sidewalk two blocks down North Alameda to Felipe's, open from 6 a.m. to 10 p.m. seven days a week. Ever since 1908, Felipe's has sold the best French dip sandwiches in the world. They burst through the doors. The place is crowded with people of every description.

Some things never change. Felipe's is one of them. On counter tops stand huge glass jars. Some hold purple pickled eggs, others are stuffed full of pig's feet. On trays behind glass the best baked apples in southern California, arranged in military rows, beg to be eaten.

Stanley loved Felipe's and everything in it. So did Violet. This comfortably run-down shop was one of their 'special places'. (From the time I was old enough to remember being taken there, it became one of mine too.) They had first come here two weeks after they met, to celebrate the 'anniversary'.

As Stanley crosses the threshold, his eyes fill with tears. 'What do you want, darling?' he asks.

'I don't know. You decide.'

He moves to the counter. At Felipe's there is never a line – just a horde of random people hoping they can place an order. Violet finds herself a seat to wait, to watch him, to discover if he has changed. She decides he looks good. Tired, but good. She smiles. Her husband has never lost his gangly boyish look. Nor will he ever lose it as long as he lives.

She looks stunning in her white sharkskin suit. Her golden hair falls across her shoulders. It shines in the streetlights that filter through Felipe's not-so-clean front window. She looks like a movie star out of a 1940s *film noir* sandwiched into a wooden booth, waiting for Sam Spade to rescue her.

Her rescuer arrives, laden with so much food they can never eat it all. Who cares! This is a celebration. She picks at her French dip sandwich with perfectly manicured nails, dipping a bird-sized portion of bread into the gravy. She never spills a drop. This is a woman who can walk though a barnyard without smudging her blue and white spectator shoes.

Unlike Stanley, who is already munching his way through a second pickled egg, Violet is seldom hungry. She has trained herself not to be. At five foot seven inches she weighs in at a meagre 120 pounds. Once, when she was on the road with nothing to do but wait for him night after night, her weight crept up to 132 pounds. She discovered this stepping on to a 'Weigh Yourself for a Penny' machine in a Cleveland drugstore while they were waiting for their breakfast to arrive. Horrified, she not only forsook the breakfast, she stopped eating for a week.

Stanley's hair is combed tonight. He has shaved too. He has carried out this ritual crammed into a lavatory on the train, which 'smelt as if it had not been cleaned for a week'. Yet, at this moment, in her presence, he looks awkward: 'I felt like a man badly in need of a wash and brush-up sitting next to the Snow Queen,' he always said.

'Monkey,' he says now, reaching for her hand, 'let's never be away from each other again.' This is short for 'Monkey Face' – a nickname he has given her. It's a name he never uses in public, a secret between the three of us.

'Stanley, we need a home.'

'Home?'

'A place that's ours – a place where we can live instead of camping out in other people's garages – a place where Leslie can grow up, where the three of us can be together.'

'A home.'

'Yes. A home.'

'Where?'

'I don't know. Anywhere. Here. Hollywood, maybe?'

'OK.'

When the meal finishes, they wrap up half of Violet's sandwich together with the baked apples for later. They both know it will be him who eats the leftovers. He always does. He hails a cab. Holding hands, they travel to the Highlander Hotel. They are exhausted. Yet it will be hours before they sleep.

Both my parents were tall. My mother was well proportioned. Not so my father. His legs were long – more like the limbs on a giraffe than those of a man. One of the first things he did when he got to any hotel was to check out the bathroom and use the toilet. Tonight he discovers that the bathroom at the Highlander is far too small. He can't unfold his legs while sitting on the toilet. Stanley's band boy, Ed Gabel, who arrived on the same train that evening, was sharing a room in a nearby hotel with trumpet player Buddy Childers. He had not been in his hotel room more than an hour or two when the phone rang.

'Gabe?'

'Yes.'

'We can't stay here. I can't sit on the toilet.'

'What?!'

'My legs are too long,' my father explains.

'OK. What do you want me to do?'

'We gotta buy a house.'

'A house?' asks Gabe.

'Yeah.'

'Now?'

'First thing tomorrow.'

Ten hours later, Ed Gabel, Carlos Gastel, Violet and Stanley were combing the Hollywood Hills with a realtor. They looked at three houses. The first one they saw was the one they liked best, so they went back to look again: 2720 Hollyridge Drive.

It sits on top of a mountain. A small, well-built house with yellow shutters, it has three storeys if you include the washroom-cum-furnace room in the basement which Stanley decides is an ideal place for him to listen to recording transcriptions. There is a rose garden to the left of the house and a small back yard surrounded by a picket fence. When you look out from the front porch you see the 'Hollywoodland' sign stretching along the mountain on the other side of Beachwood Valley. From the back you see Griffith Park Observatory – part of a panoramic view stretching eighty to a hundred miles over the whole of the Los Angeles basin and out to sea. On a clear day, you can make out Catalina Island, twenty-three miles away from the mainland. Just over the fence and aching to be harvested, avocado trees, orange trees and lemon trees – boasting lemons the size of grapefruit – grace the hill.

Since the house is empty the realtor is able to enter it into escrow that very day. Standing out front, with their suitcases in the street beside them, my parents marvel at their purchase. It could not be more perfect. Except, of course, that they have no furniture, no car, and no place to stay until they can organise things. A neighbour offers them a ride to the bottom of the hill so Stanley can phone for a taxi. From there they head back to Mom's garage. At least her bathroom is big enough for him to sit on the toilet.

What next? Money. In typical Latin fashion, Carlos comes to the rescue. He sorts out a cash advance against the Palladium booking.

They need a car, too. Not just any old car. America is still at war. Civilian defence workers and military bases are clamouring for entertainment, but tyre and gas rationing make bus travel prohibitive and train travel is not much better. Stanley and Carlos need to find a way for him to handle his own transportation. Not to be defeated by logistics just when his music is getting noticed, my father borrows yet another $300 from Carlos to buy a big, old, eight-passenger, black 1934 Buick Roadmaster. It has jump seats, luggage racks, running boards, white-wall tyres – even side wheel wells for spares. It comes with a two-wheel trailer he can attach for carrying drums and bags. My mother names it 'The Hearse' because that's what it looks like. It is meant to be both a family car and a way of transporting men and equipment from one job to another.

Having helped Violet and Stanley sort out a house and then a car, Gabe mistakenly assumed he would now be free to enjoy what was left of his days off before the band opened at the Palladium. But no. He receives another phone call.

'Gabe?' says Stanley. 'I don't mean to spoil your day off, but can you meet us at Barker Brothers downtown? They're having a big sale. Violet wants us to move into the new house right away. We need some furniture.'

Barker's – the largest furniture store in Los Angeles at the time – had nine floors overflowing with furniture to choose from. My mother made a long list of what they needed: pots and pans, linens, towels, tables, sofas, chairs, beds – the lot. The three of them met at the entrance and went to work. By one o'clock Stanley had ticked off most of the items on her list. After making sure that Barker's had a good returns policy, he told the salesman to write up the bill.

Nothing they bought that day was ever returned. Within a week they were living in their new home. For a few months that year Gabe stayed with them, as many others would in the future. Gabe smiles when he remembers his time at Hollyridge. 'Violet was a wonderful cook,' he says wistfully.

Not until almost a year later did Mom finally agree that I could become the third permanent resident at Hollyridge.

By my third birthday Mom's strict ways were taking their toll. Five nights out of seven, I would wake screaming from a nightmare. I would do whatever I could to escape the discomfort in my body, which was continually riddled with anxiety: nail biting, obsessive rocking back and forth, clutching a special toy – even physically striking out against people who probably meant me no harm. I chewed my nails despite a thousand slaps and admonitions not to do so. Mom painted bitter herbs on my fingers every morning. If I touched my face, they got into my eyes and burned badly. This didn't keep me from biting my nails anyway, so after a while she stopped.

In my outer world I pretended to be 'good', yet I trusted no one and did my best to hide what I really thought or felt. My inner world belonged to me alone. Sometimes this secret realm would be rich and wonderful to me, like when colours of drawings in books shimmered with light as I touched them. Others, it was empty, abysmally lonely, occasionally terrifying.

Sometimes Violet and Stanley come to see me at Mom's. We laugh a lot. Then they go away. Mom says it's because I'm a bad girl. I know it's true. I *am* a bad girl. That's why she hits me. I'm bad like the monsters who live in the corners of my room. When I try to be good, my monsters laugh at me. They say I can't be good because I am like them. They make fun of me. Sometimes they make me spill my orange juice down the front of my dress. Then they laugh. Sometimes they make me say 'No' when Mom wants me to kiss her friends.

I hate kissing people who smell bad. Pat smells good – warm like the dirt in the flowerbed. My-mother-in-name-only smells beautiful – sometimes like green leaves, sometimes the way stars do when the night is cold. Stanley's face is bristly, like Mom's hairbrush. I don't like kissing him. When Mom is angry she brushes my hair too hard. I don't like that either. When she pulls my hair I never want to kiss her at all.

I'm scared when Mom is angry. But I don't let her know I'm scared. My monsters say you must never let anyone know you're scared. 'If somebody thinks you're scared,' they say, 'they will hurt you.' They're smart monsters. I try to do as they say. But I'm scared of them, too.

Yesterday Mom told me, 'Tomorrow you are going to live at Hollyridge with Stanley and Violet.' She said it in an angry way. I didn't know what I had done to make her angry.

I said, 'I'm sorry.' I hoped she would forgive me for whatever bad thing I did.

She said, 'I'm sorry too, but there's nothing we can do about it.' I didn't say anything. Sometimes it's safer not to talk.

It's morning now. Mom puts my clothes in a suitcase. That means we are going on a trip. She is always happy when we go away. But today she is crying. 'You do love me, don't you?' she says. 'Don't you?'

'Don't be silly,' I say. I slap her on her leg the way she slaps mine when I am being silly. She laughs. She picks me up and hugs me. She stands me on the table. She straightens my dress. She ties my hair with a red bow. She puts on my light blue sweater. It's soft. She hands me a doll, but I don't like dolls.

We get into Pat's car. Mom lets me sit in the jump seat. I like the wind. It feels nice. I want our trip to go on for ever. I laugh at the way my hair tickles my cheek. I stand up. Mom sees me. She turns round and shoves me down. 'Don't you dare do that again! You hear me, Leslie? Don't you dare!' I don't stand up any more.

We drive a long time. The wind makes me sleepy. We come to a long, long road with tall skinny trees on it. Trees that look like they have droopy hats on. Now we turn on to a winding road that goes up and up. Mom and Pat are talking. They forget about me. I stand up. I grab leaves off a tree hanging over a wall. I pull them. They come off in my hand. I sit down before she sees what I've done. The leaves smell like pepper. They hurt my nose. They make me sneeze. I throw them out of the car.

At the top of a mountain we stop in front of a white house with a wall and a bush that has red balls on it. I point to them.

'Pomegranates,' Mom says.

'Pomgran,' I say. I run to pull one off.

'No. No. Don't touch. They're not ripe yet,' she says.

The big white door opens. Violet comes down the steps. She picks me up. Stanley comes next. He takes the suitcases from Pat's car. Mom is crying again. She's going to leave now.

'No! Don't go,' I scream.

My-mother-in-name-only takes me inside. 'This is your new home,

Leslie,' she says. 'You're going to live with Violet and Stanley now.' She tells me I must always call her and Stanley by their first names. This will make me grow up 'free', she says. I don't know what free is. It sounds hard – like being a 'good girl'.

My new room has three windows with white curtains on them and black screens. Violet says the screens are to keep the flies out. I think she is telling the truth since I don't see any flies. I keep my windows closed. It feels safer. Except for the window at the back. It has a big tree growing outside it with white flowers. Violet says the tree is 'night blooming jasmine'. Sometimes when she kisses me good-night and goes downstairs, I sneak out of my bed and open that window so I can smell the tree.

My monsters have come with me to this new house. They sit in the corners waiting for Violet to leave so they can say bad things to me. She lets me keep the door open and she leaves the light in the hall on when I go to bed. She says Mom will come to see me soon. I'm glad she will come. This place is not like Lakewood.

Violet buys me clothes. They itch. Sometimes she buys twin clothes for us so she and I look the same. But mine are smaller than hers. I tell her when I grow up I am going to be a cowgirl and ride horses. She says that's a good idea. She buys me a cowgirl outfit with guns and chaps and boots. I hide it under the bed so no one can take it away to wash it. She buys me books too. I like the books she buys. I'm learning to read them.

I was three and a half when Mom and Pat delivered me to Hollyridge to take up residence with Stanley and Violet. Moving to Hollyridge was like entering a different universe. There was so much 'freedom' I didn't know what to do with it. I had no understanding of what Stanley and Violet required of me. Living with Mom, I had known exactly what to expect. Here, because I had no idea, it frightened me.

Bizarre as it may seem, smoking cigarettes when I was four years old was part of the 'freedom' my parents were hellbent on bestowing on me. Humphrey Bogart smoked cigarettes in all the movies, they both smoked, as did everybody else in the 1940s, so why shouldn't Leslie? I hated the taste of the things but I knew being 'free' was expected of me, so I soldiered on.

Being 'creative' was another thing they expected of me. We had a little alcove downstairs where the telephone sat. One day Violet decided I should paint a picture in it. The idea terrified me, but, willing to please, I painted a tree. It was the ugliest thing you could imagine. My 'work of art' lasted about a year. Every time I walked by the phone on the way to the kitchen, I cringed. I was so ashamed of it. Happily, one day the hideous tree vanished beneath a coat of fresh white paint.

At Hollyridge, my disciplinarian training kept crashing up against Stanley and Violet's demands for *freedom, creativity* and *self-expression*. The contradictions in these imperatives threw me into even higher states of anxiety. How could I do what my parents wanted me to do – virtually forced me to do – and still be a *good girl* like Mom said I must? I found the demand to be free and be creative was even tougher to fulfil than Mom's insisting I 'be good'. I was forced to add them to the list of things I could never become, no matter how hard I tried. I was running scared. I started to get sick a lot and the nightmares escalated.

I did my best to hide my fears. A chasm began to form between my fearful inner life and the boldness of the personality I learned to show to the world. Beneath the brittle surface of my bravado lived a trembling, frightened child. But the world around me was so full of loud noises, chaos and confusion that no one suspected her existence.

5

HOLLYWOOD BRAT

Growing up at Hollyridge often felt like trying to survive in the midst of a three-ring circus. People were always coming and going.

One day a bandleader named Charlie Barnett arrived, looking like hell. He hung around for two weeks, drank all my father's whisky, then rang the liquor store and ordered more. He swallowed a lot of pills. He never took a shower. All in all, he reminded me of a dead dog.

I asked Stanley about him. 'Why is he here?'

'He's having a nervous breakdown.'

'A what?'

'It's like when somebody's life falls apart.'

'Oh.' I figured I knew about nervous breakdowns, since around me people's lives seemed to be falling apart most of the time. 'OK. But why is he here?'

My father looked at me strangely for a minute. 'I don't know.'

I think Stanley really didn't know. At Hollyridge stuff just happened, as though there were no reason behind it. Two days later, Charlie disappeared. I never saw him again.

When I was five or six I suspected that the world around me was askew. I felt like Alice in Wonderland, who could never figure out why the Queen's men kept painting the white roses red. Everybody doing it seemed to think there was a perfectly logical reason, but nobody could explain what it was. Spending most of my time with grown-ups, I seldom understood what they were talking about. Often I didn't even know who they were.

Occasionally Mom would come to Hollyridge with one of her friends to take me out. The friend might be an eccentric 'spiritual teacher', a man she met on a bus, or a movie star. One day she announced we were going to see 'The Greatest Show on Earth' – Ringling Brothers and Barnum & Bailey Circus – with a man who she said was a cowboy movie star. Now if it had been Hoot Gibson, whom I loved for his laid-back ways, or Roy Rogers, who had that neat Palomino horse, Trigger, that would have been great. But whoever heard of Ronald Reagan?

The circus: I loved the tigers. I hated the man with the whip who tormented them in the round cage. The high flyers made me shiver with excitement and I adored the tightrope walkers. Mom had forbidden me to see the Freak Show. She said it was 'not suitable for a six-year-old'.

Just as I was about to lay aside my future plans for a career as a cowgirl in favour of becoming a trapeze artist, I realised I needed to pee. Mom was busy working her way through her second cotton candy so Ronnie, her actor friend, got saddled with the onerous task of taking me to the 'Little Girls' Room'.

The circus toilets were not clean and I refused to use them. With considerable patience, 'Uncle Ronnie' held my hand while we wandered around the dusty fairground looking for cleaner lavatories. By then I was pretty sure this guy was not much of a cowboy. He didn't even wear boots or a hat.

I tried out three sets of toilets. They were all dirty. 'I can't go there,' I announced sanctimoniously. 'Mom says I must only use *clean* toilets. Dirty toilets carry *dangerous germs*. Besides, they're all too big for me to climb on. Do you know the children's toilets at Buffums?' I asked. Ronnie shook his head. 'I like them best of all,' I announced. 'I use them whenever my mother takes me shopping there. Can you ask the man in the red coat where the children's toilets are?'

I ended up behind the large tent peeing in a pile of rubbish while Ronald Reagan stood by looking embarrassed.

In spite of the dizzy social lives of my family, boredom was a major challenge for me, especially when we were away from home. I often had to wait while my father finished radio interviews so I could be let out of the tiny smoke-filled glass box where I was supposed to remain quiet as a mouse. I had to hang around in freezing garages for some guy to fix the brakes so we could drive to the next job. I would be forced to wait hours – it felt more like days – for grown-ups in restaurants to drink enough cocktails so that we could eat dinner. Then Stanley had what to me was a terrible ritual that he carried out at the end of each meal. As soon as we finished eating – even in a club or fancy restaurant – he would dip his napkin into my water glass and rub it all over my face. This practice continued until way beyond my childhood.

But there was good stuff about growing up in a showbiz family too. Like getting to hang out with a few really great human beings. When my parents went to clubs but had nobody to leave me with, they would take me with them. Whenever I had a chance to go see Nat King Cole – a man with the demeanour of a prince – I jumped at it. He was tall, shy, gentle, sweet and self-effacing. Nat King Cole was one of my big pals.

I remember going to see Nat play at Ciro's. When it comes to Hollywood glamour and nightlife, Ciro's was where it all happened in the 1940s and '50s. This was before the Sunset Strip turned into the mishmash of burlesque shows, random restaurants, tattoo parlours and assorted businesses which it later became. Ciro's had delicious food and the best entertainment money could buy. It had its own set of searchlights, as well as lots of handsome out-of-work wannabe movie actors who parked clients' cars with obsequious enthusiasm.

It was impossible to walk into Ciro's without coming face to face with the gods and goddesses of the entertainment industry. In pairs or groups, they held court night after night, each at his or her favourite table: Frank Sinatra, Marilyn Monroe, Jimmy Stewart, Cary Grant, Marlene Dietrich, Humphrey Bogart, Lauren Bacall, Ava Gardner, George Burns, Jack Benny, Judy Garland, Joan Crawford – you name it, they would show up. Cigarette girls and female photographers wandered around among them, hoping to be discovered by some not-too-offensive producer who just might – provided they slept with him – get them into movies.

That night we arrived early to see the first show: Violet, Stanley, two hangers-on, and me. My mother had poured herself into a body-hugging, floor-length gold lamé dress, topped off with an ankle-length silver mink stole, which she wore slung over one shoulder. I loved that mink. It was soft like a bunny when I rubbed my cheek against it.

When Nat came through the door, the first thing he did was come over to our table and kiss Violet on the cheek. Later that evening, I went to talk to him backstage. There, Nat taught me two important things: that even people with blue-black skin get sunburnt, and how to poke holes in the bottom of chocolates to find the cherry-centred ones, then stuff the others back in their little brown wrappers so nobody would discover they had been vandalised.

But I still yearned for a friend of my own.

In the end, my father's travels with the band brought the companion I longed for into my life. One morning, when Stanley was away from Hollyridge, my mother announced, 'I think we need a dog for protection.' I couldn't figure out how a dog was going to protect us, or from what. But I was one hundred per cent behind the idea of an animal coming to live with us – any animal. I adored animals, tame or wild.

A woman my mother knew, the wife of some Hollywood studio bigwig, owned an ocelot. Somebody had sent it to her as a kitten. When I heard about its existence I begged Violet to take me to meet him.

We had to drive down a long twisting drive behind huge iron gates to get to the woman's front door. The chimes went on for at least five minutes when I pushed the doorbell. A maid answered, dressed in black with a frilly white apron. She led us up a massive staircase with gold railings. The floors were covered in white carpet so thick that when you walked across it you felt like you were wading through a vat of whipped cream.

The woman met us at the door of her gigantic bedroom. She was dressed in silk lounging pyjamas with huge shoulder pads. Her slippers had heels so high I expected her to trip and fall on her face any moment. To my disappointment, she didn't.

In the late 1940s, there were no laws in California forcing people to keep wild animals in cages, so her ocelot spent most of its time sleeping on her big, round bed. The creature was gorgeous – yellowy-brown with chocolate blotches and a soft, white throat.

'How old is he?' my mother asked. 'It is a he, isn't it?'

'Yeah. It's a he,' the woman said, dragging on a cigarette at the end of a long cigarette holder. 'He's called Rex. He's three years old and three feet long.' She brushed back carrot-coloured hair with the longest nails I had ever seen.

My mother followed her as she teetered over to a bar made of pink mirrors at the far end of the room. She mixed cocktails for the two of them in a crystal jug using a glass wand. They sat on bar stools and began to talk. I could see they had forgotten about me.

Great. I crept towards the bed, pretending I hadn't noticed Rex. Above it was a mirror which covered most of the ceiling. I crouched down at the bed's edge and looked up. I could see all of Rex in the mirror. He didn't move except to open one eye. I stared for a long time, not daring to touch him. Then I try to make believe I am a cat. If I can convince him I am, maybe he won't get scared of me. Nonchalantly, I slither one arm over the side of the bed the way I've seen cats do. I touch his muzzle. It's wet and cool. He yawns and licks my hand.

Rex's tongue is raspy, like the heavy sandpaper my father keeps in the kitchen drawer. I stroke his head. Gaining confidence, I run my hand down his body. He purrs so loud it sounds like a car motor and his ears go flat against his head so he looks like an aeroplane about to take off. It makes me laugh.

The carrot-haired woman hears, turns and shrieks, 'No, no, dear. Don't touch him. He's *dangerous* – very dangerous!' That's the end of my romance with Rex.

'Can we get a big cat like Rex, instead of a dog?' I asked on the way home.

'No, Leslie. We need a dog.'

That night, before I went to sleep, I made a decision: if I ever got a dog of my own, it had to be a *big* collie.

'A collie? I don't see why not,' my mother said. 'You mean like Lassie?'

'Yes, but a *boy* dog, not a girl dog. Boy dogs are bigger. Better for protection,' I added with conviction.

Three days later, we drove up into the Santa Monica mountains, on a lonely winding road, in Violet's 1947 Cadillac convertible. Stanley had given it to her as a surprise, since the band had been doing well and he had some money. He had driven up one morning in a shiny blue convertible and parked it outside the house. It had a big red ribbon tied over the hood with a card on it that said, 'For my darling Violet, with all my love, Stanley.' My mother took one look at it, decided she didn't like dark blue and told him it had to be black. An hour later a little man with a thin moustache arrived in another car. The second car was a black Cadillac to replace the blue one. My mother adored that car so much she would keep it for fifteen years.

The day we went dog-hunting, she parked it in front of a dilapidated farmhouse in the mountains. We walked down a long, dusty driveway and entered a big barn. At the back of the barn, in a pile of straw, lay a fluffy collie with a row of puppies nursing from her belly. Some were gorging themselves the way Mom and I did on malts and ice-cream sodas. Others were sound asleep with their noses pressed against her side.

One puppy – the biggest one – was by itself over in the corner of the stall, rooting around in the straw. It seemed more alert than the rest. 'Is that a boy?' I asked the man in the overalls with the dusty grey hair.

'Yep.'

'He's so big.'

'Yep.'

'Can I climb over and pat him?'

'You go right ahead, little lady.'

I scrambled into the dog's nest. The puppy snuffled up to me and licked my hand. I took hold of the fluffy creature. He nipped my hand but didn't hurt. I held him up to my face and sniffed him the way he sniffed me. His body was warm against my nose.

'Please can we have this one?' I asked.

The puppy vomited all over me in the car on the way home. Then he curled up in my lap, pushed his snout against my tummy and went to sleep. I decided to call him Tuffy because that's what I wanted to be when I grew up. I didn't learn until four or five years later that I had spelled his name wrong, but 'Tuffy' he remained.

From the first day Tuffy came to live with us, he became the centre of my life. I felt safe when he was near me. All sorts of people, some with booze and drug problems, others with assorted dramas and miseries, came and went at Hollyridge. So did Violet and Stanley. Tuffy was always there.

I learned about love from Tuffy. He showed me that love is without reason, all-encompassing, not dependent on being 'good' or 'free' or 'creative' or 'smart' or anything else. He showed me that when you love someone, you delight in them and you celebrate your time together.

Tuffy kept me company during the many evenings when my mother went out and my father was away. In time, Violet even let him sleep in my room since, when he did, I didn't have as many nightmares.

He was strictly a one-child dog. I was allowed to go anywhere so long as Tuffy went with me. We roamed together through Griffith Park, which was wild – full of cactuses, hummingbirds and hawks, coyotes, snakes and cougars. In spring the earth was covered with lupins, California poppies, and wild carrot plants growing along the ground. The smells of the plants and herbs, dust and rock chippings have stayed with me all my life. So have the odours of pepper trees, wild sage and rosemary. When I smell any of them, they make me think of Tuffy.

Tuffy grew up fast. When he came to live with us he had giant paws. They never got much bigger. But the rest of him, as my mother always said, 'just growed like Topsy'. When Stanley came home a few months later, Tuffy treated him like a stranger. By the time Stanley came home a second time, Tuffy was so big he could jump against his chest, put a paw on each of his shoulders and look over his head.

Despite how important Tuffy was in my life, despite all the photographs and home movies that were shot by my family, for a long time I never had any images of Tuffy. The only memory I had of him was the one I carried about inside me of this huge, rough collie – all gold and brown and white – with a magnificent mane. I had always been suspicious about my memory because, when you are a child, just about everything looks big to you.

After his death, many of my father's papers, photographs and much of his music were archived at the University of Pacific Library in California. While researching this book, among a lot of bland publicity photos of Stanley, I discovered a photo of Tuffy which I never knew existed.

When it was taken, we had just returned from a trip abroad and a photographer had come to Hollyridge to snap a new series of publicity shots – Stanley opening the mail, talking on the telephone in the back yard, lying on a chaise-longue. He changed clothes several times that day as they moved from one location to another. In the Tuffy photo, Stanley looks like he has just changed his jacket, but not bothered with the trousers, probably because the photo was only to have been from the waist up. In Tuffy's enthusiasm – which he always had in great abundance – he leapt up on Stanley, who is obviously trying to protect his clothes from being soiled.

A few months ago, when I came upon this photo, I laughed out loud. Then I cried. There he was. My best friend in all his glory. Big? The photo showed that Tuffy was huge: so large that, had he chosen to put his paws on my father's shoulders, he could easily have licked his face.

Meeting Tuffy again this way felt like a gift of grace. In some way I will probably never understand, it brought back to me a fundamental part of myself which had been misplaced half a century before. It also gave me confidence in my memories. For Tuffy turned out to be even more glorious than I had remembered him. I propped up the photograph on my desk, where it sat for weeks while I was writing.

From the moment we met, Tuffy and I were friends, beyond words, beyond reasons and with no reservations. Not often do connections such as this get forged between two beings – man and woman, child and parent, girl and dog. When they do, it changes your life for ever. Tuffy changed mine.

6

HIT THE ROAD

NOSTALGIC, EXCITING, PATRIOTIC, romanticised – seeing the real America. Hollywood makes movies about it. It's called 'being on the road'. Chuck the demands of ordinary life. You're on your way somewhere. Follow blindly that urge to keep moving. Before long it becomes an addiction you don't know you have. Fortnighter suitcases brimming with stuffed animals, Violet's white sharkskin suits and endless pairs of shoes. Sheaves of Stanley's half-written music, my secret store of chewing gum, smuggled bottles of gin for when we travel through dry states. The black circles under your eyes never go away. You eat breakfasts of Rice Krispies piled high with white sugar at the end of the night in truck drivers' cafés. You argue over nothing for reasons that none of you can ever remember. It is the ultimate life of no responsibility. Is it Tuesday? Then this must be Dallas.

A surprising sense of safety comes from living this way. It must have something in common with being in prison. All decisions get made for you. You hold an itinerary in one hand and a road map in the other. After a while, even the jobs you rush to get to seem the same. You leave one dance hall in the early hours of the morning, jump into the car, drive 400 miles to the next one, and think no more about it.

The lion's share of the first ten years of my life were spent like this. Our trips were interspersed with weeks and months when Stanley was at home or when Violet, torn apart by conflicting desires, made him go out on his own while she stayed home with me. When we were on the road, she would spend night after night locked in a hotel room bathroom, sitting on the toilet seat so she could read without disturbing me while I slept. That was when I was still too young to be hauled off to the job every night. By the time I was five, all this had changed. I spent every night in clubs or dance halls, theatres and concert halls, drowning in seas of cigarette smoke, in which floated half-lit faces of people I would never see again.

When I was three and a half my mother had given me a camel – a yellow, two-humped, furry creature just the right size to fit into the pit of my arm with a hump in front and one in back. I can see him now: Camel travels everywhere with me. I always carry him facing forward so he can see where we are going. If I pick him up the wrong way round, he gets angry with me.

Camel is my guardian. He watches out for me. He protects me. He tells me things, like how to find the ladies' room when we are in a place where I have never been. Whenever I get sick, Camel stays beside me on my pillow. When I play on swings in a playground or we go to a museum, he comes with me. When we travel outside the United States, I make a passport for him. I draw his photo with coloured pencils. Since he can't write his name, I sign the passport for him hoping the men in uniforms will not notice that I forged his writing.

Sometimes my mother left Hollyridge at the same time Stanley did. Other times she and I would stay behind a week or two then take a train to Kansas City or Chicago, Cincinnati or Tuscaloosa and travel onwards with him from there.

The musicians always travelled on the bus. After each job they would drink themselves to sleep, play cards, or dream of being at home in bed with their wives. Meanwhile, Violet, Stanley and I would climb into his Buick Dynaflow convertible – my father loved Buicks almost as much as he did John Wayne movies – and set off, hoping to find our way to where we were supposed to show up the next night.

If we were lucky, we would get there with enough time to sleep for a few hours before work began. Often we were not that fortunate. Then we would have to find our hotel, get fed, go with Stanley to radio interviews, or to visit stores to promote his record sales. I remember one six-month period when I never saw the light of dawn, except at the other end of the day. My father's stamina and spirit seemed endless. I did my best to keep up with him out of sheer pride at being a Kenton. After all, as a Kenton, I knew it was expected of me.

Stanley's pride and joy – the Buick – had red Moroccan leather seat covers. The back seat belonged to me. Since it was where I lived, I was allowed to keep it any way I wanted. This meant lots of books, comic books, glue, crayons, scissors and assorted junk. Nobody pays much attention to what you do in the back of a Buick – especially when those in the front seat are trying hard just to stay awake. Left to my own devices, I decorated my 'room' by cutting out pictures of Donald Duck, Mickey Mouse, Charlie Chicken and Andy Panda, and pasting them on the red leather behind the front seats, using something akin to wallpaper paste which smelt awful. I put up with the stench since when I got tired of one picture I could easily rip it off and replace it with another.

Beneath these cut-outs, on the floor of the back seat, stacks of books and comics rose like miniature skyscrapers, some as much as two feet high. I never wanted to throw anything out. On days when I was feeling wicked, I would pile my comic collection higher and higher on the passenger side. I did this when I thought we would be staying at a fancy hotel for the night. My ultra-tall stacks of comics became the ultimate child's weapon against dreary, obsequious doormen dressed in foolish uniforms. We would drive up to the kerb of a hotel, the doorman would open the door to help my mother from the front seat and fifty comic books would come spilling out into the gutter. He would have to stoop and pick them up, one by one. It was perfect revenge on a world peopled by pretentious giants who made me feel I had no place in it.

When Stanley's band worked the Deep South, we used to have to play one dance or concert for whites and a separate one for blacks. I hated this. It seemed stupid. 'Aren't people just people?' I said. 'What difference does it make what drinking fountain or toilet they use or what bus they ride on?' My parents tried to explain it to me. This was tough, though, since they felt the same way I did.

When we travelled through 'dry' states, they wouldn't be able to order a drink in a restaurant or buy liquor in a store. This was of major concern to Stanley, whose very existence depended on alcohol being in good supply. He decided we would never travel anywhere without two or three bottles hidden beneath the seat of the car. When we crossed the state line, my father turned me into a mule for carrying his contraband beneath my coat or stuffed into the hollow of an old cloth bear whose innards had been removed to make a secret store for a bottle. I hated doing this. It scared and embarrassed me. I was afraid we would get caught and I would be thrown in jail. My parents teased me about my fear. They teased me about a lot of things.

Once, when we were having dinner in a restaurant in Omaha, Stanley looked at my mother and said, 'Violet, we don't have any money to pay the check.'

'Oh dear, Stanley, what are we going to do?'

'Looks like we're gonna have to wash the dishes.'

I was mortified, sure we would be arrested for our crime. 'What can we do?' I asked, tears welling up.

Neither of them answered.

'I still have the money from my allowance; can we pay with that?' Still they were silent.

'Will eleven dollars be enough?' I whispered.

'Nowhere near enough,' my father sighed.

By then I was trembling.

They laughed. Years passed before I forgave them for this.

I caught the measles on one trip, in Akron, Ohio. At least that's where Stanley said it happened. Two weeks later, on a September morning in 1948, at the Hotel Wolverine in Detroit, I woke up sweating, moaning, miserable, and covered in spots. My father didn't know

what to do, so he did what he always did in such circumstances –
hunted for someone he could ask.

Stanley's source of information and guidance, in almost every area
of his life, was whoever was at hand – be it a cab driver, some guy who
served him breakfast in a hotel coffee shop, or somebody he met at a
train station. He almost never read a book. He didn't even read
newspapers. But he liked to think of himself as 'well-informed'. For
this he turned to whoever happened to be nearby. At times, this habit
led to his expressing weird views on politics and the state of the world;
usually something he had picked up from a two-minute conversation
late at night, with someone he had just met. He would return from an
encounter to announce with conviction, 'I think we should stop
worrying about the Russians. It's the Chinese we gotta watch.' Or, 'I
just found out there's a gigantic volcano in Montana. It's a thousand
times bigger than the rest. When it erupts millions are going to die –
all the way to the Pacific Ocean. And guess what? As far away as Africa
people are gonna feel the blast.'

The subject about which Stanley needed information that day was
red spots on his kid's chest, so he pulled last night's dirty shirt over
his head, dragged a pair of slacks over his boxer shorts and without
stopping to comb his hair – something he almost always did before
going out in public – dashed downstairs to consult the best authority
he could find. Meanwhile, my mother ordered a bucket of ice from
room service and got busy rubbing down my body with a towel
dipped in cold water.

The 'authority' Stanley consulted that morning turned out to be a
desk clerk. The guy told him, 'It sounds like measles. There's a two-
week incubation period for measles.'

'A what?' he asked.

'It takes two weeks for the spots to show up. You want me to call the
hotel doctor?'

When Stanley got back to our room he announced, 'Leslie has the
measles. She caught them in Akron, Ohio two weeks ago. Remember

the kid with the runny nose at the place we stopped for breakfast? The one with the spots?' My mother said she didn't remember. I felt so rotten I didn't care. 'That's when she picked them up,' he said with certainty, authoritatively adding, 'The incubation period for measles is two weeks.'

The doctor arrived carrying the requisite bag covered in bumpy black leather. Despite my misery he made me laugh. He looked just like the doctor in a comic book I had been reading except that he didn't have one of those silvery disks strapped to his head. He said 'Umm' and 'Ah' a lot. He told me to open my mouth. He pressed a fat ice cream stick against my tongue and told me to make sounds. Then he stuck a thermometer in my mouth, made a few sounds himself and declared, 'It's measles. Keep her cool in a dark room and protect her eyes from light. Call me if you get worried.'

The band was supposed to play only one night at Eastwood Gardens in Detroit. The doctor said I couldn't be moved. My mother said she would stay in Detroit for a few days to look after me, then we would catch up with Stanley in Canada where the band was going next. My father agreed. He said he would leave us the Buick and travel on with the band on the bus.

That decided, he gave the bellboy $5 and told him to look after me while the two of them went shopping. As soon as they got back they plopped a pair of dark glasses on my nose and told me I was not to take them off. Then they handed me a flat box wrapped in bright paper. The card on top had a cartoon of a panther on it all covered with red spots, just like me. When I opened the box I found a game. It was Monopoly.

After Stanley left, my mother and I played Monopoly, and played Monopoly, and played Monopoly. Eventually, she got so bored with gaining and losing fortunes that she left me alone and went out. I called room service and ordered everything on the menu that sounded good, then ate none of it. Next I rang the bell captain, got a bellboy on the end of the phone, and talked him into playing

Monopoly with me as soon as he finished his shift. We played until I fell asleep.

Two days later my mother and I left in the Buick. With me in my dark glasses, this time sitting in the front seat, we set off for Canada to meet up with Stanley.

Some of the roads we would have to take from job to job were little more than dirt tracks, especially when we were in the Deep South and the Midwest. Others were turnpikes where you had to pay money and couldn't get off for miles if you missed a sign. In the autumn in New England, these turnpikes would be lined with giant trees shedding red and orange and purple leaves.

Sometimes if we were driving down a lonesome road, Stanley would announce that it was time to clean out the car. There was never any attempt to put rubbish into a bag and dispose of it later, say, when we got to a town. He would just put the top down, and we would throw out everything we no longer wanted. I don't know where my parents thought it would disappear to. It didn't matter, I guess. The United States was a big country then. You could drive a long way on a lonely road without even meeting another car. Pollution was a word nobody had ever heard of. Worrying about stuff like that was as silly as worrying that all the deer would disappear from Wisconsin or all the tigers from India. Everybody knew that could never happen.

There were arguments – sometimes between Violet and Stanley, sometimes between them and me. Often nobody knew who was angry with whom or about what. I think we frequently argued just for the sake of arguing or because we were so worn out.

Once, when I was seven, my father borrowed $5 from my savings to buy a carton of cigarettes. Two weeks later, driving through the Southern States, along a bumpy country road, I asked him to pay it back. 'You owe me five dollars,' I said.

'I don't owe you anything.'

'You do too. I want it back.'

The dispute went on. My mother chimed in, 'Stanley, if you owe Leslie money, pay it to her.'

'I am not going to be held to ransom by her fantasies,' he snapped.

'Don't be silly,' Violet replied. 'You borrowed that money from her. It was the day we stopped at the run-down gas station where the old guy was drinking applejack. Don't you remember?'

'Now you're both making it up,' he said. The argument went on for several minutes during which I became more and more frustrated. I could never stand what I saw as injustice. It is a personality trait that at times, throughout my life, has cost me dearly. But still my father refused to repay the money. Furious, I took hold of a heavy wooden coat hanger hooked over the back window on the driver's side and cracked it over Stanley's head as hard as I could. He was stunned. We were all stunned. Violet began to laugh hysterically. He joined in. He sounded like a donkey braying. The three of us laughed for a good ten minutes. When it was over, he apologised and paid me the $5 he owed me.

In the 1950s, Hollywood started making 'realism' movies. I remember watching scenes in some of them where a father would come home from work and slam his newspaper down on the kitchen table; then the mother would tell her children, 'For God's sake, don't disturb your father. He's had a hard day.' I never experienced any-thing like that in our family. There were no covert resentments. The three of us said whatever we thought to each other, with no holds barred. I have always been grateful for this. It wasn't until I was in my late twenties that I learned how unusual was the direct way we related to each other.

Every time life on the road got to be too much for my mother, she would take me back to Hollyridge, leaving my father to fend for himself. When I was five or six years old, Lockheed's Constellation hit the American skies. A stunningly beautiful plane, it was the first aircraft to fly coast to coast non-stop. It sat a then unheard-of one hundred people. As soon as it came on the scene, we forsook its puddle-hopping predecessors, which landed in Salt Lake and Kansas City on the way, and took the Connie. She cruised at an astonishing speed of 380 miles an hour. Her passengers were dressed as though they had just stepped off the pages of *Vogue* – Violet's favourite magazine. All meals were cooked on board. You could choose what you wanted to eat from lots of great stuff. I always ordered steak. When I was a child, steak and frogs' legs were my favourite foods, but they never offered me frogs' legs.

We flew east to west, west to east on the Constellation. Once, on the way from Los Angeles to New York, one of her four engines caught fire.

I remember sitting in the window seat right over the wing. Some pilot has told my mother that it is the safest place on any aeroplane. I look out the window. Flames are pouring from the engine. 'Look, look. We're on fire!' I shout with enthusiasm.

The captain's voice on the intercom says 'Ladies and gentlemen, we are experiencing a minor problem with a port engine. It is nothing to worry about. However, I am going to make an emergency landing in St Louis.' I can see that none of the passengers believe what he says about 'nothing to worry about'.

People start murmuring. I can hear them all the way down the aisle. A fat man across from us shrieks. Pretending to be calm, stewardesses rush around making people fasten seat belts. 'I repeat, there is nothing to worry about,' says the captain.

I'm surprised at how scared everybody is. To me this feels like a great adventure. When finally we land three fire engines are waiting for us and lots of men are running around squirting big hoses. It's even better than a movie.

On one of our trips home, my mother made a grim announcement. 'It's time you went to school,' she said. I hated the idea. What formal schooling I received in childhood could not have been more *ad hoc*.

My so-called education had started when I was four during a period when Stanley was away. A woman who lived down the street told my mother, 'Leslie should be in a nursery school. There's a good one nearby.' So my mother sent me.

The man who ran this 'good' school had a bulbous nose with acne scars all over it. He was sneaky – all smarmy when parents came to deliver us or pick us up. But as soon as the parents were gone, he ruled with an iron hand. He said we needed discipline and that we had to do exactly as we were told. These were not empty threats. I once watched him knock a little girl around for not doing something he had told her to do. He also said that if we so much as hinted that we had been 'punished', our parents could die in a terrible accident.

I hated his threats. Most of all, I hated him. I went home one afternoon and told my mother what I saw happening and how horrible the man was. She called the police. After that, I didn't have to go to nursery school. She said that 'the authorities' had investigated the school and closed it down. Thus ended the first phase of my formal education.

However, I had been reading from an early age. On the road there was not much else to do. I read one book after another, in dance halls, jazz clubs, and in restaurants. Like my mother, I loved books. Violet believed that books were essential to bringing up a child. She had begun to read to me on my first trip East, even before I was a year old. After Mom and I returned to Lakewood, she tried to convince Mom to read to me too. My grandmother was against the idea. She preferred taking me to the kitchen and showing me how to pluck chickens or can peaches. But Violet was always rummaging in bookstores, buying books and sending them home for me. Given Mom's lack of enthusiasm, I was forced to wade through most of them on my own, but by the time I was four I could read simple books out loud, even though sometimes I didn't know the meaning of the words.

After that, I read everything – train and bus timetables, road signs, menus, newspapers, cereal boxes – whatever I came across. Words were magical. Through the magic of books, especially stories about the Greek gods and their ambivalent morality, I escaped into a world of my own making, away from the adult craziness around me. Already a confirmed atheist when it came to the Christian god, I had absolute belief in Greek and Roman gods, since they behaved the way people in Hollywood behaved. Violet preened like Aphrodite to make her great beauty even greater. Stanley seemed like a cross between Prometheus, since he was long-suffering and heroic, and Hephaestus, god of the forge. The Hephaestus connection was obvious since, like him, Stanley loved making beautiful things, mostly music. But like the lame Hephaestus, I sensed my father was crippled in some way – not in body like the god, though he was certainly uncoordinated and gangly – more in the way he felt about himself. These gods made more sense to me than tales about good little angels and Santa Claus.

When I was six, my mother gave me a book called *The Country Bunny and the Little Gold Shoes* by DuBose Heyward. It was about a little bunny with a big dream: she was determined to become an Easter Bunny. All the other rabbits laughed at her. But Cottontail just folded her arms and said, 'Wait and see.' And she proved them wrong.

Like Cottontail, I was a little girl with big plans. Unlike Cottontail, I was not at all sure I would ever amount to anything, so I dared not speak to anyone about my dreams. But I had fallen in love with the idea that, one day, I too might become *wise, kind* and *good*. Each time I read Heyward's story I would bask in the belief that the people who told me I wasn't good enough could be proven wrong. What I didn't know then was how strongly myth can take hold of a child. I could never have imagined the effect it would have. It was to become almost a blueprint for my future life.

In the story, Cottontail gives birth to twenty-one babies whom she raises with great care. Now she has all these babies, the other rabbits are sure that her dream of becoming an Easter Bunny will never amount to anything. Like Mother Cottontail, I would give birth to my own brood very early on. I would have four children by four different men and raise them on my own. Like her too, I would be able to say the equivalent of, 'Yes, they do carry their ears rather well.'

And the parallels would not stop there. Another thing I was sure of as a child – although I could never have put it into words then – was that there was some other mysterious purpose to my life, which had to do with a gift I would be able to give to my children and to other people, and to animals as well. I couldn't imagine what this gift might be. I was only sure of one thing: this gift was something I would never be able to give *alone*.

When I was six, the inevitable happened. My mother sent me to school for real: first grade at Cheremoya School on the corner of Beachwood Drive and Franklin Avenue in Hollywood. I was adamant I wanted nothing to do with school ever and I protested vehemently the morning she delivered me to Miss Feeney's classroom. A middle-aged spinster, Miss Feeney was forced to endure my curses. 'I'm not staying in this goddamn school,' I shrieked. 'I hate it. I hate you. Get away from me!'

Within two days Miss Feeney had me eating out of her hand. I think she took one look at me, saw a ball of wild, undirected energy and decided to channel it by saddling me with as much responsibility as she could. She made me 'Hall Monitor', which meant I had to leave the classroom to take messages to teachers all over the school and to the principal's office – a privilege usually granted only to fourth-, fifth- and sixth-graders. She also gave me arithmetic problems to solve which were far beyond my abilities. She knew I was stubborn and that I wouldn't stop working on them until I succeeded.

I had never been happier. I developed a passion for school so strong that I begged to be taken early each morning so I could hang out with Miss Feeney. She really was the wisest and kindest person I had ever met.

I was only in Miss Feeney's class for five months before Stanley arrived unexpectedly from the East, to take my mother and me away.

He wanted us on the road with him. Lonely and afraid of living up in the hills on her own with me (in spite of the 'protection' offered by Tuffy), I think Violet was finding motherhood more daunting than she bargained for. She called Mom, asked her to come and look after our house and, with me in tow, hit the road again. I did not see the inside of a school again for several years.

A week after Stanley arrived to take us away, I had to say goodbye for ever to Cheremoya School and to Miss Feeney. She came to school especially early that morning. So did I. In her hand she was carrying a package wrapped in newspaper tied in string. 'This is for you, Leslie,' she said. I cut the string and tore off the paper. In my hands lay four books: Hugh Lofting's *The Story of Doctor Dolittle* and three sequels. 'They were mine when I was a little girl,' she explained. 'These were the books I loved most. I want you to have them so you can take them with you on your trip.'

I had never been given anything so precious. I carried those books with me through forty-eight states, Canada, South America and Europe. To this day they sit in a place of honour in my library. My children have all read them, as well as some of my grandchildren. I would read Miss Feeney's books over and over again – sitting in truck-driver cafés, under the red lights of nightclubs to the sound of my father's theme song, 'Artistry in Rhythm', crammed into the wings of a theatre while tap dancers did their thing on stage.

Uncertain about my own worth and living day after day from a suitcase, I never knew when I was supposed to sleep or when the next meal would arrive. The books acted like talismans for me. Each time I read about John Dolittle, Gub-Gub the pig and the Pushmi-pullyu, they reminded me of what I had learned from *The Country Bunny* and from Miss Feeney: I had a right to live. I was allowed to dream of becoming whatever I wanted to become, no matter what anybody else said or did.

7

ENTER THE DARK

F ROM A VERY early age, I was angry with my mother. I hated it when she 'messed' with me – which she did often. I had straight blond hair, almost white. She insisted it be made curly. Violet had seen Ingrid Bergman in *For Whom the Bell Tolls*. Soon after, she met Bergman at a Hollywood dinner, fell in love with her, and was dazzled by her beauty. 'She was wearing no makeup at all,' she said the morning after they met, 'except a little lipstick. She has got to be the most beautiful woman in the world.'

In the film Bergman's hair had been cut short and curled softly. Following my mother's new-found enthusiasm for her, she took me to the hairdresser. She told him to cut off all my straight hair and give what remained a 'permanent wave' so that I would look like a miniature Bergman. At the age of four, I hated sitting in a chair for hours with foul-smelling rollers that looked like the bones from chicken wings wrapped in my hair. Afterwards she had a photographer come to the house and photograph her and me with my phoney curls.

As a worshipper of Beauty, Violet had superb taste in all things physical and dressed in wonderful clothes which she wore with a grace and style that literally made Hollywood stars from Joan Crawford to Ava Gardner – even Bergman herself – envious.

Everything she touched became beautiful.

Naturally, she was determined to work her magic on me too. She would go shopping for clothes for me and come home with all sorts of tailored suits, little bolero jackets and wool sweaters. I hated all of them. I could not bear wool against my skin. It itched like crazy. I preferred dresses with ruffles and sashes that took half an hour for the maid to iron, and which tied in a huge bow at the back – as different from tailored suits and sweaters as you could get. We even disagreed over colours. Violet loved browns and beige. I loved red and pink and white. I have memories of the endless arguments we had over clothes from when I was five or six onwards. She often lost her temper with me. While violently pulling a striped wool sweater over my head, she would scream, 'I don't care what you think, you will wear this, like it or not!'

One day the argument between us became so heated that I tore off the sweater, picked up a knife from the kitchen and ran out the back door. No more than six years old, I was in such a rage I had no fear of anything. I ran along the road, which twisted through the mountains until it came to a steep stairway leading from the top of the hill all the way down to Beachwood Canyon. I sat down on the highest step. The dry dirty stains on my face betrayed the tears I had shed. In my heart a silent, deadly rage reigned. It was no longer towards my mother. It was not towards anything. It was just *there*. By then, my rage had taken on a life of its own.

I can see them now: a thin, black line of ants making their way across the top step. I sit and watch them, mesmerised by the trail they follow. How do they know where they're going? How do they get there in such order?

These ants become the focus of my rage for no reason other than they exist. I still hold the knife I took from the kitchen in my hand. With deliberation and full awareness of what I am doing I begin to cut each ant into pieces, watching with abstract curiosity as it writhes in agony and dies. I and the hatred have become one. I enjoy the killing. I love the feel of the knife in my hand and I like being able to destroy them. After murdering a dozen ants my rage disappears.

While I sat there, cutting up insects, another being within me had taken over. Shocked, I realised what I'd been doing and, in a few moments, she, I, we, began to feel again. Years later I would realise that, in that moment, I had come face to face with the nature of evil. I was shocked by how dangerous the lure of power can become.

'Killing ants?' you might laugh. 'Why, that's nothing – everybody kills ants, don't they?' Had someone asked me that question then, my answer would have been that it's one thing to kill insects but another to experience the kind of impotent rage that makes you enjoy having so much power over another being that you choose to kill it. It matters little what it is you are killing. The evil that takes you over when you do this and enjoy it is just the same. Knowing that I was capable of deliberate violence changed my six-year-old life.

That day marked the beginning of a realisation that each one of us is both light and dark. Only when we become aware of this can we begin to make conscious choices about what we choose to do and not to do. Until then we remain at the mercy of unconscious urges from within which drive our behaviour.

This knowledge has remained with me ever since. Of course we all love the light and want to live in it. Yet the quality of our life is greatly determined by how we relate to the darkness both inside us and in the world around us. Sooner or later, each of us has to come face to face with a major challenge: can we learn to love and bless both the light and the darkness? Not an easy task for any of us.

When I was seven, my mother spoke to me about the Holocaust. It was dusk. We were standing against the white picket fence in our back yard, looking out over all of Los Angeles and the sea beyond, eighty miles or more in three directions. The sun was setting. One by one, the lights of the city flickered on. I always loved dawn and dusk. I used to call them the 'in betweens' – in between day and night, in between what you see and what you think you see, in between something dying and being born.

'How did the Holocaust happen?' I asked her.

'Well,' she said, 'there are good people in the world and there are bad people – like light and dark. You and I are good people. The Nazis are bad.'

I thought that one over, as serious seven-year-olds do. Remembering the ants, I said, 'I don't believe you. People are all the same. We are all good and bad.'

'Where on earth did you get such an idea?'

'I saw it.'

'Saw it?'

'When I close my eyes I see a line of soldiers with guns in their hands. They're going to shoot somebody. I'm standing beside them. I've got a gun in my hand too.' My mother stared down at me. She looked frightened and angry at the same time. I knew I'd said something wrong. 'Well, that was what I *saw*,' I said in my defence.

I didn't know it then, but my experience with the ants, together with my vision of myself as part of a firing squad, presented me with the first inkling that my life was going to draw me into a wild and dangerous dance with light and dark. My own dance with the dark began early. What I came to understand about light and dark, good and evil, at the age of seven, has always stayed with me.

I was sure, even then, that each of us is both perpetrator and victim, rapist and raped, creator and destroyer. Later on I would come to see that, in some miraculous way, the dance between light and dark is akin to a passionate love affair: light hungers for the depth and richness of soul that darkness holds, while darkness longs to have its deepest pain seen, blessed and transformed by illumination.

It is not easy to come to terms with the powerful dance between light and dark if you happen to be someone born with strong polarities of both. My father was such a one. His radiance dazzled. It fostered his creativity, power and charisma. It made him an exceptional leader of men. His darkness was equally intense – so intense that in time it would destroy his life force because he so feared it and tried to hide it, especially from himself.

His mother, Stella, had behaved in erratic ways towards him while he was growing up. One minute she would praise him to the skies; the next she would spurn him, telling him he was a 'bad boy' or 'nasty child'. She made Stanley the scapegoat for her own miseries and frustrations – a practice that continued all through his life. My father feared how 'bad' he was, how 'wrong' he might be, how 'inept' – in perfect keeping with Stella's judgements of him. Her judgements seemed to have a kind of demonic power over him. Even though he did his best to drown out her insidious insinuations with activity, with meaningless affairs with women he cared nothing for, and with alcohol, these pursuits only shoved the whispers deeper inside him. The harder he tried to run away, the more what he always called his 'demons' pursued him.

My early memories of my father are a conflicting mixture of images and events. He was big in every way. He had hands twice the size of anyone else's. Reach an octave on the piano? That was nothing. He could manage a tenth with ease. Sometimes he was so full of angst that being with him was like being with someone I didn't know. Then, without warning, he would rage with terrifying force. I was scared of him when he shouted at me for not eating my dinner or for chewing my nails. Other times he was distant: towering above the rest of the world, sequestered behind the glass at the front of our car, the Hearse, or 3,000 miles away playing piano on some bandstand. He lived a lot in his own world. One moment he would behave like a lost animal who couldn't find his way home. The next he would become a playful child, making up nonsensical stories to make people laugh. He also had a will of steel when he wanted to use it.

I remember how big and insistent he had been the day he showed up unannounced in Miss Feeney's classroom and announced that he was taking me away from school. He stands still as a statue in the doorway, staring down at me. His head almost touches the top of the door frame. At first I don't recognise him. I haven't seen him for months. The last thing I expect is to find my father in my classroom. Then all at once I know it is Stanley. Nobody else smiles at me that way. No other man is that big. I lay my head down and rub my cheek against the desktop. It makes a funny sound. I pretend not to notice him.

Partly I was shy. Partly, I suspect, at some deep level, I knew even then that there was a powerful connection between us and it frightened me. My instincts told me this was something never to be made public.

Who knows how or for what purpose the lives of two people become inexorably bound together in a powerful double helix born out of our shared DNA and destiny? Seldom are we aware of the unknown choices we are making, or when we make them, or why. Yet somewhere deep in that sea of unknowing, choices must have been made, planting the seeds of a hidden union, that allowed it to grow.

Throughout his life Stanley was much loved and much maligned – sometimes by the same people. He was unpredictable, charming and good at almost everything he tried, except basketball and dancing. When the powers that be handed out talent, he got a lion's share. Yet he was terrified by his own brilliance and he abhorred criticism. Sometimes he would meet it head on with all the power of his six-foot-four frame. But no sooner would his curses fade to silence, than he would visibly shrink in size. 'Is that critic right?' he would say. 'Am I nothing? Less than nothing?'

He was often afraid. Out of the blue a dark shadow could appear over him. His blue eyes would glaze over and he would become another person. He even *looked* different. If I asked him a question when he was in this state, he wouldn't answer me. It was as if he had not even heard me. When I needed permission to do this or that and he paid no attention to me, I learned to walk away and do what I intended without it.

Sometimes when he changed in this way, it made me angry. I'd shove my elbow as hard as I could against his leg to make him wake up. He would look at me. Then his long arms would swing down to lift me up so we would be face to face. 'For God's sake, Shortstuff, what the hell do you want?' he would say. Then we would laugh. He knew I hated being tickled, more than anything, so he would tickle me. But there were times when not even my punching him could bring him back. I hated it when I couldn't reach him.

The times I liked best were when he and I took on a challenge together and pulled it off. One holiday he decided we needed to make our back yard wider. 'Let's build a retaining wall,' he said. The fact that he'd never built a retaining wall was of no concern to him.

'How do we do it?' I asked.

'We mix some concrete,' he said. 'Get some wood, dig a ditch, scrounge some soil ... I don't know. We'll figure it out as we go along.'

He was right. We did figure it out – just like the following year we figured out together how to rewire Mom's house. In the process we bickered, grumbled and giggled. When the retaining wall was finished, it seemed to me like the best retaining wall in the whole world.

In addition to building retaining walls and rewiring houses, my father and I shared other passions. One was music: from jazz to Rachmaninov, Prokofiev, Ravel, Janáček and Richard Strauss – anything so long as it had not been written before the beginning of the twentieth century. He was adamant that seventeenth-, eighteenth- and nineteenth-century music was 'not relevant to today'. He would not let me to listen to it. But Stravinsky or Ravel? We filled our house with their music. It had to be loud – loud enough that we could drown in it. If addiction is carried in the genes, this was certainly an addiction we shared. Left to our own devices, he and I would listen to music day and night, turning up the volume so high that my mother had to leave the house.

I developed a particular passion for Stravinsky. I couldn't get enough of him. I would lie on my belly at the far end of our living room, listening to *Rite of Spring* for hours at a time, mesmerised by the intricacies of it. Petrouchka and the Symphony *in* C touched lonely places inside me and awakened longings I didn't understand.

His music said to me, 'This is the real stuff of life – the sun around which everything revolves.' The music resonated with joy and grief, light and dark, tenderness and courage. Above all, it nourished me.

Another fascination Stanley and I shared was with the elements: blizzards, fires, violent winds, the sea. In the mountains above Los Angeles occasionally the winds turned into gales. When others retreated to the safety of their houses, he and I went out to play. Branches broke. Rain came and went. We stayed out in it, shouting and laughing, until we were drenched to the skin.

My father was, and probably always will be, one of the most complex human beings I have ever known. 'Stanley was going in so many directions at once that sometimes he lost himself altogether,' says Noel Wedder, who travelled with the band as its publicist in the 1960s. He is one of the few men still alive who *knew* Stanley (at least during that decade of his life) and loved him – warts and all. 'Stanley had a tendency to talk off the top of his head,' Noel says. 'At times he could be very malevolent and cruel. If he found an opening in someone, he would tear into them, opening it up until it became a real wound.'

I know what Noel was talking about. My father hated anything he perceived to be weaker than he was. This would come out in irrational anger when you least expected it. Some of the things he said with no apparent provocation used to horrify me when I was a kid.

'I despise those skinny little dogs,' he said to me one morning on our way to a recording session at Capitol Records.

'What skinny little dogs?' I asked.

'Oh, you know, those Mexican things that shiver all the time.'

'Chihuahuas?' I said.

'Yeah. Right. Chihuahuas. They remind me of rats. Whenever I see them I wanna kick them.'

And yet I recall a night at Hollyridge when I woke up to the sound of someone crying and tiptoed downstairs. Stanley was sitting at the kitchen table, his head slumped over something lying on a towel. As

I came close I could see a little dog half wrapped in the old towel he always carried in the back of the Buick to clean the windshield. The terrier's eyes were closed and, except for the blood on his hip and leg, he looked like he was sleeping.

'I've killed him,' Stanley tells me. 'He ran in front of the car. I couldn't stop,' he sobs.

'That's terrible.' I reach out to stroke the dog's muzzle. I have never touched anything dead before. It feels strange, as though he is no longer a dog at all but an empty shell. 'Do you know who he belongs to?' I ask.

'I carried him up and down Beachwood until I found his owner. He belongs to an old woman. She cried and told me he always chases cars. She said his name is Otto. She asked me to take him away.'

'We better bury him. I'll get the shovel.'

By now it is around 1 a.m. The three of us – Stanley, me and the dead dog – go through the gate that leads down the hill from the back yard. We dig a grave. We wrap Otto in a clean white towel I have stolen from my mother's linen cupboard and we tuck him into the earth.

We didn't tell my mother about Otto. She never figured out what happened to her missing towel. From as early as I remember, Stanley and I had secrets between us that were always kept.

8

CRISIS

MY PARENTS' STRUGGLE to blend being on the road with marriage and family went on for eight years. Neither was willing to give up the marriage, yet neither knew how to make it work. At one point they decided to set up 'ground rules' for periods when they were apart from each other. Stanley would do his work. They would speak at least once a week. Violet would go out with friends and entertain herself any way she pleased so she did not get bored on her own. This she did four or five nights a week – dinners, clubs, theatres, parties.

At one such party she met a man who would change our lives for ever: Dr Bernie Gindes. Bernie presented himself as psychiatrist extraordinaire. He was a Freudian. From the day Violet met him, he was constantly at our house. Bernie, who was never to be seen without a cigar in his mouth, analysed everything and everyone – dreams and attitudes, behaviour, values, ideas: you name it. On meeting him, my mother became devoted to psychiatry. She read every book she could get her hands on about it.

She shared her new interest in psychiatry with Stanley, and together they became hooked by this latest Hollywood fad – a cure for all their ills: 'Nothing is impossible through the miracle of psychiatry,' they insisted. They not only talked about psychiatry and read about it (something pretty amazing for Stanley since he seldom read anything); they decided to get into analysis immediately as a way of resolving their problems.

The deeper Stanley got into psychoanalysis with Gindes the more fascinated he became with the human psyche. My father was smart but his mind was undisciplined so he was always a bit of a sucker for a quick fix. He loved the idea of learning to control the mind – his own and other people's.

Before long Stanley was analysing everybody he met. Anyone who did not agree with him or who wouldn't do as he wanted them to, he decided was 'sick'; that is, mentally ill. I suspect he lost a few good friends from having told them – for their own good, of course – that although they didn't realise it, they 'needed psychiatric help' to sort out their problems. As such proclamations were not usually well received, he began to be more circumspect with his pronouncements on mental health. Instead of telling the people to their face that they were crazy he started telling other people that they were. My father also had a tendency to project on to whoever happened to be around him whatever he didn't want to acknowledge in himself.

So excited was Violet about the glories of psychiatry that she tried to get everyone she knew who had any money (it was an expensive pastime) to be analysed. It would not be until a few years down the road that she would discover that Gindes-the-Magnificent was not even a doctor. Nor did he have any training whatsoever in psychology or anything related to it. Nonetheless, for the next two years, this hairy-chested, cigar-chewing phoney became my parents' 'guru'. He told them how they should handle home and family conflicts. He guided Stanley in the band business. He advised them to live 'separate lives' for a while, which they did.

Long before Bernie came up with the separate lives agenda, Stanley had been living his own 'life of freedom'. He had been through a string of affairs with other women, some of them my mother's friends. But now, following Gindes's suggestion that they create an open marriage – under the good doctor's guidance, of course – men began to appear at Hollyridge. They took my mother on dates and courted her favours. Sometimes they courted me too in an effort to get closer to her.

One of these men was my mother's second cousin – a favourite of

Mom's. He was the son of Mom's father's sister. Violet had first met him when they were still children. I was instructed to call him 'Uncle Jimmy'. Her other suitors included an endless stream of not very interesting people, with a few exceptions such as the singer-bandleader Billy Eckstine. During this period she became pregnant by one of them. One day, out of the blue, she said to Audree, 'I've just had my first abortion.' No further words were spoken.

During the psychoanalytic phase of my parents' lives, inevitably Violet decided that I also needed *help*. As she pointed out, I stored my clothes in heaps under my bed, frequently refused to comb my hair and insisted on wearing sundresses in the dead of winter. So she looked for, and found, a child psychologist. The guy was probably a friend of Gindes. Thankfully, he was nowhere near as revolting. She introduced him to me as a 'friend'. He came and went at Hollyridge, watching my every move. He gave me test after test in the guise of games. In the end, he told my mother that my IQ was over 160 and advised her not to worry about my storing clothes under the bed. He said that she had two choices: either she could turn me into a child prodigy – a musician, a dancer, a mathematician – or she could help me lead 'as normal a life as possible'.

My mother opted for having me live the 'normal life' – not the easiest of tasks given the family I had been born into. That decided, the next thing she did was take me to the Hollywood dance studio of Adolph Bolm, the most respected and acclaimed teacher of ballet in the United States.

Bolm was like no one I had ever met. He did the same things my parents and everybody in Hollywood did, like drink and smoke. But he never became addicted to anything. When he found himself craving another drink or cigarette, he would stop until all his cravings disappeared.

I loved learning to dance under Bolm. I was quite sure that, for him, psychoanalysis held no fascination. Only the body mattered. Movement mattered. *Doing* mattered, not sitting around analysing stuff. I longed to have more people around me who lived the way he did.

I showed up for my first lesson expecting to meet lots of gorgeous little girls in pink costumes. My candy-floss notions bore no resemblance to what he had in store for me. Not only was each lesson carried out alone with Bolm, the reality of what we did together was not at all what I had expected. Bolm had brought the discipline and dedication of his training with the Russian Imperial Ballet to his Hollywood studio. He would work me at the *barre* until my body ran with sweat. He treated me the way horse trainers break horses, except without the lead or bridle. He would stand in the centre of the floor and make me walk around him again and again until every movement was co-ordinated – right arm forward, left leg backward, and on and on. My head had to be carried as though it were suspended from heaven on an invisible cord. My feet were to be placed as simply as possible one after another.

He insisted there be no drama or showiness to any of my movements. If, given my theatrical bent, I tried to introduce them, his kindly manner and warm humour would be replaced by a fierce voice telling me that *everything* I did was wrong.

One of the longest and most painful hours in my life was spent with Bolm trying to carry out one of his 'simple walks'. There was no way I could get it right. The harder I tried, the more tears I shed. I ignored them, knowing that he too would pay them no attention. I was afraid he would get angry with me for being such a wimp.

After an hour of this, sweating like a racehorse, I finally got it right. Everything became easy. It was no longer me doing the movement, but the movement doing me. Amazing. Exciting. Wonderful. I gathered the courage to ask if I would be able to wear toe shoes soon.

He laughed out loud. 'Absolutely not,' he said. 'It will take four years of hard work – maybe longer – before your body is strong enough to even think of points.'

'Oh,' I replied. I didn't dare ask about tutus or if one day he would let me join a class with other girls.

Three months after my beginning work with Bolm, Stanley summoned us to go on the road again. That meant leaving Bolm. Part of me felt relieved. For, next to Mom's disciplinary training, working with Bolm was the hardest thing I ever had to endure in my young life and the first thing I had actually chosen to do myself. Until then, I had been used to spending time on my own keeping out of everybody's way. The bigger part of me missed Bolm terribly. The day we left again to go on the road, I felt that I was letting myself down as much as I was letting him down. He died two years later; his death marked the end of my dream of becoming a dancer.

Over the next couple of years, the Kenton music continued to gain recognition and popularity, while my mother grew ever more frustrated about the way the all-encompassing world of being a public figure had engulfed Stanley. Stanley was often on the road, leaving Violet unhappy at home yet unwilling to join him on tour. In his letters and phone calls home, Stanley often blamed Carlos Gastel's bookings for the band – and Carlos himself – for keeping them apart, but despite Stanley's complaints about Carlos, three years would pass before he dealt with the issues he worried about.

The band's burgeoning success, coupled with mounting tensions in his marriage, had my father in a frenzy. He began to work even harder, to sleep less, drink more and take far too many pills, just to keep going. He often fell ill. My father's illnesses were almost always violent. The symptoms would vary – from pain in his liver to uncontrollable vomiting, fever, an inability to sleep and what he called 'the shakes'.

These sicknesses were accompanied by distortions in his thought processes and feelings. He would flare up in anger for no apparent reason. He would tumble into despondency, believing not only that the world did not appreciate his music but that it was actively trying to destroy him.

Given the intensity of Stanley's life force and his almost total lack of concern for his body, his ill health was not surprising. He treated his body ruthlessly, as though it were a machine on which he expected to be able to rely no matter what he did to it. No sleep – why worry? Alcohol? Well, of course he drank. Didn't everybody?

Then there were the pills. Our bathroom cabinet was full of them. On the road they travelled with him in a little bag stuffed into the pouch of his suit carrier. He once explained to me that each pill had a different 'personality': opiates, stimulants, antihistamines, narcotics. He told me he got to know them by experimenting. He had learned to mix them into even more potent potions depending on his needs: a central nervous system depressant swallowed with a short-term hypnotic, such as pentabarbital, calms convulsions, he said. It helps you sleep a few hours. Can't wake up? No problem. Get the hotel operator to ring several times, then pop a Dexedrine to make sure you don't go back to sleep. No time to eat? A little Dexy and you forget all about food too. Take one more and you fly.

'Benzedrine helps keep my wits about me,' he said. 'It makes me confident. It keeps me awake. I can keep going on it, even when I think I'm going to drop. Dexedrine helps me kick the blues.' But mix too many of these magic cocktails together, add alcohol to the brew, and the results can be devastating. For him, they often were.

Drugs affected my father physically, mentally and – it appeared to me – even psychically. It would sometimes seem as if his body had become invaded by the foreign energies he called his 'demons'. He would start to move repetitively in meaningless stereotypical ways, known by mental-health experts as 'knick-knacking' or 'tweeking'. At times, convinced he'd been infested with parasites, he would pick at his skin and wash his hands again and again, trying to get rid of them.

To Stanley, Violet had always been the cure for whatever ailed him. So long as he had her by his side, so long as she still loved him, so long as she never left him, he knew that, sooner or later, things would be all right. The moment she arrived and opened the door to his hotel room, having crossed America to be by his side, he felt he could breathe again. Life was safe.

He was wrong. On her birthday, 30 December 1946, my mother told my father she was going to file for divorce. She said she was going to take me to Las Vegas with her, where we would stay for the six weeks needed to finalise the divorce. Two weeks later, we arrived at a dude ranch in Nevada, where we went on picnics with the other guests and my mother learned to fly light aircraft. Then, one afternoon in early February, my mother got a phone call from Kansas City. It was Stanley. He pleaded with her not to go through with it. He was on his way home. He loved her. He was sorry he had always been so self-obsessed. He would change now. He promised. She gave in. And life carried on much as it had always done.

The strain of being on the road was taking a vicious toll on my father's mind and body. By the middle of April 1947, he was on the verge of collapse. Without warning, while playing at the University of Alabama in Tuscaloosa, he disbanded the orchestra, paid his musicians two weeks' salary, gave them their train fare home, and disappeared. Nobody knew where he had gone.

He told me, years later, that when all this happened, he had felt betrayed and deserted by everyone – by my mother, who was still refusing to go on the road, by a singer who had fallen sick and by dozens of others. That night, after finishing the job in Tuscaloosa he had climbed into his Buick and driven away.

'I felt like I was losing everything,' he said. 'I was sick of music, sick of the road, sick of fighting to keep my life from breaking into a million pieces.'

He drove aimlessly around, thinking. He decided he would quit the band business altogether and get himself an 'ordinary job'. Two days after his disappearance, he drove past a lumber camp. He decided he would apply for a job there. He turned the Buick around, got off the main road and headed down a long dirt track leading to a foreman's hut.

'I want a job,' he said to the man.

'What can you do?'

'I can do anything.'

The man looked at Stanley's hands. 'You never done a day's work in your life.'

'I can learn!'

'Not here you can't, Mister.'

With nowhere to go, in a state of complete exhaustion, he stopped at a gas station down the road to ask if he could use their phone. From there he placed a collect call to my mother. 'I'm beat,' he said. 'I've fired everybody. I don't want anybody to know where I am. I want to come home – but not yet. Can you and Leslie meet me somewhere? Then, in a few weeks, we can all go home together.'

They agreed that we would meet in Texas. The next day, Violet and I climbed on a plane. Stanley drove non-stop to get there. The three of us spent two weeks together in Mineral Wells. My parents slept a lot and walked on the land together. I rode horses. Sometimes Stanley rode with me.

When we got back to Hollyridge he made us both swear we would tell no one he was there. For the next four months, he stayed at home and spoke to nobody. It took weeks to clear the drugs, the booze and the exhaustion. After that he became a different man – peaceful, calm and happy – at least for a time.

Friday, 30 May 1947 – Memorial Day weekend. We woke at dawn and drove from Hollyridge to Balboa for a few days' vacation on the beach – Violet, Stanley, Mom, me, and Tuffy, since I refused to leave him behind. Three hours down the road, we passed a sign saying 'Boats for Sale'.

'Boats. Hey, let's buy a boat!' Stanley says, turning the car around.

'Great, a boat!' I echo. 'Can we buy one now?'

'Sure.'

The boats beneath the garish sign turn out to be 35-foot Steelcraft cabin cruisers, as ugly as sin. Made of heavy-gauge steel, they're lethal weapons in the hands of amateurs.

'How much are your boats?' Stanley asks. The little man who runs the boat yard tells him they cost several thousand dollars. 'We'll take one,' says my father. 'That one with the white line around it.'

'Yes,' my mother says. 'I do like the white line, Stanley.'

'Good choice,' the little man replies. 'When would you like to pick it up?'

'Now.'

'Now?'

'Yeah.'

'No, no. She has to be weather stripped. She should be fitted with an automatic bilge. You'll need a dinghy . . . and bedding, and dishes, life jackets and . . . How about next week?'

'Nope. We want to take her out this afternoon.'

'How are you going to pay for it?' the man asks, sensing he is beginning to lose ground.

'Cash,' says my father.

Fearing the loss of a sale, the man shakes his head. 'OK, I'll do the best I can. Give me two hours.'

'Right,' says my mother. 'That'll give us time to buy what we need and get back here after lunch. Let's see: food, dishes, paper cups. Did you say life jackets? We've got Tuffy's dog dish and some canned food. Leslie, get me a pad of paper from the glove box so I can make a list.'

First we go to the bank. Stanley withdraws a big wad of $100 bills. The customers and cashiers stare at him. I stand by, delighted that they might think my father is a bank robber. From there we head for the ships chandlers where everything looks inviting. My parents pick out captain's hats, life jackets, ropes. I don't think Stanley was quite sure what ropes were for, but he knew you were meant to have ropes on boats, so he bought a big selection.

Like invading hordes, we descend on a food store, coming away with enough food to fill three galleys. We pile it all into the back of the car together with the ropes and life jackets: bedding, potato chips, beer, whisky, paper cups, a waterproof jacket for Mom. We head back to the boat yard.

Mom is not at all sure we are making the right decision in buying a boat. 'Stanley, you're bound to get seasick,' she says. 'What do you know about boats anyway?'

'Don't worry, we'll figure it out,' he says.

A couple of hours and one purchase of a boat later, we set out on our first adventure. The water is as smooth as glass. By 3.30 p.m. the swell has risen to ten feet high. The boat is swamped. Dressed in new marine gear and captain's hats, Violet and Stanley try desperately to clear the water that, by now, is flooding the deck. They use whatever they can find – a bucket, a pitcher, their cupped hands. All the while they're vomiting into the wind. It takes them a long time to figure out which side is the right side of the boat to throw up over so the vomit doesn't return to cover them. Before long Tuffy vomits too – all over me. Mom sits stone still at the table in the galley, holding on and shouting, 'Stanley, for God's sake, stop rockin' the boat!'

We didn't drop anchor until 2 a.m. My parents swore they would never spend another night on the damned boat. We agreed to head home first thing in the morning. In the end, we did no such thing. What none of us knew then was that the boat bug had already bitten us bad and there is no escape once it gets hold of you. Thus began my father's and my shared obsession with this tub-for-a-boat and, more importantly, with the sea on which we floated her. For Stanley and me, being on our boat in the sea turned into another passion akin to the one we had for playing Ravel at full volume. We spent every weekend that summer on our boat. I learned everything I could about how to handle her.

As soon as Violet and Stanley found their sea legs, we stayed clear of afternoon crossings when the Pacific got too wild for small boats. I had never seen my parents as happy. Floating in this steel tub in the Pacific Ocean, Violet forgot about being perfectly groomed. She treated boating as a light-hearted romance. She stuffed her bleached blond hair beneath a captain's hat and wrapped a sarong around her body. She laughed with Stanley and me. Her laughter was very different to the hysterical outbursts I was used to, which often turned to tears or anger. It was a magic time. Like all magic times, it did not last.

Within a few months, for reasons I never understood, our boat became invaded by a lot of people. Maybe my parents were *afraid* of being happy together. Or maybe they wanted to share their happiness with others. I don't know.

At first the 'invaders' were fun. Except that, as always, the alcohol flowed fast and furious when they came aboard. In the beginning my parents invited one or two couples from the band. But the quality of guests hit rock bottom when Dr Bernie Gindes and his mousy wife arrived. By that time he was being paid a small fortune to direct my parents' lives. Each day he would drink his way through a dozen gin and tonics, while making pompous remarks about *complexes* and *repression* and analysing everybody's dreams. Naturally, whenever he approached me, I told him I never had any dreams.

Eventually my father's family – Stanley's mother Stella, her daughter Beulah and one or two of Beulah's children, such as my cousin Barton, and some of the other Kentons – began to show up too. Then my mother's laughter, which a few weeks earlier had been so infectious, turned shrill and took on an edge of desperation.

Stella hated me. I knew this the way an animal 'smells' an enemy and does its best to avoid it. My parents pooh-poohed me when I brought the subject up, but I believe they knew she did too. It would just have been inconvenient for them to admit it.

It was late morning the day after we arrived in Catalina. We were tied up to somebody else's buoy. My parents had taken the dinghy to a nearby boat for drinks. I was lying on the top bunk in the galley reading. My cousin Barton, who was a year or two older than me, got into the bunk beneath me, put his feet against the bottom of my bunk and kicked as hard as he could. Propelled into the air, book and all, I came smashing down on to the galley floor. I screamed. The pain in my shoulder and collarbone was excruciating. Stella was on deck. She rushed into the cabin, grabbed me by the arm, and yanked me to a standing position. I kept screaming.

'Stop it, Leslie! Right this minute,' she bellowed. 'Do you hear me?'

I couldn't stop. I hurt too much. I was terrified. I'm not sure if I was more scared of the pain or of Stella. Her face, at the best of times, looked like an ageing bloodhound. Now, it was so twisted up that it resembled the head of a rabid dog.

'I want my father,' I cried.

'Be quiet!'

'I want my mother!' I screeched, pulling away from her and running out on deck. 'Help,' I cried, 'help, help!'

No one heard.

'I'll have no more of this nonsense,' Stella growled. 'You'll do as I say or you'll have me to deal with. Sit down.'

Even through my tears I could see I'd been trapped. I tried hard to stifle the sound, but the tears wouldn't stop. My body began to shake. Barton was standing behind Stella at the entrance to the galley looking down at me. It seemed to me that he was smiling. I don't know how long I lay slumped against the stern, cold and trembling, even though my head was burning in the California sun. Eventually I fell asleep.

My parents returned in the late afternoon to find me there. Stanley asked what was wrong.

'She just had a little fall,' said Stella.

'That's not true,' I said. 'Barton shoved me off my bunk with his feet. I landed on the galley deck. It hurts awful. I can't move my arm.'

'Stop behaving like Sarah Bernhardt,' snapped Stella, echoing something she had heard my parents say to me from time to time. She pulled me to my feet. My mother took one look at the strange way I was holding my shoulder and mumbled in a voice saturated with alcohol, 'Stanley, we need to find a doctor.'

'Don't fuss so, Violet,' snapped Stella in a shrill voice. 'You always spoil the child. Where on earth are you going to find a doctor here?'

'You're sure she's all right?' Stanley said.

'Of course she's all right. She doesn't need a doctor. We can have her seen to when we get back to the mainland if she doesn't straighten herself out by then,' Stella replied, glaring at me with steely eyes.

Two days went by before we returned to the mainland – two days in which my parents went here and there while Stella babysat me and my cousin. My shoulder swelled so badly I could not bear to touch it. I lost the use of my left arm. Before long the pain became so familiar it seemed like I had lived with it all my life.

Having to stay on that boat with Stella felt like I'd been thrown into hell. The worst of it was when she decided I had to go swimming with my cousin. She made us put life jackets on. The life jackets were filled with cork which, when wet, became unbearably heavy. She lifted a wet orange life jacket and ordered me to put my arms through the opening. I could not even lift my arm. The pain was so bad I felt I was going to vomit or pass out. She pushed me into the water. Once there, the cork floated, taking most of the weight of the jacket off my shoulder. The water was so cold my body went numb but I stayed in as long as I could. I knew when she pulled me out, the weight of the jacket would bring back the horrible pain.

The third day after the accident we crossed back to the mainland. By then my parents were sober. They could see that something was seriously wrong. They dropped Stella and Barton at her home in South Gate. From there, my mother called Dr McCarthy. He, in turn, rang the Queen of Angels Hospital and spoke to the chief surgeon. By the time we arrived at the hospital, Dr McCarthy was there waiting for us. He personally took me into X-ray.

My collarbone had been broken in two places. My shoulder had been dislocated. Because children's bones knit quickly, mine had already begun to set askew. They rushed me into the operating theatre. The surgeon re-broke the bone, reconnected my shoulder and packed me into a cast. It looked like a white bolero and itched like crazy. As I lay in the recovery room at the hospital, vomiting and trying to shake off the effects of the anaesthetic, I worked out in my child's mind that all this pain had been a punishment for something I must have done. I kept asking myself what it could have been. I vowed that I would never trust Stella again.

9

VALE OF TEARS

Stanley's success had soared from 1946 to 1948, but they were tough years for him personally. He had been able to salvage his marriage by pleading with my mother at the last minute not to go through with the Nevada divorce. Yet the push-me-pull-you conflicts continued. So did his reliance on her love and attention and his dependence on prescription drugs. From the day in Alabama when he broke up the band and disappeared into the wilds of Arkansas, even he had begun to suspect that the tensions had become more than he could safely manage. 'My life is coming apart at the seams,' he kept saying. After those months during which he refused to answer the telephone or tell anyone where he was, and all the time we spent on the boat, the process of recovering his equilibrium had been progressing. But this did not solve the marriage problems.

The demand for his music had grown exponentially and he worked himself harder and harder as a result. As his reputation grew and his innovative Progressive Jazz began to win more admirers, he decided that 'Stan Kenton' had become someone too complex for Carlos Gastel to manage any more. He decided to manage the band himself.

By the autumn of 1948, the band had become the hottest box office draw in the country, but Stanley was in a state of continual frustration over where to go next. Yet he continued to become embroiled in conflicts with promoters after Carlos's departure. He was frustrated by a public whose traditional tastes, he believed, prevented him from creating a new kind of music. Most troubling of all, he had grown more and more afraid he would lose Violet.

All this brought him to breaking point. He did the only thing he knew to do: during a sell-out stint at New York's Paramount Theater in December 1948, he quit the music business, 'for ever'. He sent a telegram to each musician in the band saying he was going on 'an extended holiday' with his family. After that he would be entering UCLA to get a degree, he said. Then, having developed a fascination with psychoanalysis, he would go to medical school and become a psychiatrist. Leaving behind dozens of bemused and angry people whose lives his announcement had turned upside down, he remained adamant that this was how it was going to be.

We returned to Hollyridge for several weeks. Then one day we got into the car and headed for New Orleans to begin the first, last and only real holiday we ever had together. It was an amazing time: at last, my parents seemed genuinely happy; we laughed our way through the shimmering streets of New Orleans, and danced in the exhilarating Mardi Gras Carnival in Rio. I drank champagne for the first time and learned to play poker like a professional card shark.

By the middle of June we were back at Hollyridge. Stanley was still undecided about what he wanted to do with his career. He loved the Latin rhythms and music he had heard in South America, but he didn't want to get into the same old rut – beating himself up on the road as he had done in the years before. He was still not playing the music he wanted to play. He didn't know how to convince the guys at Capitol Records and GAC (the General Artists Corporation), nor his public who adored him, to let him do that. They wanted him to go on playing the same stuff he had played a thousand times before.

He was mostly worried about two things: first, he knew he had got so caught up in making his career a success that he had written nothing of his own for years. Second, he kept saying, he didn't believe he could write anything good. He needed more training. He said he was also scared that if he followed his heart and tried to do something innovative, he would lose his public success and not be able to make a living. So he waited and he wondered what to do next.

*

While my father continued to juggle possibilities and consider the shape of his future career, I went through my own personal crisis. During our long trip to New Orleans and South America, we had left Tuffy in the care of a couple my parents had hired to live-in and look after Hollyridge. When we finally got home from the trip, we discovered that the people who had been house-sitting for us had been beating Tuffy. As a result, he bit the postman.

Two days after we returned home Tuffy disappeared. It was as if he had vanished into the ether. My mother said she had to send him away to live on a farm so he wouldn't hurt anybody else. When I lost Tuffy, I lost any sense I had developed about who I was. With him gone, there seemed no point in my living any more. Tuffy was not only my best friend, he was the only real source of security I had ever known – the one creature in the world I could rely on. Now Tuffy was no more. When tears came, I hid them, trying to appear tough. I could no longer bury my head in his beautiful ruff when I felt scared or lonely, no longer whisper my troubles to him knowing he understood.

With Tuffy gone I stopped hiking in the hills. My mother would probably have let me go alone by then, but that didn't matter since I had no desire to play and there was nowhere I wanted to go without him. For weeks I closed the door of my room, lay on the floor and took refuge in solitude. I read one book after another. When Violet went out, I would go to the living room to play records – Rachmaninov, Debussy, Prokofiev, Stravinsky, Mussorgsky, Aaron Copland, Ravel, Gershwin – as loud as our speakers would let me. When she was home I would go back into my room to listen. I began to drown myself in music, the way I had once drowned myself in Tuffy's fur. Music and my bedroom – with the doors locked – became my 'safe places'.

In a way, so did Hollyridge itself. I loved that house passionately. It was *my* house – my *home* – and always would be. When nobody else was there, it became transformed into a world of magic for me. Just about every dream I ever dreamed that was not a nightmare took place in that house. I dream about it to this day.

One morning, at the beginning of December 1949, my mother and father went out together for a late breakfast at Du-par's Restaurant. 'Best place for pancakes in the world,' Stanley always said. Du-par's was on Vine Street, next to Capitol Records. We often went there.

That morning, a bomb exploded the future he had been ruminating over for more than a year. Violet told him point blank she'd had enough of their marriage. 'She said she wants no more of it,' he told me. 'She said she's gonna marry Jimmy Foster. I never thought that would happen. Never.'

I think her announcement shook him as nothing had done before. The impending loss of my mother not only left Stanley bereft, it plunged him into a maelstrom of fear and despondency. For fifteen years she had been there whenever he needed her, even when they had been thousands of miles apart physically.

There was something more to his sense of loss as well. From the time he was born Stanley had taken direction and sustenance from a woman. In the beginning Stella had served as his guidance system, controlling his life. She taught him what to be, what to think, where to go next. She urged him to become a 'good boy' – not like his father, Floyd, whose image she had blackened to such a degree that all her children came to look upon their father as an outcast and to treat him as such.

As a result of his upbringing, complete with Stella's praise and calculated punishments, my father grew up with a belief that, without her, he was worthless. He believed that her strength and her savvy would forever supply the guidance and power he needed to become great. He would never be successful without her. This was how an insidious pact got made between them: so long as he stayed close to Stella, listened to her and followed her guidance, she would make sure his life went well. The bottom line was that she had taught him that he had better remain dependent on her, since he had no power of his own.

Despite all his analysis and rebellion, I don't think my father ever became fully conscious of the hold his mother had on him. He would struggle for independence from her one moment, while placating her wishes and demands the next. He despised her, yet felt powerless before her strength. He did everything he could to break away from her, yet, from the time he left high school to make his way in the world, their pact remained in force.

Having been brainwashed in this way he was impelled to seek power outside himself – from another woman. And the woman would dedicate herself to his success. This is, after all, what women are supposed to do for the men they love, are they not?

When, at the age of twenty-three, he met Violet, he sensed a different energy in her. Unlike Stella with all her dark machinations, Violet was radiant – clear as a fountain. Although she was stunningly good looking, the purity of her spirit transcended her physical beauty. Her energy was clean, as far away from Stella's cold-hearted controlling as you could get. He responded to this in Violet as he responded to no one else he ever met. Nor, he told me before he died, did he ever meet it again. Violet became his tuning fork. Her light vibrated with his own at a level even deeper than the heavy programming Stella had carried out on him.

When they got married, Stanley's dependence on Stella as his power source shifted to Violet. She filled the emptiness Stella's machinations had instilled in him. It was perhaps not surprising that Stella's hatred for her daughter-in-law came to know no bounds. She did everything possible to undermine the closeness between them. Six years later when Violet gave birth to me, Stella transferred a good portion of her hatred for my mother to this fruit of her union with my father.

The day my mother ended their marriage, a vast repository of self-recrimination and fear which had been locked away exploded into Stanley's life. Broken open by Violet's desertion, he began to rage. She had betrayed him. He hated her. He needed her. He loved her.

Did her leaving him mean he was worthless? He feared he had failed as an artist – failed as a husband. He felt impotent. The implications of this were unbearable. So he sought refuge in what he knew best. 'That morning at Du-par's I made a decision,' he told me. 'I was going back to music. I had no choice.' The future on which he had counted and on which he believed he could rely was gone. There was nothing he could do about it. His ambition to write 'new music' was all he had left.

Before Christmas that year he made a public announcement: 'I'm putting together a forty-piece orchestra. It's gonna have strings – sixteen of 'em. And lots of other instruments foreign to jazz but at home in concert halls: English horns, oboes, bassoons, maybe a tuba.' By New Year's Day, 1950, my father had begun to rehearse musicians at El Capitan Theatrer in Hollywood. His passion for the pioneering venture, called 'Innovations in Modern Music', inspired one musician after another to join his quixotic quest.

My parents kept their divorce secret from me until a few days before my mother and I were to leave Hollyridge. Meanwhile, the tears had been flowing in our house ever since our return from South America. When Stanley's came, he pretended they were not there. He would wipe his face and leave the room. Violet's ran silent, like the tears of a woman walking in the rain who pays no attention to anything around her. I was submerged in my own grief over the loss of Tuffy.

It was Violet who eventually gave me the news of their break-up. It was early morning. Stanley had gone to a rehearsal or was working on new arrangements for Innovations with Pete Rugolo at Capitol. She and I were alone at Hollyridge. I remember everything about that morning: the smell of her perfume (it was called Tabu), the way the sun pours through the French doors of the dining room like corn syrup, the heavy shadows from the table and chair legs falling across the rose-coloured carpet.

I'm piling a mountain of white sugar on half a grapefruit which sits in front of me. Sugar crystals stick to the silver spoon. They tickle my tongue as I lick them off – something I am normally forbidden to do. I find it strange that my mother doesn't tell me off for doing this. Nor does she tell me off for eating the soft parts of my white toast and leaving the crusts.

'I have something to tell you, Leslie.'

'OK,' I say, paying no attention. I'm trying to figure out what to do today.

'Leslie?'

'Umm.'

'We're going to move.'

Still lost in plan-making, I hardly hear her.

'Leslie, we're leaving Hollyridge. We are going to Visalia to live with Uncle Jimmy.'

The sweet taste in my mouth turns sour, sickening, hateful. 'What? When?'

'Soon.' Her eyes are brimming with tears.

'No!' My face has turned the colour of a well-cooked lobster. 'What about Stanley?' I ask.

'We're not going to live with him any more.'

My own tears flood my face, my neck, my blouse. 'You can leave if you want to,' I snap. 'I'm not going anywhere. I'm staying here.'

'Don't be silly, you can't stay here alone.'

'Yes, I can! I like being alone.' I stand up. By now the green and white stripes of the Dorothy Draper wallpaper are starting to wave back and forth like flags in the wind. I throw my spoon on the table. 'I'm not going. I'm not, I'm not!' I screech, running out of the house and slamming the door behind me.

*

Two days later we went. It was 7 February 1950, the day before Stanley was to leave for Oregon. When interviewed by the Press Club there, he told the world about the 'revolutionary' Innovations music he intended to play. A day or two later he executed a document at the offices of Alvin P. Jackson, Attorney-at-law, of 8272 Sunset Boulevard, Hollywood. In this new draft of his will, he mentions the divorce proceedings, yet names my mother as the executrix of his estate and the heir of his estate in the event of his predeceasing her. The document reveals the depth of his bond with my mother – a bond that remained unshaken in spite of his rage and pain.

What the will doesn't show is that this depth of commitment was by no means one-sided. Despite love affairs on both sides, despite forthcoming marriages to others, despite my father's hope that one day a new woman would release him from his need for Violet, and despite vitriolic denials of her existence and her importance to him, the bond between the two of them remained unbroken until the end of their lives.

As for me, the day my mother told me she was taking me away from Hollyridge felt like the end of my life. I had lost Tuffy, my home and my father, all at once. I needed someone to blame for it. So my child's mind turned my mother into the 'bad guy', forcing her to take the rap for everything. After all, she was also the one who sent Tuffy away, wasn't she?

I began to wonder if she had really had Tuffy killed. Had she lied to me about the farm? From that day on, I often looked upon Violet as though she were some kind of monster who had not only destroyed my best friend, but ripped me from my home and devastated my father. It had to be her fault. Everything had to be her fault. To my young mind, she had treated Stanley horribly. It was obvious how much he needed her. In spite of his bravado and his big feet, anyone could see he was not as much like Superman as he pretended to be.

Thus did my father become the 'innocent' one – the 'wounded' one

– the victim of a callous woman who had torn us asunder. The morning Violet and I climbed into her car to leave Hollyridge, I made a dangerous vow: 'Stanley, somehow, somewhere, some way, I'll do my best to make it up to you.'

10

A DIFFERENT LIFE

THE MARRIAGE WAS over. Violet had had enough. 'I want a husband who lives with me,' she said. 'I want a real home.'

I learned years later that – most importantly – she wanted a sexual relationship that worked. Despite the lifelong bonds and the force of feeling that united them, making love with Stanley had been a dismal experience for her. It was during one of our many woman-to-woman conversations, when I was in my late twenties, that she confided this to me.

Audree, a loyal friend to both my parents, had stood beside Violet for several years while my mother tried everything she could think of to make the marriage work. 'It's little wonder it didn't work,' says Audree. 'Stanley had no idea what to do with a woman. I think he had been too damaged by the fear and self-loathing embedded in him from life with his mother. To Stanley, engaging in sex was being a bad boy.'

Jimmy Foster was as different from Stanley as any man could be. A far cry from my father's unpredictable moods, manners and movements, Jimmy was dependable. He was patient and determined. Discharged from the Marine Corps following World War Two, Jimmy was handsome and physically fit.

Because he was related to Mom through his mother, Mom had long looked upon Jimmy as an alternative husband for Violet. With Mom's encouragement, 'Uncle Jimmy' had come time and time again to take my mother to nightclubs or dinner while Stanley was away. Eventually, his persistence and his willingness to hang out behind the scenes paid off. Yet right up to the moment he and Violet were married, he was scared to death that he would lose the woman he had worked diligently to capture. 'I remember the day your mother and I were married,' he used to say. 'Standing in that gingerbread chapel in Nevada, I was terrified she'd change her mind at the last minute and walk out. I heard the man say, "And do you, Violet, take this man, James, as your lawful wedded husband?" There was a silence you could cut with a knife. My shirt got drenched in sweat.'

Despite the pause in the ceremony, Violet did say yes. That's how she and I came to live with Uncle Jimmy in a two-bedroom, nondescript track house at 1500 East Noble Avenue in Visalia, a cow town in the middle of the San Joaquin Valley, California. There, my mother's new husband ran a lumberyard. He left each morning at quarter to eight and walked back through the front door at five past five every evening.

The house we moved into was bland, makeshift and soulless. But the new marriage, with all the promise it held for my mother, inspired her to transform it into something beautiful. She seemed truly content for the first time in her life. She had a sexual union with a man who satisfied her. She cut short her shoulder-length platinum hair and let it revert to its natural colour, a mousy brown. Inspired by the stability of the new relationship and glowing with a womanly radiance not seen in her before, she got busy turning this boring house into a vibrant, charming place for us to live. She bought bolts of material, designed sofas and sewed curtains and bolsters in colours and textures that reflected her newly discovered enthusiasm for life. She cooked gourmet meals using wild mushrooms gathered from cow fields nearby and strawberries grown in the garden.

I did my best to accept the circumstances in which I found myself but I resented Jimmy. I saw him as an invader who had destroyed our family and torn me away from my beloved Hollyridge. At the same time, I despised my mother. I believed she had turned against my father who, I knew, loved and needed her; and it must be said that

Stanley did nothing to dissuade me from this view. Each night when I climbed into bed in Visalia, I would lie awake longing for my own bed in Hollyridge, and worrying about Stanley. What would happen to him without my mother? Why did he let her leave at all? I fantasised about the terrible consequences that his being on his own could have. Somebody needed to be there to look after him – someone who could let him know that everything would be all right – especially when he had one of his night fugues or when, scared or pushed too far as a result of no sleep, too many pills or too much booze, he believed his life was falling apart again.

When at last I succumbed to sleep, I slept fitfully. My nights were riddled with confusing, fragmented, frightening dreams, one after another. When I woke up shouting, Jimmy or my mother would come to my room. I was desperate to feel safe, but if they invited me into their bed, I always refused. I did not want to be in a bed with Violet and some man who was not my father. What safety could there be in that?

I began to have migraine headaches. My mother suspected, and she was probably right, that they were being caused by unhappiness. Knowing my passion for animals, one day she asked me if I would like to have a pet. Leaping at the chance, I acquired hamsters and parakeets, which roamed and flew freely around the house.

During the first year they were together, Jimmy was so in love with my mother that even she, with all her need to be loved, was not large enough to hold it all. Some of his love overflowed on to me. This did not go on for very long, but while it lasted Jimmy expressed his affection for me in two ways that I have been forever grateful for. He once nursed me like a saint through the worst headache I've ever known. And, knowing how little confidence I had when it came to sports, one day he taught me how to swing and hit a baseball so hard I could knock it not only over our house, but over the neighbours' house too. His encouragement was responsible for turning me into an accomplished athlete. I would get good at softball, which they played in school, and I learned to play football with boys so well that I became an important member of any team. Eventually I would break the record for breaststroke for under-twelves without realising I had done it.

Jimmy Foster understood something about me that nobody had ever seen. Despite all the boldness I pretended to have, I had no belief in my ability to do much of anything. He knew different and showed me how to achieve the things I had once thought impossible.

A few days after my pivotal baseball lesson with Jimmy, my mother made a terrible proclamation: 'Soon you'll be going to a new school.'

A week later, trembling like a wild rabbit, I walked through the gates of Conyer Elementary School. Totally out of my element, I had no idea what was expected of me. Because I had spent so little time with children, I didn't know how to get on with them. If they had been horses or goats or dogs, it would have been OK. The girls in the class didn't seem too bad but the boys paid too much attention to me and I hated that. Within my first few days at Conyer, I devised two not very intelligent plans for dealing with the uncomfortable situation I had found myself in.

The first involved a method for handling boys. It turned out to be simple. When one came near me or tried to talk to me, I would kick him in the shins. Apparently this was a technique which none of the other girls had thought of. But it caught on fast as my female class-mates joined me enthusiastically in the practice. Within a week the legs of every boy in the class had turned black and blue.

When it came to finding a way of getting a foot in the academic door – if the word 'academic' can be used to describe the activities of fourth-graders – I was more at a loss. Reading was not a problem. I had been doing that since I was three or four. But I had never read anything anybody else in my class had read. However, I was determined to impress them, and impress them I did – by writing a book report on *Hamlet*.

I had seen the movie with my mother and knew there was a copy of the play in *The Complete Dramatic and Poetic Works of William Shakespeare* that I had given her as a Mother's Day present. As a rookie fourth-grader trying to make an impression, I reasoned that nobody in this class would ever have heard of *Hamlet* or Shakespeare, especially since Shakespeare was not one of the authors listed on our book report chart, pinned to the classroom wall. He was probably some unknown Englishman since the actors in the movie all talked in that weird English way. Anyway, I knew he was long dead and England was far way from Visalia. In my mother's copy of the complete works, *Hamlet Prince of Denmark* started on page 998 and ended on page 1140. I wrote my report and handed it in. Boy, were the other kids impressed to hear that I had read a book 1140 pages long! My wise and kind teacher never betrayed me.

The day fourth grade ended, I left my birds and hamsters in Violet's care and flew to Los Angeles to spend the summer with Stanley. He had just done the final Innovations concert for the year at the Hollywood Bowl and was doing some recording at Capitol. I was glad to be back with him – and even more glad to be back at my beloved Hollyridge.

As soon as Violet and I left Hollyridge, Mom had moved in to keep house for Stanley. Now she arranged a ninth birthday party for me. Afterwards, my father and I spent most of the summer together, shuttling back and forth between Hollyridge, where Mom stayed, and Balboa, where my father had rented a beach house. After losing hundreds of thousands of dollars on the Innovations tour, Stanley had decided to form a smaller jazz /dance band for clubs and dance halls while still playing concert dates with the Orchestra. The new, smaller band played a week at Club Oasis in Los Angeles, then went back and forth playing a few days there, and weekends at the Rendezvous Ballroom in Balboa, where my parents had first met.

Just as we were getting ready to leave for Balboa the first week, Mom said something to me that I found strange: 'Now Leslie, don't go walking around in your pyjamas with men in the band around.' Why would she say this to me? I was just a kid. I never paid the least attention to whether I was in pyjamas or not. Still, I didn't ask her why, since I didn't want to get into another argument with her. But it worried me.

Each night in Balboa, I go to work with Stanley. While he works, I hang around the soda fountains in the ballroom drinking Cokes, or go up on to the balcony to read my book. In the daytime we go to the beach. I build sand-castles while he sleeps. We spend a lot of time laughing.

'God, Shortstuff,' he says, 'it's good to be with you like this. I'd forgotten how to have fun.' He grabs me around one of my knees and squeezes hard. He always does this on the beach, and when we go to a movie together. Then I screech and leap out of my chair. He laughs.

In one of my father's many modes, he would behave like an enthusiastic dog, leaping at me without warning, as though he would eat me up. This happened when he became so full of manic fervour that he couldn't contain himself. Or he'd put his arms around me and squeeze so tight I couldn't breathe. If I tried to pull away, he'd pull me back to him and laugh.

That summer, he kept thanking me for being his 'best friend'. I thought this was strange since he was not my *friend*, he was my *father*, but if he wanted to think of me that way, I figured that was OK. The only best friend I had ever had was Tuffy.

That summer Stanley also began to buy me jewellery – a solid gold charm bracelet, a gold chain for my neck, a big gold sunburst with a ruby in the middle of it. I loved the red stone. It made me feel more alive. That summer too he talked more than ever before about things that worried him: the money he had lost with the Innovations Orchestra, his fear he would never write music again. He said he wanted to study composition but he had to make more money.

When summer ended, I went back to Visalia and Stanley left Los Angeles to go on the road for six months. I didn't see him at

Christmas that year. He would ring me every couple of weeks and he sent lots of telegrams. Some of them were funny. He loved sending telegrams. They were signed: 'All my love, Stanley.'

Back in Visalia I entered another new school where I knew nobody. The day I arrived there, to begin fifth grade, I met Seiko Kawasaki. If such as thing as a 'soul mate' really exists, the closest I have ever come to having one is Seiko.

Both of us were new to Sierra Vista School. The previous year, Seiko, who was Japanese and the daughter of a Buddhist minister, had been in a school that was 90 per cent Hispanic. There were no Asian kids at Sierra Vista and so she felt uncomfortable being thrown together with a lot of kids of well-to-do WASP townspeople.

I sat in the row just behind her. 'Every time I looked back at you,' she says, 'you'd be sitting up straight with your hands folded on the desk. I found this very weird.' Stranger still was the way I wore my blond hair twirled around on both sides of my head. 'You looked like a co-pilot or like you were wearing earmuffs,' she said.

As for me, when I scanned the kids around me, I saw nobody who interested me. Nobody, that is, but Seiko. I asked her if she liked roller-skating. She said yes.

Over the following weeks and months, we became such close friends that Seiko's parents adopted me – metaphorically at least – as a fourth daughter. I spent as much time with them as I was allowed. Each time my mother would come to pick me up, Seiko and I would hide for as long as we could. I always wanted to stay longer in the home of my adopted family.

When Seiko first saw my mother wearing giant dark glasses, driving her black Cadillac convertible, she said Violet looked like a movie star. Seiko loved my mother's house and the way she had decorated it: her Charles Eames chairs, which were so comfortable, the beautiful fabrics, the hardwood floors. The floors in the Kawasaki house were covered with linoleum.

The first time Stanley came to the Kawasakis' house, he unfolded his body from his Porsche the way a clown gets out of a miniature fire engine at the circus. He was full of warmth when he greeted them. For years afterwards Mrs Kawasaki would speak about how considerate and charming he had been. Since he was so big and she was so tiny, he got down on his knees to talk to her. She never got over that.

Mrs Kawasaki, whom I called 'Mommy', was always amazed that Violet and Stanley were divorced yet seemed to be such good friends, and at the way he visited her so often. She said to Seiko that my mother had told her the reason they were divorced was because she wanted to make a home for me. I suspect this was something my mother came to believe herself after awakening from the first flush of sexual joy at marrying Jimmy, when she began to realise she had chosen for herself an existence that was less than inspiring.

Before long, I came to like school and I settled into some kind of what you might call normality – a word nobody would ever have used to describe my life until then. Thanks to the kindness and stability of my adopted family I had begun to see the world through new eyes. Being with Seiko's family was so different than living in the crazy environment I was used to. There was a sense of integrity about everything they did and an acceptance of life in whatever form it presented itself. They never analysed or explained anything. They never demanded that I believe in anything. Gradually I began to feel a little confidence in myself; and to think that one day I might turn out to be something more than the mess I felt myself to be. Thanks to this, I began to excel at school.

Seiko and I did everything together, including getting straight As on our school reports. The first year we hand-made Valentine cards for everyone in the class, then borrowed bikes and delivered them to homes all over town. At Christmas, we gathered mistletoe, made wreaths from cottonwood trees, and gave them away. We liked to wear identical tartan dresses – blue with red stripes running through them.

Every morning we would ring each other to work out how we could dress alike.

For the first time in my life, I began to feel like I knew where I belonged. I would join in the day-to-day Kawasaki family activities – from the polishing of Mr Kawasaki's shiny black car before he drove us to school each morning, to washing dishes and household chores. I would go to all the Japanese festivals with Seiko's family, dressed up in a traditional silk kimono to celebrate the Buddha's birthday, or on picnics held in farmers' fields. I had my hair cut (rather badly it must be said) in a classic Japanese bob. I was often the only Caucasian among hundreds of dark-haired Orientals, but slowly I came to feel that I was one of Seiko's family: clean and solid, instead of the chaotic misfit I'd felt myself to be for so long.

In March of 1951, during our Easter holidays, Stanley's band was playing at the Palladium. Seiko and I flew to Los Angeles on tickets my mother gave us, to spend our vacation with Mom and Stanley. When the stewardess served our dinner, we took out child-size chopsticks to eat it. At Hollyridge, we picked flowers from neighbours' gardens, then we went up and down the street selling our bouquets to the same neighbours to raise money for the Red Cross.

We wrote a play based on the fairy tale 'Rapunzel', sold tickets to it and performed it in the back yard at Hollyridge. I was Rapunzel. We worked out a way to throw a flaxen rope over the balcony and make it look like my hair. Some nights we spent at the Palladium, listening to Stanley's music and dancing together. Others we stayed at home with Mom and baked cookies.

Being able to share my first *human* friend, whom I loved more than anything in the world, with Stanley seemed to bring together both the worlds I lived in: Visalia and my life with him. For a time I felt like I was living in a magic place. But magic times never last for ever.

11

OUT OF THE FRYING PAN

MY PARENTS' DIVORCE SUITEd Mom's purposes. She wanted security. For her to feel secure, she had to exert as much control as possible over the life of anyone she thought might provide it. For many years that person had been Pat. He held down a steady job and he provided her with a large and useful house, plus the rental properties. Now she was divorcing Pat, so she needed a new home over which she could exercise her will. With Violet gone from Hollyridge, she earmarked Stanley to provide it.

By the time Mom took over at Hollyridge, her divorce from Pat was a done deal. This new position of authority brought her a sense of freedom she had long pined for. She announced that she would now be able to move deeper into her 'spiritual studies' – which meant reading endless books and making connections with a wide variety of people she looked up to as teachers.

While she ran Hollyridge, Mom made good use of her cooking and housekeeping skills while offering much 'spiritual advice' to my father. These were tools for insinuating herself deeper into Stanley's life. He was her current hub of power. Struggling to reinvent himself, Stanley was highly vulnerable to Mom's influence. She willingly embraced her role as his adviser and guiding light. She introduced him to the esoteric in all the books she read; she opened the door for him into the bizarre world of gurus, bringing into the house a hodgepodge of Hollywood's finest. Some were notorious. Many were self-proclaimed 'enlightened beings', 'philosophers' and 'holy men'.

Amongst Mom's spiritual stable were L. Ron Hubbard and the bestselling writer Ayn Rand, author of *The Fountainhead* and *Atlas Shrugged*. Rand's message soon inspired Stanley. 'I am not primarily an advocate of capitalism,' said Rand, 'but of egotism, and I am not primarily an advocate of egotism, but of reason. If one recognises the supremacy of reason and applies it consistently, all the rest follows.' While Rand's insistence on 'reason' felt reassuring to Stanley, Hubbard's quick-fix solutions appeared even more hopeful.

Mom knew L. Ron Hubbard from our many visits to the Parsonage, a redwood mansion in Pasadena which was always overflowing with the sorts of people who fascinated her. They seemed like characters in a movie and made the visitors at Hollyridge seem bland by comparison. From the time I was five or six, Mom often took me with her to the Parsonage. There I would wander from room to room as they argued about books and rockets and war and bombs and freedom.

The Parsonage was ruled by Jack Parsons, a brilliant, warm, wild and funny, yet – in many ways – tortured human being. John Whiteside Parsons was his real name. He was – still is – called 'the father of rocket science' by men much more famous than him, such as Wernher von Braun and Theodore von Karman. Scientists even named a crater after him on the dark side of the moon. He was also immersed in esoteric magick practices.

One day Jack told me something I have never forgotten. 'Freedom is a dangerous thing,' he said. 'But so what. After all, not all of us are cowards, are we?'

'Are you a coward?' I asked.

'Sometimes,' he said. 'But I'm learning not to be.'

I was pretty sure I was a coward too, so I asked him, 'Can you teach me too?' He laughed. For some reason he always seemed to find me funny.

'Freedom is like that sword,' he said, pointing to a long silver sword with brown tassels hanging from its hilt on the wall of his huge bedroom. 'It has two edges. Both are sharp as razors. One edge can carry you across the Universe with the wind in your hair. The other is there to remind you that you must be responsible for everything you do.

'No, Leslie, you are not a coward,' he said. 'If you were, you wouldn't be here. But if ever you believe yourself to be cowardly you must never take up the sword of freedom.'

I didn't fully understand what he was saying but I nodded my head, because his words felt right to me.

Another day, while I was reading a book at the back of the mansion (where I spent a lot of time by myself while Mom did her thing with people inside), Jack came out of the house to find me sitting in the branch of a big oak. He grabbed hold of my legs, shaking me from my mesmerised state. He smiled.

'You like to climb trees,' he said.

'More than anything,' I said, 'except maybe riding roller coasters.'

'Aren't you afraid you'll fall?'

'Yeah, sometimes. But that's part of the fun, isn't it?'

He laughed again. 'Good. Then they haven't ruined you yet.'

'What?'

'Ruined you – hypnotised you with the vicious lies people hand down from one generation to another to keep children from seeing beyond the illusions of the world so they will become afraid.'

I didn't know what he was talking about. 'But I *am* afraid,' I said.

'What are you afraid of?'

'The dark. The monsters that sit in my bedroom at night and tell me to do things I don't want to do. Stanley, when he shouts at me. I'm scared I might not ever be able to do the things I want to do when I grow up.'

'I see. You don't know it yet, Leslie, but I think you're one of the lucky ones. You're still wild.'

'Yeah, people tell me that. Some say I'm wicked too.'

'That's because they haven't been able to crush your spirit, which is what they try to do. You remind them of the freedom they have lost and they hate you for it – freedom that has been ripped away from them by inhibitions and rules and regulations. Man's built a terrible world out there. His blindness to what he's done prevents him from knowing it. Whenever he gets even a glimpse of how horrible it is or a whiff of the freedom he's given up, he becomes so scared he retreats deeper into the little prison he's made for himself and prays to some phoney god outside of him that it will bless him for his cowardice.'

I liked the sound of what he said. Nobody had ever said anything like that to me. To my child's mind, it rang true.

'I don't ever want to be like that,' I said.

'Then you gotta listen to your inner voice and tell your monsters to go to hell when they try to spook you. Put faith in what you know in your own heart. It will always beckon you to more life. Follow its call, no matter what anybody says or does and no matter how much anyone tries to stop you. Remember that and you won't go wrong.'

I will never forget Jack. He was not only different from the people who hung around Hollyridge, he was unlike anyone I have ever known. He was incredibly brilliant. That didn't stop him falling foul of one of L. Ron's scams. Initially, Jack and L. Ron Hubbard hit it off famously at the Parsonage, until Hubbard conceived a 'sure-fire business deal', which left Parsons financially and emotionally destitute.

Along with the philosophies of L. Ron Hubbard and Rand, Mom introduced my father to a pot-pourri of conflicting ideas. He got caught up in some of them. It was as though he was clutching at anything that might help him. At one point Stanley even started to parrot John Wayne's simplistic description of reality, dividing the world into heroes and villains, good and evil. 'They tell me everything isn't black and white,' John Wayne said to Stanley one day, 'I say why the hell not?' My father agreed wholeheartedly.

My father was any self-promoting guru's dream. 'Stan Kenton' was a famous man; therefore he must have money which would prove useful to any spiritual teacher's ministry. One after the other, at Mom's invitation, they visited Hollyridge for the next three years, displaying their wares. Many promised to guide him, help him, both personally and professionally. All he had to do to reap the rewards offered was to follow the teachings and make a contribution to their cause.

While all this was going on, the economics and logistics of moving the forty-piece Innovations Orchestra around the country were crippling Stanley. He paid for most of it out of his own pocket. Two buses were needed. One carried jazz men and the other string players who thought of themselves as the classical musicians. Constant rivalry between the two groups undermined morale. Unloading the equipment and setting up each night took more than two hours.

Almost every performance was a one-night stand. Attendance at the concerts was generally poor, even though the new music had received some positive, influential reviews. A *New York Times* correspondent went so far as to describe Innovations in the way Stanley had hoped it would be received, as 'the first successful attempt to bridge the gap between classical and jazz music'.

My father continued to drive himself in the Buick he kept for going on the road instead of riding in one of the buses, so he could arrive in a town early enough to do promotional record signings, radio and press interviews, in the hopes of drumming up more business before they opened that night. This exhausted him. The more tired he felt, the more determined he became. He had to keep going, no matter what the cost. His use of amphetamines and barbiturates escalated to the point where his body had trouble coping with what he was putting into it. Yet he dared not stop. 'I've got wolves at the door,' he told me one night. 'I gotta keep 'em at bay.'

When I stayed with him during the holidays, he didn't sleep. As he had done often in the weeks before my mother and I left Hollyridge, he started coming to my bed again in the middle of the night. He would lay his head on the bed covers and talk for hours. It was not just a financial beast that he was battling. His 'demons' had finally broken their tether and they were chewing away at him from inside out. This triggered one fugue after another.

In his eyes, psychiatry had failed. He turned his back on the idea of becoming a doctor after Bernie Gindes was proved to be a fraud, and now he insisted that any form of psychiatry was 'a bunch of crap'. Nevertheless, he continued to apply the ideas and techniques he had learned from Gindes, analysing the men in the band as well as every woman he knew. My father looked upon his analyses as a way of helping people guide their lives. He often used psychological mind-bending to manipulate his musicians in whichever way be believed necessary 'for their own good'. While a few of them resented this, most looked upon it with gratitude, believing that 'the Old Man' cared deeply for them.

Meanwhile, Stanley continued to reassure himself and everybody else that he'd 'never suffered any problems from this divorce thing'. Beneath these vociferous assertions, his inner demons chuckled. And Mom was always there to hold his hand and point the way forward. While he was on the road, she was never further away than the end of a phone, willing to lend an ear, while cementing her position of authority. He relied on her clairvoyance, her will and her wisdom. During the first year or two after the divorce he continued to turn to her for guidance and reassurance – especially in regard to highly personal matters, like his growing anxiety about the jitters he was experiencing as a result of taking so many 'uppers' and 'downers'. After all, he kept saying, 'Mom was a registered nurse. She knows about these things, doesn't she?' Maybe she could keep the demons at bay too: the feelings of guilt, despondency, rage, shame, loneliness, and fear of failure. Since she was connected with some pretty powerful people, she might also be able to help him find the strength and power he needed to achieve greater success.

Eventually, the fascinations Stanley developed during the years Mom guided him, and the distortions of belief that accompanied them, would contribute to the unravelling of large parts of his life.

PART TWO

BLOOD

ROOFTOPS OF MANHATTAN

THE YEAR I turned ten, at the end of the fifth grade, Stanley had arranged for me to spend my summer vacation with him. The band was scheduled to play a week at the Marine Ballroom on Steel Pier in Atlantic City. I loved Atlantic City. When he worked there, we could spend our days on the beach, drink lots of freshly squeezed orange juice and play together before the one-nighters would begin.

By that age I had spent a great deal of my life on aeroplanes, yet my mother was concerned about my travelling across America by myself. My grandmother Stella offered to make part of the journey with me and deliver me to Stanley in Atlantic City, before going off to visit friends on her own. She suggested that we could both spend a few days in New York 'sightseeing' on the way. While I disliked Stella a great deal, I had not seen her since my mother and I had left Hollyridge. I had forgotten what she was really like and so our trip was arranged.

On 17 July, I said goodbye to my mother and climbed on to a United Airlines plane at Visalia airport to fly to Los Angeles, where Stella was to meet me. The plan was to spend one night at her home in South Gate, then to take a plane the next day to New York, where we would stay at the Taft Hotel for three or four days before meeting Stanley.

Stella was waiting for me when my plane landed. I looked at her and felt afraid. I didn't know why. And when we walked through the front door of her house, I began to tremble. 'Are you cold?' she asked.

'Are you sick?' I was neither. I think being there reminded me of the days I spent in torment with her on our boat after I broke my collar bone. Yet it was not just that. Something else bothered me. I didn't know what it was.

It seemed as though the warm, safe, solid world I had been living in with Seiko and her family was being overshadowed by something threatening, even sinister. My grandmother's house looked dirty to me – and not just physically dirty. It felt as though the very air and everything in it was covered with cobwebs. I found it hard to breathe and the place smelt like something old and dead.

When she went into the kitchen to prepare dinner, I asked, 'Can I make a collect call to my mother to let her know I got here?' She said I could. I went into the hall, picked up the phone and dialled zero.

'I'd like to make a collect call,' I said, 'to Visalia.' My voice sounded odd – as though I was hearing someone else speaking from far away down a long corridor. 'Mother?'

'Leslie? You sound strange. Are you all right?'

'I want to come home,' I explained.

'What?'

'I don't want to stay here. Can I come home?'

'Why?' she asked.

'I don't know. It feels dirty. I hate it. Please can't I come home?'

'Leslie, it's all arranged,' my mother sighed. 'You are going to New York with Stella and then on to Stanley.'

'Can't I go to New York on my own? I don't want to sleep in this house. I'm scared.'

'That's ridiculous. What on earth are you afraid of?'

'I don't like her. I don't want to be with her. Please.'

'Don't be silly,' she said. 'There's nothing we can do to change things now. You always make such a drama out of everything.'

'But . . .'

'You're going!'

When, in my twenties, forgotten memories started to come back of what happened to me in the years following this trip, my mother would remind me of this conversation. She told me she recalled it word for word because she found it so strange that I would react to anything the way I did that day.

That night I slept little. The curtain in the window next to my bed reminded me of a shroud. I lay there imagining that it was growing bigger and would wrap itself round me so I could never get away. I couldn't shake the feeling that engulfed me. Yet, the next morning, as Stella busied herself getting ready for our flight, I wondered why I had felt so apprehensive.

The plane trip to New York was uneventful. We arrived in the early evening. Instead of taking a taxi from Idlewild airport to Manhattan the way Violet and I always did, Stella insisted we take a bus. 'Taxis are too expensive,' she said. We arrived at the Taft Hotel after dark, having missed dinner.

'I'm hungry,' I complained.

'It's too late to eat now,' Stella replied. 'Wait until tomorrow.'

The next morning we went down to the coffee shop. I ordered French toast, which the waitress brought without butter. I asked for some butter. 'You don't need butter,' Stella said. 'Butter costs extra.'

The Taft was a massive, spooky building on the east side of Seventh Avenue between 50th and 51st Streets. I don't know why my grandmother chose that hotel. Maybe it was because our room there cost only $7.50 a night.

During the next couple of days, Stella dragged me all over Manhattan to 'see the sights'. Everywhere we went – from the top of the Empire State Building to the golden statue of Prometheus at Rockefeller Plaza – she demanded I take a photograph as a 'souvenir of our trip'.

The second day, after forbidding me to order freshly squeezed orange juice at breakfast, she announced, 'Today we're going to do something special. I thought I would take you to meet some dancer friends of mine at a theatre. Would you like that?'

I was sure anything would be better than more sightseeing, so I said yes. What was to happen later that day I will never be able fully to explain and the horror of the experience remains hard for me to put into words.

After buying some tacky souvenirs to take home to her friends and her other grandchildren, Stella took me two or three blocks up Seventh Avenue. This surprised me since all the theatres I knew were down Seventh Avenue near Times Square. We turned right into what I think was 54th Street and entered an alley. At the end of it, iron steps led up to a stage door. We climbed the stairs and went inside. The office, where the stage door man usually sits, was empty. Maybe this was because it was too early in the day for anyone to be there.

'Wait here,' she said. She disappeared down a corridor. I heard knocking on doors, and voices. Then everything fell silent. There is nothing quite like the silence of an empty theatre. It feels like a tomb.

I didn't wait for Stella to come back. I made my way through ropes and sandbags on to the stage. It was huge with a pit big enough for a full orchestra and trap doors in the floor. I was trying to open one of them when Stella came up behind me. There were two men with her. One was tall with a long pointy face. The other was little. He had blue-black hair cut in a funny way so you could see lots of white skin around his ears. His hair had been slicked down with Brylcreem or maybe it was axle grease. He seemed like a miniature bad guy from a silent movie. I didn't like silent movies.

Stella told me their names but I didn't pay attention. I have always had a habit of forgetting the names of people I don't much want to remember.

'Would you like to see the dressing rooms?' the tall guy asked. By then I had seen so many dressing rooms that the idea of looking at another one didn't grab me. Still, it sounded better than being dragged along on another of Stella's shopping expeditions so I said yes.

'I'll be back around four,' Stella said. Then she left me alone with the two men.

The little guy took me by the hand and led me down a passageway with lots of doors in it. On one of the doors there was a sign saying 'Miss Channing'. I remember wondering who Miss Channing was and hoping, no matter who she was, that she was there in the theatre that morning, so that I wouldn't be left alone with these guys.

We went into a big room with lots of costume stuff in it – tuxedos on hangers, shoes, makeup, feathers, photographs.

'Your grandmother says you want to learn to dance,' said one of the guys. 'Tell you what, let's have some fun. We'll put some makeup on you, then see what we can teach you.'

These two men made me feel strange. It was something about the way they moved around and how they touched each other. They sponged pancake makeup on my face, glued false eyelashes on me and covered my mouth in bright red lipstick. They put a tight net on my hair and pulled a red wig on to my head.

'Not right,' the little guy said. He took the red wig off and put a silver-blond one on instead.

'You look neat,' the skinny one said. Then he made up his own face so he looked like a girl. So did the little guy.

When they were finished, the tall one said, 'Come on, we'll find something for you to wear.' We went into another room filled with men's suits, hats, a full-length mirror and metal rails overflowing with dresses and gowns. Around the walls there were umbrellas, a clown suit, dressmaker's dummies, hatboxes, shoeboxes and other stuff. A dozen or more wigmaker's dummies and lots of hats were stacked in rows on wooden shelves. Masks and shimmering materials hung from the rails, along with full sets of costumes, each on its own hanger, labelled with a name.

They told me I wasn't allowed to touch the costumes with names on them but I could play with anything else I wanted to. It was a child's dream come true. I tried hats on, one by one – a tiny one like flappers wore, a huge one with pink feathers on it, a man's top hat, a helmet that looked like it belonged to a Roman soldier, a dusty green Robin Hood hat.

Entranced by the costumes and the mirrors, I got lost in my dressing-up games, so I didn't pay much attention to what the men were doing. In a big box I found the bottom half of what looked like a jester's suit. It had huge diamonds in bright colours all over it. The gigantic waist was wired with braces attached to it. This made the trousers, hung from my shoulders, stand way out from my body.

When I turn to look at them, the two men are busy undressing and dressing themselves. The guy with the weird haircut puts on a tight gown made of red sequins that's too long for him. He stuffs something down the front of it to make him look like he has a bosom. The skinny one takes off all his clothes and puts on the tiniest pair of underpants I've ever seen – they're more like strings tied together – and a garter belt with long black stockings and a pair of platform high heels. He glues glittery tassels over his nipples, then puts the red wig they have taken off me on his head. He grabs an enormous fan and starts twirling it round.

'Let's have some music,' he shouts. On a bench at the side of the room there's a record player with a pile of 78s next to it. The skinny one puts a record on the turntable. The music is kind of like blues but very slow. It has a pounding beat. They start to dance.

'Come on, dance with us,' the skinny guy says. I try to dance but the big jester's trousers prevent me from moving. They laugh.

'Take them off! Take them off! Take them off!' they chant, whirling round me. I take off the trousers so I'm in my underwear.

'Come on,' the small guy says. 'We'll show you how.' He pulls off my undershirt and fastens a bra with tassels around my ten-year-old chest. He has to pin it at the back because it's too big. He drapes a robe over my shoulders and ties it round my neck. Still dancing, they start covering me with frou-frou – pieces of lace, scarves, necklaces, paste jewellery, earrings, bracelets, arm-length gloves.

I'm fascinated by what's happening, but frightened too. One of them puts a large floppy hat on my head, pink stockings on my legs with a red garter belt, then a pink ostrich boa around my neck. I suddenly think, they're smothering me in stripper's gear.

Then they show me how to gyrate my hips and take some of the clothes off. They egg me on, applauding. I do my best to follow instructions. I think I'm learning something very 'grown up'.

They begin to laugh again, to tease and to shout at me. They call me 'Salomé', 'Sadie Thompson', 'Whore of Babylon'. The room starts spinning. They take masks from the rails and put them on, one by one, then throw them off again. Jeering at me, they poke at my body and tear at my clothes, piece by piece. It feels as if I'm in a swirling nightmare, but I can't make myself wake up from it. I throw up. This makes them laugh more. 'Look what you've done,' one of them screams. 'Naughty, naughty.' I have vomited on some costumes. 'What a bad girl you are! You'd better get out of here before someone finds out.'

'Come on,' says the little guy. He grabs me by a shoulder. The other one takes hold of my other arm. They hold me tight so I can't get away. They drag me into the corridor and they shove me against a heavy door at the end of the hall next to a stairwell with concrete steps and metal railings.

'Up,' shouts the tall one, poking me in the back with his fingers.

'Up, up, up,' screeches the little guy.

I run up the steps. They follow behind me but I can run faster than they can. The stairwell is damp. It smells of men's urine. The walls are pushing in on me.

'Faster, faster,' they scream.

When I get to the top of the steps I run up against a door with a bar across it – the kind you push down on to open. I push. It leads on to a huge flat roof. I can see other flat roofs all around. I think that maybe I can jump from this roof to another. I run to the edge but the roof next door is lower and too far away. I turn to the adjacent edge.

There is nothing there. Only the street below – no way out. I fall backwards then everything goes black.

When I come to I'm lying naked on a dark red couch that must be leather since my skin is stuck to it. My body is covered by a brown hairy blanket. It smells damp and it itches my skin. I sit up and look around. I seem to be in an office. I can see a desk with papers on it and a telephone. There are wooden filing cabinets. My clothes are in a heap on an old brown chair. I put my feet on the floor. It's cold like concrete. I stand up. The wooziness is gone.

So are the men.

By the time Stella returned I was dressed in my own clothes. I still had globs of cold cream at the edges of my hair. Somebody had tried to scrub off all the horrible makeup. I was too afraid to cry. The men came through the door, dressed in their own clothes. They told Stella I had been 'a bad girl', then they laughed. Stella pretended to be shocked. Then she laughed with them.

'She's going to be a wicked one,' said the skinny man.

'She was born that way. It's her mother's blood,' said Stella.

I felt I had done something wrong – so wrong I would be damned in hell for it if anyone ever found out. I was not really sure what it was, but that didn't change my certainty that I would never, ever be forgiven.

That day, Stella began to weave a web of secrecy and shame around me. It would surround me, like a fetid mist, for decades. Not until much later on in my life would I realise that she had deliberately and carefully planned the entire incident at the theatre in order to entrap me, as she had long before entrapped my father and been entrapped herself in a mire of guilt, shame, secrecy and nastiness.

Neither of us said a word on the way back to the hotel and we ate dinner in silence. When we finished, she said, 'Unless you do as I say from now on, I will tell your mother and your father what an evil child you are and all the nasty things you do.'

I did not know then that my grandmother's life was full of dark secrets, nor that her night-time activities were kept hidden from almost everyone who shared her daytime existence. Later I learned that she often hung out with outsiders, with risqué dancers, carnival people and freak-show entertainers at Venice Beach and other places in California. She also took part in weird Hollywood parties and occult gatherings. Late at night, she liked to spend time with strange people who shared her appetites.

By the time we boarded the train for Atlantic City, my paternal grandmother had successfully persuaded me that I was 'damaged', 'bad' and 'filthy', and that everything that had happened in New York was my own fault. 'You must never tell anyone, but don't worry, we'll let this be our little secret,' she said, patting me on the knee and binding me to her in a conspiracy of silence.

Guilt is a bitter sauce. Feed it to someone long enough and it can destroy his life. Stella had made it Stanley's daily fare from the time he was a child. She also nourished him on shame, fear, addiction and deception. Now she was beginning to work on me.

Among her grandchildren, I was the odd one out. The two daughters of Stanley's younger sister, Irma Mae – Janis and Shelley – tolerated Stella with superficial equanimity. Jan, then very young, and her parents even lived with her for over a year after returning from abroad. The three sons of Stanley's older sister, Beulah – Gary, Barton, and 'Little Stanley' – lived only a block and a half away from Stella. They spent much of their childhood in her pocket. Only Gary despised her. Barton, the grandson Stella was closest to, adored her. He stayed with her for two years while he was enrolled in East Los Angeles College. When I asked Barton recently about his memories of his grandmother he told me, 'She was the most caring, loving person you could ever imagine.' Like her Stanley, Stella was more than one person. The Stella that Barton remembers was not the Stella I knew.

When I began to work on this book, I was determined to learn as much as I could about my paternal grandmother and the family she came from. I was trying to figure out what made her the double-sided person she was. Quite apart from not understanding what motivated her behaviour towards me, I had never been able to fathom why she did so many other strange things or how she came to live two distinct lives.

During the day Stella was a middle-class member of the Church of Religious Science. She gardened, raised parakeets, collected coffee tins, played canasta with her women friends and ping-pong with her grandsons. During the night she travelled. She would show up where Stanley was playing or arrive at Hollyridge either late at night or at dawn for no apparent reason – always uninvited. Stanley said some nights she went to strange parties where, according to him, guests never called each other by their proper names.

Although drawn to misfits and outcasts on the fringes of society, Stella was nevertheless fiercely proud of her bloodline, which she could trace back to pilgrims on the *Mayflower*, and which included veteran officers in the American Revolutionary War, Huguenots and a handful of United States presidents, as well as businessmen and wealthy ranchers, of which her own father was one. She worshipped her father, Silas Edgar Newcomb, even though there is much evidence that she had been both neglected and quite damaged by him.

Silas and his brother, Daniel Ephphatha Newcomb, were ninth-generation Americans and respected as leading citizens in La Jara, Colorado. Silas owned two huge ranches as well as a fancy house in town. He was admired, lauded by local newspapers and journals. He and his brother were the region's most influential figures.

Silas looked upon his four children and his wives – he had three in succession – as *possessions*. The wives were expected to work hard, bear children, look decorative and not interfere with their husband's affairs. His sons were expected to grow up in their father's image and to bring more money, social prestige and political prominence to the family. His daughters were tutored in 'female pursuits': embroidery, music, cooking, maybe writing. They were also cautioned to keep out of Silas's way.

While growing up I heard many reports about Stella's family from my paternal grandfather, Pop, especially when I went to visit him on his goat farm in Corona. Pop had known Stella as a girl, long before they were married. Apparently, the whole Newcomb lineage was steeped in hierarchical beliefs. Pop once told me that as Stella's brothers grew, they were initiated into the secret practices of a provincial elite – elaborate rituals linked to Freemasonry, which took place behind closed doors and were off-limits to women and children.

There was also a completely different kind of ritual, which took place in the farmyard or the barn and which was intended to bring about a good harvest or to stem the danger of disease spreading through Silas's herd of prize mules or his cattle. Unlike those carried out behind closed doors in the town house, the farmyard rituals were not considered off-limits to women. In fact, women and children were considered essential for them. Somebody had to clean up the mess of an animal sacrifice afterwards.

Pop said that while she was growing up, Stella shouldered the lion's share of such chores on the farm. She did this to try to win her father's favour. Her conscientiousness was never rewarded. 'She was a good girl,' said Pop. 'A bit like the scullery maid in that fairy tale. Always tryin' to please Mr Newcomb. Don't think he ever noticed.'

What Stella did experience in no small measure was the control her father exerted over her. By all accounts, it extended to every aspect of her existence. He told her what to wear and what to do. And he ignored every daughterly approach she ever made towards him, every bid for affection. He criticised her for climbing trees like a tomboy. He browbeat her into learning the 'graces pleasing to others' so that she could earn herself a good husband. 'I never once heard him praise her,' Pop said.

It was not an easy family for my grandmother to grow up in. Although she was intelligent and, in accordance with Silas's wishes, eventually became accomplished at playing the piano, Stella was a sickly child who lacked physical beauty. This diminished her value to Silas. By the time she was born, the role of favoured daughter had already been bestowed upon Stella's older sister Gertrude. Whatever she did, Stella would never be good enough for Silas.

Similarly, Floyd Kenton was the last man on earth to be acceptable to Stella's father. Six foot four inches tall, with show-stopping china blue eyes, he had so much charm that, everywhere he went, people took to him. Gifted with vitality and his Lincolnesque stature, he radiated the magnetism that one day he would pass on to his son, Stanley. He played guitar and was a superb storyteller, a valued gift in the days before radio or television. He could even dance a mean jig. He was inventive and free-spirited – a fundamentally good man. Stella became infatuated with his charm. Not only was he dashing; unlike Silas, he *paid attention* to her. Unlike the men of the Newcomb lineage, Floyd was entirely self-taught and lived his life from his heart, not his head.

On 16 July 1910 Silas Edgar Newcomb died. By March the next year, Stella was pregnant with Floyd's child. Stella and Floyd married hurriedly and left for Kansas City, where he picked up a job as a butcher. On 15 December 1911, in a small white house at 120 South Fern Street, my father – Stanley Newcomb Kenton – was born. Not until 20 February 1912 did Stella and Floyd, my Pop, write to family and friends in Colorado to announce the birth of their son – claiming he had been born the previous day. Months later, when they returned to La Jara, Colorado with their child, they were greeted with the same comment again and again: 'My, he is certainly a big boy for his age.'

The marriage of Stella and Pop turned into the disaster you would expect between two people as different as they were. She was ice, steel and calculation, hellbent on organising the future. She saw Floyd as a possession and believed it her duty to direct and control him as Silas had controlled her. But how can anybody control a will-o'-the-wisp? Floyd was all fun and dreams. He lived from one moment to the next and loved all of it without reason. Unlike Stella, he cared nothing for social standing or money. He loved everyone. More than once he gave away his last sawbuck to some guy on a street corner he would never see again.

Stella's marriage to Pop quickly turned sour. Angry and disappointed, she turned her attention towards Stanley, making him the focus of all her hopes and dreams. She groomed and indoctrinated him, hoping he would bring her the rewards she longed for – social prominence, money, connections with the right people. There is a photograph of my father at the age of thirteen dressed in a knickerbocker suit, knee-high stockings, starched shirt and tie. On his left side stands his sister Irma Mae, then aged seven, on his right sits Beulah, who was ten. Not one hair on my father's head is out of place. He is smiling gently. Already he has become Stella's 'perfect son'.

The first time I saw this picture, it brought tears to my eyes. The pubescent male which Stella so carefully moulded and manipulated was so far removed from my father's essential nature that, even now, when I look at the photo, it makes me shiver.

What was done to Stella by Silas Edgar, she, in her way, did to my father. The deeper I delved into the bloodline from which they came, the more I was sure that the controlling behaviour and obsession with secrets in the lives of Stella and Stanley had not begun with them. Such things formed a leitmotif in those who came before them. Researching my family tree on my paternal grandmother's side, I found that two major themes ran through the Newcomb and Bradford family trees. The first of these was that many of Stella's ancestors appeared to live double lives, like her. On the surface they were upstanding, privileged, *noblesse oblige* members of society – people to be admired and emulated. They considered themselves arbitrators of morality by Divine Right. They believed it their duty to make judgements about lesser mortals and then to carry out whatever punishments they deemed necessary – even when this resulted in great cruelty and the exploitation of others, the dark side of their seemingly virtuous behaviour.

Stanley talked to me about Stella's double-sided streak several times. In private he often expressed contempt for what he called 'my mother's split lives'. Yet, every time I asked him to tell me more about it, he would always change the subject.

Like Stella, her ancestors played ritual games to amass power – the second theme to run through her family tree. While appearing to be upstanding citizens, they were leading secret lives. They must have spent a lot of their lives not only concealing their own darkness from others but hiding it from themselves beneath a membrane of lies, deceit and justification. Unless some of them were psychopaths they, like my father, must have continually had to do battle with self-loathing, fear and frustration. None would have been able simply to allow themselves to trust in their own spirit to guide them and nourish them. They too probably attempted to get what they longed for from others by seeding illusions in them, perpetrating traumas and manipulating them.

Stella sometimes indulged in ritual involving Stanley, using plant substances or drugs. Audree recalls visiting my paternal grandmother at her condominium towards the end of her life. She explained, 'I went there several times with Stanley in the years before Stella died. She always spoke to him in a little private language they had together which made me feel very uncomfortable.

'She would say, "Would you like to come out in the kitchen and I'll make you a little goop?"

'He would say, "I'm not ready yet."

'Then she would say, "Would you like a little blood transfusion?"

'Stanley would laugh a bit then just accept it. I felt very out of place – like I was being made privy to a nasty practice no one else was supposed to know about,' Audree concluded.

At first, when I learned more about the Newcomb family bloodline,

I was sickened by the thought that generation after generation had passed on these dark machinations to their children and their children's children because this was the only way they knew how to live. Then a great sadness welled up in me as I began to gain some understanding of where the horrors that my father had been living with all his life might have come from – horrors that were soon to become part of my own life.

13

ROAD TO NOWHERE

Stella stayed in Atlantic City for two agonising days. Every time she looked at me, I felt dirty, ugly – full of shame. I wondered if she was keeping her promise or if she had already told my father what happened. Even after she left, I felt afraid.

Two changes had begun to take place in me: I developed a strong sense that I had become *contaminated* and therefore *dangerous*. I felt like I was carrying a virulent disease; no, it was more as if I *were* the disease. I became afraid to let anyone close to me lest they catch it. Yet my memory of what happened in the theatre and on the rooftops had already begun to fade, the way the screen at the end of a movie does. This occurred in direct proportion to my growing sense of contamination.

Some protective mechanism inside me was turning the memories into disconnected sensory fragments, filing them all away in some primitive area of my brain. Walled off and divorced from conscious awareness, before long they would become completely inaccessible to me, to resurface only years later. Yet the effects of trauma remained in my body like an energetic static producing physical symptoms and uneasy emotional states. I began living much of my life between the shifting poles of emotional numbness and alarm. But alarm over what, I had no idea.

In spite of my growing sense of shame and self-loathing, I was glad to be in Atlantic City. It was a favourite place for both my father and me. When the band was working the Marine Ballroom at the end of Steel Pier, we would have a week or more of lazy days to ourselves.

We always stayed at an old hotel on the boardwalk. It had huge windows overlooking the sea and all the charm of a fading Victorian photograph. We drank our beloved fresh orange juice until it felt like we were swimming in it. I ordered French toast for breakfast and asked Stanley if it was OK to get butter for it.

'What?'

'Butter. Is it OK if I get some butter to put on it?'

'What else would you put on it? Ketchup?'

I laughed.

'You better have some maple syrup too,' he added.

Every afternoon in Atlantic City they would hoist a man on the back of a beautiful white horse, high above the end of Steel Pier. This terrifies me. I love horses. I don't want to see this magnificent creature hurt. Up, up, up, the pulley hauls them, until it seems they are a hundred feet above our heads. The horse quivers on a platform just big enough for his hooves. My body starts to shake.

The man urges the horse forward. I swallow hard, close my eyes and turn my head away. The crowd is hardly breathing. My father squeezes my hand. 'Watch, Shortstuff,' he says. 'Open your eyes.' I know the man is going to make the horse leap off and I don't want him to. 'Watch, Leslie, watch,' my father says.

'No!' I cry. 'Oh no, no!'

Bold and trusting, the horse leaps into space. Down, down he plunges, disappearing into the sea. Waves spread out in all directions. My body is pouring with sweat. I am sure he is dead.

Seconds later he surfaces – the man still on his back. I begin to cry. I'm grateful the horse is still alive. I long to be strong and not afraid, like that horse.

My father looks down at me. 'What is it, Shortstuff?' he wonders.

'I was scared he would die.'

Stanley's huge hands grasp me under the arms and raise me up, just the way the crane picked up the white horse, until I am lying against his chest with my heart pounding. He hugs me so hard it takes my breath away. He laughs. Pushing hard against his chest, I try to get my breath back. I laugh with him. He puts me down. We clap and shout with the people on the pier as we watch the horse and the man swim back to shore.

When we left Atlantic City, we seemed to drive all over – from Pennsylvania to Canada – before heading West. The jobs were far apart. Sometimes we'd be in the car for six or seven hours a day. We spent more time alone together that summer than ever before. We told each other stories. He would start a story. I would take it over and finish it, and vice versa, until we ended up in stitches at the absurdities we had made up just to pass the time.

In the car, he talked a lot. He said how disappointed he was with psychoanalysis, that it hadn't helped him. I was glad to hear him say this since everything I knew about psychoanalysis made me feel it was generally useless. He confessed that there were things that happened to him – especially when he was a child – which, although he couldn't remember most of them, he had always felt were holding him back.

'Back from what?' I asked.

'From writing great music,' he said. 'From being happy and making Violet happy. From lots of things.'

He seemed sad. I didn't like him to be sad. When he was sad, I was sad. I asked if he was sad because Violet went to live with Jimmy. He didn't answer.

He began to talk about something else too that summer; something he read about in a book that Mom had given him. It was a really good book, he said. It was called *Dianetics*. It was so good that it had sold hundreds of thousands of copies, which sounded like an awful lot of copies. According to the book, all people's problems are caused by things called *engrams*. Engrams, he said, are memories of bad stuff that has happened to you. They get stored away in your unconscious mind. 'These bad memories are what keep you from being really healthy and doing all you want to do in your life,' he said.

I wondered if Dianetics was like taking an eraser and wiping words off the blackboard.

'Yes, it's like that,' he said. 'It's called "clearing". When all the engrams are gone then you become "clear". Dianetics is a great way to do this,' he added. He told me he had done some work with a guy called an auditor. 'He asks you a lot of questions so, eventually, your reactive mind gets destroyed.'

'Then what happens?'

'Then you can do whatever you want. You get supranormal powers.'

'Ugh. It sounds awful,' I said. 'I wouldn't let anybody destroy my mind no matter what was in it.' He laughed.

Later I learned that the creator of Dianetics had been none other than L. Ron Hubbard. He had introduced the idea for Dianetics in an article published in the spring of 1950 in *Astounding Science Fiction* magazine. Within months his book, *Dianetics: The Modern Science of Mental Health*, was published.

Hubbard put forward the hypothesis that mental and physical problems are the result of traumatic memories stored in someone's 'reactive mind'. The goal of Dianetics was to take control of the mind and get rid of this part of it altogether – wiping away unwanted emotions and banishing physical illness, most of which, Hubbard claimed, were psychosomatic in origin.

Having introduced Stanley to L. Ron Hubbard's writings, Mom had invited Hubbard to Hollyridge where he spent days with Stanley, initiating him into the process of 'auditing' and helping him confront his own 'engrams'. Stanley and Mom even spent time on Hubbard's boat which he kept anchored offshore. Where once 'Dr' Gindes had promised Stanley all the answers, Dianetics had now taken over and he was as obsessed with it as he had been with psychiatry.

On the road that summer, Stanley was working so hard and sweating so profusely that he got into the habit of carrying a big towel with him. He kept it on the piano, so he could wipe away sweat while he was playing. I read book after book those weeks, waiting for him to finish work each night. He often seemed sad. I wondered if not all of those engrams had got pulled out yet. Or maybe Dianetics would turn out to be, as Stanley always concluded about anything he came eventually to reject, 'nothing but a load of crap'.

My father drank a lot after each job, even if we had to drive on to the next night's work without sleep. I didn't like it when he drank. He was always 'different'. Then he didn't remember things and he was never funny. He never called me 'Shortstuff' when he drank.

We raced from job to job, diner to diner, hotel to hotel. He made me navigator. He would tell me where we were supposed to be and it was my job to work out the fastest way on the map to get there. I was always scared I'd be wrong and we'd get lost. When I made a mistake, we'd stop someone at the side of the road and ask the way. Most often it would be some old codger who would say that the place we were looking for was 'only down the road apiece'. That was OK. But if he added, 'You can't miss it,' Stanley and I would look at each other and laugh since, each time anybody said that, we always did miss it.

By the end of August we had worked our way across America and back to Hollyridge, in time for me to start school again. Stanley drove me from Los Angeles to Visalia, then stayed the night in the new house my mother had designed. He loved it. It was all glass and steel with a big yard and a swimming pool and a gigantic indoor planter filled with nine-foot tropical plants separating the front door from the living room.

Violet was always glad to see him. They would sit in the living room and spend most of the night talking while Jimmy poured their drinks and lit their cigarettes, one after another. When Stanley and Violet started talking really loudly – as they often did – or hugged and kissed each other, Jimmy's response was always to hand them another highball.

Two days after my return to Visalia, I entered sixth grade. I had a new teacher with a weird name: Mr Widger. He turned out to be the best teacher I ever had. Mr Widger was big – an inch and a half taller than Stanley – and he was loved by everybody. Within a couple of weeks, he had even brought the class troublemakers into the fold. He was the first man I met whom I felt I could rely on. I felt safe around him and this sense of safety nourished me.

Thanks to Mr Widger, I loved being in school. After all the crazy years on the road it was wonderful for me to show up each morning. Learning was a never-ending game. I would leave home at 6.30 or 7 a.m. to make the thirty-minute walk to school, arriving before anybody else. I liked hanging out there, cleaning blackboards, talking to Mr Widger – it didn't matter what.

I was also glad to be back with Seiko and her family, even though the sense of contamination I had carried since New York made me feel strangely distant from them. Although we both got into mischief as often as we could, the rest of the year passed fairly uneventfully.

In the Christmas vacation, Seiko and I flew to Los Angeles to spend it with Stanley at Hollyridge. He had a lot of time off at the end of 1951 and the beginning of 1952. He had played the final Innovations concert in early December and then recorded 'City of Glass' at Capitol. Written by Bob Graettinger for the forty-piece orchestra, this strange suite of non-jazz, non-classical music was, for Stanley, the culmination of his attempt to create music that would bridge the jazz-classical gap. Yet he lamented that he could not write the music himself, believing he lacked the necessary training.

When that Christmas vacation came to an end, Stanley drove Seiko and me back to Visalia. The drive took four hours. The three of us sang songs together. Seiko and I teased him because he could never carry a tune. We got to Visalia at dinnertime. Violet had prepared beef stroganoff with wild mushrooms and lashings of sour cream, one of his favourite dishes.

Stanley had never looked on Violet and Jimmy's new house as a place belonging to them. He just made himself at home and stayed as long as he liked. If Jimmy resented this – and I am sure he did – he hid it well. When it came to my mother, Jimmy looked upon himself as the knight in shining armour who had rescued this golden-haired Rapunzel from the tower in which her marriage to Stanley had imprisoned her.

When Stanley came to Visalia again a few weeks later, he stayed with us for three days to celebrate his fortieth birthday. The three of them were well on their way to becoming soused. Stanley and Violet were in that place of self-assertive coherence that precedes the blotto phase, which comes two or three drinks further on.

Stanley started talking about Dianetics – about how he knew how to 'clear' people through 'auditing' them, and how he himself had been 'cleared'. Violet in particular asked a lot of questions about it. Stanley, who I think expected Violet to join him in his enthusiasm for his newly discovered passion, became furious with her and Jim for having 'no goddamn imagination'.

The next thing I knew he got up out of his chair, walked out slamming the back door and took off down the road. Two hours later we got a call from the police who had picked him up for drunk driving after he ran his car into a tree on Highway 99. They put him in jail where he spent the night drying out.

In June of 1952 I celebrated my eleventh birthday by inviting the entire sixth-grade class to a swimming party at our house. It was important to me that everyone be there.

Except for somebody pushing Victor Chan, a classmate who couldn't swim, into the pool and my having to dive in and pull him out, it was a wonderful party. It ended my best year at school yet. I looked forward to entering junior high school the coming autumn.

By then the memory of my days with Stella in New York had been locked away in the darkest recesses of my psyche. Even my free-floating feelings of guilt and shame had eased off somewhat. I was sure this summer with Stanley was going to be the best ever. I could feel it. I was on a roll.

14

BLOOD ON WHITE TILES

IT WAS THE middle of July 1952. We were on the road in and around New England, playing lots of dates at amusement parks. I loved it when the band played ballrooms in amusement parks since I adored roller coasters. During the previous five years, I had ridden roller coasters every chance I got – once I got tall enough to lie about my age to the guys who operated them so they would let me on. I knew most of the big dippers in the country, from the Comet at Crystal Beach in Ontario to the Blue Streak at Conneaut Lake Park in Pennsylvania.

I loved the way riding a roller coaster made me feel. It was like listening to music real loud or running in the wind. I liked their unpredictable nature. Back then most of them were made of wood. Some were so old that, when you gave the man your ticket and climbed into a car, you were never sure if you'd make it to the end of the ride or if the ride would be the end of you.

When the band played amusement parks, Stanley always gave me money for the rides and told me to be back in the dance hall by 10.30 p.m. He warned me never to talk to strangers. I thought this was a stupid thing for him to do, since wherever we went – except for the guys in the band – everybody I met was a stranger. I would nod my head, feigning obedience, then dash away to check out the territory.

I liked hanging out with the people I met. I liked the way when, if I did talk to 'strangers' – the man with the baseballs and the stuffed bears, or the Ferris wheel operator – they let me have free throws and free rides. As for the woman who looked after the spinning barrel, she might let me run back and forth through it for free, hoping this would attract more customers.

All these delicious possibilities depended on my being able to talk to strangers long enough to make pals of them. In all the nights I spent by myself in nightclubs, dance halls and amusement parks while my father worked, I never met a stranger who was unkind to me. At times somebody would be grumpy, but when this happened, I would just wander over to the next stall, the next stand, the next table, in search of somebody more friendly.

That night the band was playing the Starlight Ballroom at Lake Compounce in Bristol, Connecticut. The ballroom was big enough to hold 5,000 people. It was almost full. However, the amusement park itself was quite empty and felt creepy.

Its roller coaster was called the Wild Cat. It would have been better named the Tame Cat since it was too mild for my taste. Because the ballroom was packed there were not too many clients for the Wild Cat that night and the man who looked after it had time on his hands. I talked to him a lot since I was hoping he would let me have some free rides.

He told me the whole place was 'haunted' – especially the ballroom. Lots of accidents had happened on the roller coaster, he said. Once, a workman even had his head chopped off by it. He also said that lots of people had drowned in the lake. But the ballroom was the worst place of all. Workers in the park had seen dancing ghosts float in and out through its walls after the doors were locked and everybody had left for the night. I didn't know if he was telling the truth or just trying to scare me.

I rode the Wild Cat eight times, although the man only made me pay for five rides. I knew it was eight because eight was my magic number.

When the job finished, Stanley and I drove back to the hotel. On the dresser of the room lay the keys to his Buick. Next to them, my furry camel stood proudly, a sentinel on guard. The first thing I did whenever we checked into a new hotel was to stand Camel on the highest surface in the room. This was often the centre of a dresser – where he stood that evening. So long as he was there, with his noble stance and his soft snout overlooking the room, the place became home for the night.

That night, Camel's scratched glass eyes reflected the coming and going of neon lights shining through the open window. On the chair next to the dresser on which he stood, a pair of size 13½ men's shoes were lined up like soldiers at attention. My father always put his shoes side by side before he went to bed. Certain things had to be just so, or he didn't feel right. I understood that. This was why I made Camel stand guard over me.

Stanley's shoes were stuffed with the takings from a job that evening. We had carefully counted the money together. I loved doing this. I liked the way American money smells – different from any other money in the world. Stanley made me carry the cash takings out of jazz clubs and dance halls when a job was over. 'The best way to keep money safe,' he always said, 'is to stuff it in a paper bag or a pair of old shoes and give it to a kid.' He believed nobody would think to rob us as we made our way down dark alleys or across a trash-strewn amusement park.

I loved carrying the money. I liked that final walk through the amusement park on the way to the car. There is something mysterious about the way crushed peanut shells and hot dog wrappers get scattered by night winds as the carnival lights are being turned off one after the other. The roller coaster – all locked up – waits patiently for tomorrow. But that night the deserted grounds had seemed eerie as we walked through them. I didn't like it. I wanted to get out of there before we met any of those ghost dancers the roller coaster guy had told me about.

By the time we got back to the hotel room and I wrote down the takings, Stanley was high on alcohol. He never drank before or during a job. But the moment the last strains of 'Artistry in Rhythm' faded away, he would open a bottle of bourbon or Scotch and drown himself in it. For the next forty-five minutes, he could talk happily about nothing in particular or tell stories. During this time he made sense. After that, I would begin to lose him as the alcohol switched him on to automatic pilot. He would say the same things over and over, or become maudlin about something that had happened in his past. Booze took him through a swing door out of this world into some other – a place where I could not go with him.

Tonight was no different. He went to the closet where he had stashed a bottle of Scotch on the shelf above his suit bag. He opened it, took a glass from the bathroom, filled it, and drank it down in one gulp. Then he made a nasty face. 'Jesus Christ, the damned maids have been watering my Scotch again,' he said. 'What's wrong with these hotels?'

I trembled. The maids had nothing to do with it. It was me who poured half his whisky down the drain and topped up the bottle with water when he went out of the room, in a futile attempt to protect him from drinking too much. I missed him when he disappeared into that foreign world. I figured if I could get him to drink less he'd stay with me longer. I didn't think he'd notice if I replaced half of his bottle with water. After all, the bottle was a dark colour so it didn't look all that different. He did notice, of course, but for some reason he never figured out that I was the culprit and until the day he died I never confessed to my crime.

As usual, Stanley and I slept in the same bed. We always did when I was with him – at least we did after my mother left Hollyridge. I loved curling my back up against his. He was long and broad and warm. His feet were never cold like hers. I didn't like his snoring, but, like most kids, once I drifted off I slept like the dead, so it didn't matter.

That night, before we crawled into bed, he got me to cut open a cyst at the back of his neck. Acne pursued him in one form or another all his life. So I was used to playing surgeon. I would grit my teeth, take a single-edged razor blade, and do as he asked, cutting into the offending lump to release its virulent contents. I carried out this request with some skill, since I'd had a lot of practice. I mopped up the mess with toilet paper and we nestled down to sleep – back to back.

I don't know if I ever went to sleep or not. The next thing I knew his massive body was on top of mine. In a rough voice he started to repeat my name: 'Leslie. Leslie. Oh, Leslie.' His hands stroked my body in ways that frightened me. It felt like he was trying to take me with him into a strange universe – a place where I didn't know the rules. What was he doing? What did he want? What did he expect of me? I reassured myself that it must be OK. After all, he was my father. He was my pal. Didn't we laugh together? OK, sometimes we fought, and sometimes he would take a swing at me, like when I bit my nails, but he was my protector, my friend.

Then came the pain, the sweat and the heat, the weight of his huge body on mine. Searing pain – the lining of my life being ripped apart. There was none of the moving of one body into the body of another, of getting lost in the flesh of another, lulled by heartbeats and an ecstasy of dissolution. That I would only come to know much later with other men – after I had grown up. Now there would only be a searing pain. Like the shell of an oyster, I was prised open. My soft insides spilled out everywhere. In one moment, my entire existence becomes unglued.

Out of here. I'm out of here. From the ceiling I look down at the bed, at the floor, at the bodies of the two people beneath me, twisted on each other. I am curious. Indifferent. What do I care? It is cool up here and light. Here there's no sound, no sweat, no pain. Here everything's made of crystal. A fairyland with castles of ice – not hot and horrible like those people down there. Up here I am a princess going about my business, making children happy – handing out pink cotton candy that melts in your mouth. And ribbons – lots of ribbons blowing in the wind.

I go further out, beyond the room, beyond the night, beyond the stars. I go to a secret place at the centre of the Milky Way. That's where I come from. That's my home. Not this little room. What little room? There is no room. Only light and angels singing.

I look down again. It's finished. Over. The man has fallen away from the child. The child's eyes are dry. The room turns quiet except for the sound of heavy breathing and a wind that has turned the glass curtain into streams of red seaweed. That's funny. Now the whole room has turned red.

I lie still. I'm afraid to move. I might wake him. The wind grows stronger. I have to go to the bathroom. I pull myself up to a sitting position, swing my legs over the side of the bed and move as silently as a cat. I do the best I can to ignore the pain in my belly and between my legs. I make my way across the room into the bathroom.

I turn on the light. Too bright. Go away, light. I want to go back into darkness – back into the time before, the time when night is my friend and I can lie safe against my father's back, suspended in velvet blackness.

Blood drips on the shiny white tiles beneath my body. One drop, two drops . . . seven.

That's it. That's what I need to do. If only I can wipe up all the blood then everything will be OK. It must have been a dream. Anybody can see that. If only I can make those angry red spots go away, then everything will be white as snow again.

Cleaning the floor becomes the focus of my life – the only thing that matters. I can do it. I know I can. After all, I've done lots of things before. Naked except for my pyjama top, I work hard – harder than ever before – wiping up blood and washing out towels.

Later – I am not sure how much later, maybe fifteen minutes, maybe hours – I open the bathroom door. The room is still. Even his snoring has stopped. Tomorrow everything will be all right, I tell myself. I know it will. I make my way back to my side of the bed. Slowly, oh so slowly, I crawl beneath the covers. I look up. Camel is no longer standing sentinel. The wind has blown too hard. He lies on his side. He looks defeated. But I am frozen – too scared to get up and put him back in place.

I don't know what happened to Camel after that. I don't remember losing him, yet a week later I realised that he had gone.

15

SECRETS OF FORGETTING

THE MORNING AFTER. I wake up to the sound of Stanley coughing. It's how every morning begins: with this deep hacking from his having smoked thirty cigarettes a day all his life. Dark, resonant, it goes on and on. He staggers into the bathroom. That's where the Alka-Seltzer lives. I hear *plunk, plunk* – two tablets dropped into a glass. He comes back into the room holding the fizzing water. He sits on the edge of the bed, pulling his boxer shorts together the way he always does. He swallows his morning brew in one gulp. Today is the same as any other. He shows no signs of remembering what has taken place only hours before.

Huddled against the head of the bed, I pull the covers around me. I am crying.

He notices. 'What's wrong with you?'

'How could you do that to me?'

'What're you talking about?'

'Last night.'

'Last night?'

'How *could* you?'

'How could I what?' There is a long pause. Then he growls, 'Don't you come crying to me. Anything you got you asked for. Put that in your pipe and smoke it.'

I can't believe my father is saying these things to me. My eyes go dry. Fear takes over. My body freezes. I try to work out what is expected of me. Is he telling the truth? Does he really not remember? This idea frightens me even more than the horror of what happened last night.

I think back to other times and other things he has forgotten: like when I asked him if I could go to the Metropolitan Museum in New York. We were staying in an apartment on Fifth Avenue almost across the street from it. He said, 'Sure. That sounds fun.' An hour later I was dressed and heading out the door. 'Where the hell do you think you're going?' he shouted at me.

'I'm going to the Met,' I said. 'You told me I could.'

'I said no such thing,' he snapped.

I was furious. 'You did too!' I retaliated. 'You did too.' I hated him when he was like that. I walked out and slammed the door behind me.

Then there was that day in Chicago when he asked me to go and buy a packet of Camel cigarettes. When I came back with them, he exploded in anger. 'I won't have you sneaking around smoking cigarettes!' he bellowed. And I remembered that day in the car with my mother, in the middle of nowhere, when he swore he had never borrowed $5 from me – the day I became so frustrated that I bashed him over the head with the wooden coat hanger. My father was always forgetting things.

Now, in this room brightened by morning light, there was no more laughter. I felt nothing but a hot tearing in my belly as though a monster had plunged its paw inside me and ripped out my guts. Violet was not there to remind him how he'd torn me open. Nor did I have a wooden coat hanger I could hit him with to make him remember. Now it was all too scary. I felt trapped with no way out.

Alone, in an ugly place, sitting on a bed I hated, I was staring at a man I didn't know. With his face covered in stubble, he looked like the tramps you find near railroad tracks with their skinny dogs.

This stranger goes back into the bathroom. I hear the shower – then the sound of shaving. What do I do now? What do I say? Is it my fault, like he says? Did I do something to make it happen? If so, what? What does he want me to do now?

It feels like I'm going to throw up. I'm filled with questions to which there are no answers. Does he want me to *pretend* that nothing happened? Maybe that's the game he wants to play. But I can't. I don't know the rules. I'm shaking with cold, yet I know the room is warm.

The stranger comes back, opens the closet door and pulls out a pair of slacks. He looks different now, more like my father.

'Get dressed, Shortstuff,' he says. His voice is warm. It always is when he uses his nickname for me. 'Let's see if we can rustle up some fresh orange juice.' I try to smile. This is a ritual I know – something familiar – something we share – something I can hold on to. I remember that it's easier to find freshly squeezed orange juice in New York or New England than in California and Florida, where all the oranges grow. Maybe orange juice will make things better.

At that young age I had no understanding of the emotional conflicts I was experiencing, nor of the psychological consequences that night would have on me. Experts on incest say that every girl who has been raped by her father makes excuses for his behaviour. Supposedly, the child does this to protect the untarnished image she has of her father, which she needs to hold on to. When it comes to me I don't think this was the case. Although I loved Stanley more than anything in the world, I don't think I ever had an untarnished image of him; at least not from the time I was three or four years old, when I began to know him. I had spent too much time with him in difficult circumstances. I had too often witnessed what took place when his public persona dropped, revealing a frightened, self-centred man – sometimes cruel, sometimes greedy – hidden beneath his boldness and his charm. I had been trained throughout my childhood to witness such changes in him and to treat them as normal. I knew them well. All of his different moods and identities were OK with me. *He* was OK with me. My reasons for believing that Stanley was only dimly conscious of what he had done – if he was conscious of it at all – are quite other. They have to do with the tortuous blood he inherited from his mother's side of the family and all the dissociation that went with it.

*

The next few days were chaotic, fragmented, surreal. I had no sense of what he wanted from me. Stanley may have been as confused as I was. He acted as though nothing had changed between us – at least he *tried* to act that way. Yet he was nervous; distracted. Every time he looked at me he would look away again. It felt like he wanted me to say something, do something – anything – to make it better. But I had no words to speak. Every night before we went to bed he drank so much that he would fall into a kind of coma.

Before that night we had always carried out a little litany together at bedtime:

'Good-night,' he'd say.

'Sleep tight,' I'd answer.

'Don't let the bedbugs bite.'

This used to make us laugh because, once or twice, there really had been bedbugs in a hotel bed and we had to move to another room. Now there was no laughter, no bedtime ritual. Just a frightening hollowness inside me that nothing could fill. I felt like a pariah – the scapegoat responsible for ruining our life together. But I had no idea how I'd done this.

I'd lie awake in darkened hotel rooms, my back against Stanley's as always. But now there was no warmth the way there used to be. His body was icy, even in the hottest part of the summer.

One night, maybe a week after Lake Compounce, I got out of bed, put on a pair of his socks – the long kind that he held up with garters – wrapped myself in a coat and curled up on a big chair with a blanket over the top of me in an attempt to get warm. There I fell asleep.

I woke up next morning to find him standing over me in his shorts. 'Shortstuff, are you all right?'

'I'm cold.'

'Are you sick?'

'I don't know. I don't think so. Just cold.'

'Come here.'

Pulling the blanket around me, I got up and tried to move towards him but I had wrapped it so tightly around my body that I tripped and fell. He grabbed me, lifted me up and carried me to the bed. He laid me down and covered me with the bedspread. He put one hand on my forehead. 'I think you have a fever,' he said, tucking the bedclothes around my body. 'Are you still cold?' I nodded my head. 'Come on, let's get you into a hot shower.'

He carried me to the bathroom, turned on the shower and then went out, leaving me alone, standing in the middle of the bathroom floor wrapped in bedclothes. Shivering, I peeled away the stuff and climbed into the bathtub. Water poured down my skin. Too hot? Not hot enough? I didn't know. I stayed there a long time. Maybe the water would wash everything away.

When I came out of the bathroom he was not in the room. I rummaged through my suitcase, hunting for something clean enough to wear. My body was hot now but it might not stay that way. I found a quilted tartan skirt and a creased white cotton blouse with a big cowl collar. I put them on with white cotton socks and loafers. I wrapped the gold charm bracelet he had given me that summer around my wrist – gold animals hanging from a heavy gold chain – a circus horse, a lion, a turtle. I sat down on the chair I had been sleeping in, wondering if he would come back. I watched dust particles swirling in the light that spilled through the window on to the threadbare carpet. I moved my hands to make them writhe like the heap of snakes I had seen in a movie at the Natural History Museum.

The sound of a key in the latch. The door opens. He stands in the doorway the way he often does before coming into a room – the way he did the day he came to my school to take me away.

'Are you warmer now?' he says.

I nod.

'Leslie, I . . .' he begins, then stops. He is staring at me. I look back at him. I wonder if he is still angry. He knows what I am thinking.

'I'm not mad at you, Shortstuff,' he says.

He comes into the room and shuts the door. 'I'm mad at myself.' He sits on the edge of the rumpled bed. 'I love you so much, Leslie. It's just, maybe I love you the wrong way.'

Now I know what he is talking about. I say nothing.

'I . . .'

'It's OK,' I say. 'It's OK.'

His eyes fill with tears. He shakes them off violently as though the shaking will remove every thought from his head. 'Are you hungry?' he says.

'Starving.'

'Me too. Let's go eat.'

That was all that was ever said. It would be twenty years before we would speak openly about what took place at Lake Compounce and the sex that would happen between us again and again during the next three years. I have often asked myself how it could have been that these were the only words spoken between us about it, when both of our lives had been altered beyond all recognition for ever.

This was the middle of July. The rest of the summer lay head. That morning – the morning of the shower, the fever and the tears – a morning of unspoken agreements and unspoken terrors – marked the beginning of a new, wild, unpredictable existence we began to live together. It marked the start of a different life in which secrets had to be so tightly held that they became secret even to ourselves.

16

FORBIDDEN HONEYMOON

WITH EVERY DAY that passed our secret became hidden more deeply. Our minds had pushed the pain, the shame and the guilt far beneath our conscious awareness. So long as they remained there we were 'safe'.

At the same time we had both been strangely opened up to exchanges of energy, feeling and experience so vast it is hard to describe them. It was as though we were drawn into a multi-dimensional Universe. The intensity of emotional exchange between us and our connection – moment to moment, wherever we were and whatever we were doing together – became so all-encompassing it often felt as though Stanley and I *were* one another.

Breaking the taboo of incest had breached the boundaries of acceptable reality, forcing us to journey into unknown territory. We turned our backs on the rules and regulations of the world. Sometimes we faced each other with the kind of raw presence soldiers in trenches must experience as, together, they face the enemy's assault. Even when separated by thousands of miles, the pact remained. Judging by Stanley's communications with me – especially during the last years of his life – this was as true for him as it was for me.

Apart from the months I spent away from him at school, from that time onwards we hardly left each other's side. Up till then – except for his music – Stanley had been preoccupied with everything from his short-lived relationships with women to mind-controlling techniques such as Dianetics. Now, he became obsessed with me: my physical presence, my opinions and my feelings, as well as his thoughts and feelings about me. It started with his insistence that he know my whereabouts at every moment of the day and night.

A couple of weeks after Lake Compounce, the band was playing at another amusement park. As usual, I had left the ballroom to check out a roller coaster. I could not have been gone more than half an hour when Stanley showed up. He had forsaken the bandstand, leaving the band to play without him, to dash around the amusement park in a frenzy, searching for me.

Finally spotting me swinging in a chair at the top of the Ferris wheel, he shouted at the man in charge of the ride, 'What the hell do you think you're doing?' The sound of his voice scared the guy so he shoved the brake on hard, making the chairs swing wildly. My father took hold of the poor man by his collar and, pointing at me, yelled, 'Get my kid down from there!' In less than a minute I arrived at the bottom. Stanley did not even wait for the man to lift the bar so I could get out. He reached over, grabbed me under the arms, and pulled me free of the chair as though my body was no heavier than air. Then he plonked me on the ground.

'I never said you could go on that thing,' he said.

'You never said I couldn't.' I was embarrassed to have my father following me around, making scenes – especially when I was trying my best to appear grown up and independent.

'Come here.'

'I won't.'

I turned away from him, in a futile attempt at pretending I didn't know him. He grabbed me again, and lifted me up to eye level.

'What's wrong with you?' I snapped. 'You worry about me on a Ferris wheel, but you don't care how often I ride the roller coaster?'

Stanley began to laugh. He pulled me so hard against him that it knocked the air out of me. I squirmed, trying to free myself from his bear-like grip. He loosened his grip enough that I could laugh with him. 'I do care,' he said. 'I don't like this place, Shortstuff. Let's get out of here. Come back to the ballroom.'

One day followed the next. We spent them like wild children – stubborn, enthusiastic, fighting, laughing, teasing. One moment he'd be furious about something, real or imagined. The next we'd be caught up in insane laughter, triggered by nothing more than looking at each other. We looked for adventure wherever we could find it.

He and I shared an unpredictable, mercurial streak, often unsettling to the people around us. It showed itself in him when he was in one of his silly, funny moods. In me it was most often triggered when I felt adults were looking down their noses at me or whispering clichés such as 'children should be seen and not heard'.

Towards the end of July, the band had two days off near Cape Cod. One of Stanley's fans offered him the use of a private house on the beach where we could stay. We arrived there so late on the first day we decided to stay up for the rest of the night to watch the sunrise.

Unusually, that night Stanley had had nothing to drink. When we arrived at the house we had trouble finding the key. It was supposed to be under the eaves by the back door. We searched for half an hour before locating it under the eaves of a tool shed at the rear. It was caked with sand, which made it hard to unlock the door.

The place turned out to be such a homely cottage that when we walked into the kitchen it felt like there should have been a pot of home-made soup waiting for us. We found an old patchwork quilt in a wooden chest in the bedroom. We took it and headed for the sand dunes. Snuggled together beneath it, sitting in tufts of prickly beach grass, we waited for dawn.

The coast was deserted. The air was cold – much colder than the water – so a mist had formed. It lay across the ocean, not on the water itself but a few feet above it so we could look both beneath the mist and over the top of it at the same time. When the sun did come up, it turned the mist into a three-layered sandwich in fiery ice-cream colours.

The waves were small; not like the crashing breakers of the Pacific that we loved so much. The sun rose higher. The mist faded. We took off our shoes and socks and hid them with the quilt under some driftwood. Stanley rolled up his trousers. This always made me laugh. He looked like a white-fleshed chicken with scrawny legs. We walked, then ran, along the beach at the edge of the water.

The higher the sun rose, the worse the infestation of sand flies became. To get away from them, we splashed each other. As each wave ebbed, we would run towards the sea to see how far out we could go, then race back up the beach before the next wave could catch us.

People began to appear. By then we'd made our way so far along the beach that we ended up in a village where shops were beginning to open. We got coffee-to-go in a paper cup for him, an ice-cream cone and hot chocolate for me. Then, from a tiny bakery, we bought a big bag of home-made Danish pastries to take with us.

When we got back to the beach house he went to take a shower. Left alone, I seized the moment by turning the bed into a trampoline. My mother strictly forbade me to jump on beds, but I loved doing it. Anyway, now she was three thousand miles away. Unfortunately, this bed turned out to be a less sturdy piece of furniture than I had hoped. After a few jumps, one of its legs gave way with a horrible cracking sound. I slid off the thing, afraid I was going to be punished.

'What the hell was that?' Stanley shouted from the bathroom.

'I think I broke the bed.'

He came into the room with a towel wrapped around his waist. 'What were you doing?'

'Jumping.'

He got down on his hands and knees to look at the broken leg.

'I'm sorry,' I said.

'We can fix this,' he said. 'It's been broken before.' I remembered the retaining wall we made together at Hollyridge. I was glad I broke the bed. Now we could fix it together.

We pulled the mattress off the bed frame on to the floor. As usual, it was nowhere near long enough for my father's body. 'Are you hungry?' he said. Pulling the curtains to shut out as much light as possible, we flopped down in the middle of the mattress. In five minutes we had covered the sheets, the blankets, and ourselves with flakes from the Danish pastries. They were yummy.

'I'm tired,' I said, curling up against his back. I wasn't afraid any more. Whatever had happened that was horrible was all finished for the moment. He turned his body towards me and slid his left arm under my head. I lay in the crook of it, my head against his chest. My father had little hair on his chest. But the hairs that were there were long. They tickled my nose.

Although we'd been up all night, we stayed awake, talking.

'What were you like when you were my age?' I asked.

'I don't remember.'

I jabbed him in the side with my elbow. 'I want to know!'

'You want to know, do you?' he said, tickling my ribs with his knuckles.

'Stop it. Yeah. I want to know.'

He went quiet. I think he was hoping I would let him sleep, but I wanted to talk. I wanted to know everything about what he was like before I was born. He could see there was no escape.

He sighed. 'I don't remember much. My mother used to send me to the corner shop to buy food.'

'Was that fun?'

'God, no! I hated it. Mr Woolsey, the guy who had the grocery store, was suspicious of me. We always owed him money. It was my job to convince him to let us buy more bacon and flour and eggs on an account that never got paid off.'

'How awful.'

'Yeah. I felt like a criminal – I had to lie all the time.'

I turned away to play with a dust ball that had rolled across the floor to the bed. 'What else?' I said.

'My mother made me join the Boy Scouts. But the scoutmaster acted like a Nazi and I quit.'

I sat up. 'I joined the Brownies once when you were away for a long time. The woman promised to put me in a Thanksgiving play.'

'So what happened?'

'The woman wouldn't let me play a pilgrim,' I scowled. 'They wanted me to play a turkey. So I left.'

He squeezed me and laughed. 'Stella was always angry with me for hating Scouts,' he said. 'She'd pull a long face. She kept making me go, so I went for a while. Then I'd get dressed in my uniform and go down to the river instead.'

'What did you do at the river?'

'I sat by the bank and daydreamed.'

'About what?'

'Anything. Getting out of there. Being a different person. Having an adventure. Leading a pack of wild horses down the mountain.'

'Did you tell anybody your dreams?'

'Never – not until I met your mother. There was nobody to tell.'

His saying this made me sad. I kept thinking he must have been lonely. I knew about that kind of loneliness. I asked, 'What else did you do?'

'Once I built myself a go-kart from a box and some two-by-fours that Pop gave me. I used to ride on it down the hill near our house. I got in trouble for going too fast. Stella made me give it away.'

'Did that make you mad?'

'Not really. If I couldn't go fast, I didn't want to ride it at all.'

'Were you sick a lot like me?' I wanted to know.

'I guess so. My tonsils used to swell up like golf balls, till the doctor cut them out with a pair of scissors. My sore throats stopped but I still got bronchitis every winter – pneumonia too, once or twice.'

I liked learning that my father had been sick like me. I had always felt guilty about being sick so often.

'What else did you do when you were a kid?'

'Well, I went to the movies with Freddie Ames who lived across the street.'

'Can we go to the movies tonight?' I murmured, finding it hard to keep my eyes open.

'If there is a theatre in this godforsaken place.'

I wanted to go on asking questions but my body was already tingling. It sank into the bed. I passed out with visions of a movie I hoped we'd see – a Superman serial in black and white with lots of good and evil in it.

When we woke up the sky was growing dark. It was much too late to find a hardware store. We had eaten all the Danish pastries and we were ravenous. We drove twenty or thirty miles to a town where someone said there was a movie theatre. The film started in fifteen minutes.

Stanley grabbed my hand and dragged me to the counter of the drugstore next to it. 'What can we get in five minutes to take away?' he said to the man behind the counter.

'A tuna sandwich?'

'Great. We'll have four tuna sandwiches and two vanilla malts.'

I bought the tickets while Stanley waited for the guy to wrap 'dinner' in waxed paper. We hid it inside my sweater and slipped into the theatre just as the lights were going down.

The movie began with great billowy mists on screen, an ocean of clouds in constant motion. 'How did they do that?' I whispered, taking a bite of a sandwich.

'They dropped dry ice into buckets of water, I think,' he said. I was proud to have a father so smart that he could figure it out. Maybe one day, I can get to be as smart as he is, I thought.

We didn't know this at the time but the movie we saw that night echoed aspects of what was unfolding in our lives. Called *Portrait of Jennie*, it was the haunting story of impossible love between a painter called Eben Adams, played by Joseph Cotten, and a child, Jennie Appleton, played by Jennifer Jones. In the film, Jennie first meets Eben in Central Park and makes him promise to wait for her until she grows up.

The man and the girl meet again and again. She keeps entering his life and leaving it. Each time they meet, Jennie is a little older. Eben has tried, unsuccessfully, to make a living from painting landscapes. He decides to paint a portrait of Jennie. The painting not only makes him famous, it eventually hangs in the Metropolitan Museum in New York. The story builds into high drama as the impassioned Eben finds, then loses, Jennie – who is by then a young woman. The movie ends with the most magnificent violent storm at sea I have ever seen on film. The storm takes place at Cape Cod – not far from where we were watching the movie.

Given the weird bond that was developing between us and our shared obsession with the powers of nature – especially storms at sea – Stanley and I would go back to see the movie again and again. Stanley would turn to me suddenly in Chicago, or Atlanta, Los Angeles or Boston, and say, 'Jennie?' I always knew what he meant.

'Right,' I would say. 'Let's go.'

When we were in New York, we'd search through Central Park for the locations where the movie was shot.

As for the storm at the end of the film, I began to see it in dreams. By the time I turned fourteen, it would become, for me, a symbol of the violent end of everything – a loss so great I could not face the grief of it. By then I would feel like I was dreaming the dream in a half-dead body. I would watch from a great distance as giant waves destroyed what had once been my life.

17

CASTLES IN THE SAND

OUR DAYS AT Cape Cod strengthened the connection between us – a closeness which bore little resemblance to the horror of Lake Compounce. Yet had the rape never happened, I doubt that this bond would ever have developed as it did.

We were near Chesapeake Bay in Virginia and that day Stanley had some free time. He had asked somebody the night before, 'Where can I take my kid tomorrow?' The chosen destination turned out to be the ugliest lighthouse I have ever seen. It was called 'Old Henry', 'Old Cape Henry' or something like that. Constructed from cut stone two hundred years earlier, it skulked miserably on a mound of sand overlooking the bay.

When we got there we were met by a man whose task it was to look after the light. It didn't seem that he was doing a great job of it, since it looked to me like it might fall apart in a gale. He asked if we wanted to climb to the top. I couldn't wait. I charged up the stairway, shouting to Stanley, 'You'll never catch me!'

'Oh, yeah?' he hollered. 'Just wait until I do!'

I won hands down. Even though his legs could take three steps at a time when I could only manage one, my father got out of breath easily because he smoked so much.

After exploring the lighthouse, we headed for the beach. I built a castle in the sand. My father slept in the sun, his huge feet and long legs covered with a towel to keep them from burning. After maybe an hour the tide turned. The surf rose, threatening to wipe out my construction, which I had wanted him to see before it dissolved. But

I also liked the idea of letting the water flow up over his body to wake him up. He'd been asleep too long. I felt bored and lonesome. I sat there, looking out to sea, watching the waves gather power and trying to guess how long it would be before the rising waters would swamp him.

The Atlantic Ocean played out the drama perfectly. A big swell rose far out from the beach. It rolled in without breaking, until it was no more than ten feet from us. I got to my feet and watched. The water not only flooded the lower half of Stanley's body, it came all the way over his chest before receding. He leapt up like a circus clown with his bottom on fire and started stumbling around in a daze. He was probably still asleep.

It made me laugh. He looked so funny with his bright red chest and his chalk-white legs. He grabbed his towel, now sopping wet, twisted it into a whip, and snapped me with it in mock rage.

'Why did you let me sleep so long?' he demanded.

'I'm not responsible for you,' I retorted. 'Why should I care what you do? I was working on my castle. If you're too stupid to get off the beach when the tide comes in, it serves you right to get washed out.'

'Looks like your castle got washed out too.'

'Yeah, but it was worth it.'

He picked me up and threw me over his shoulder like I was a piece of meat or a sack of flour. 'You want a pineapple rub,' he shouted. Making a fist, he ground his knuckles into my scalp.

'Put me down,' I shrieked, laughing. 'I hate you.'

He carried me back to the hotel and up to our room. He turned on the shower and shoved me into it. There was sand everywhere. It had even found its way inside my ears. I thought we'd never get rid of it all. Afterwards he plonked me on the bed and smeared me in lotion. Then he made me do the same for him.

We got dressed, and went downstairs to the hotel dining room. He was wearing a loose black shirt, open at the neck. What I could see of his chest was fire-engine red.

The *maître d'* showed us to a table on the terrace. 'Would you like a cocktail before dinner?' he asked.

'Why not?' Stanley said. 'I'll have a J&B on the rocks – a double.'

'And the lady?'

'You want a cocktail, Leslie?' my father said. Having been asked this question a hundred times before, only to be offered a disgusting concoction of cherry juice and goo called a 'Shirley Temple', I was about to refuse. Before I could say anything, Stanley said, 'Bring the lady a champagne cocktail.' The *maître d'* took our order and disappeared.

'What's a champagne cocktail?' I asked.

'I don't know,' he replied. 'I think it's champagne with Angostura bitters and syrup or something. It's what women drink.'

The syrup sounded OK. I liked sweet things. I figured I could probably manage the champagne since I had drunk champagne in New Orleans and that was OK. But 'bitters' sounded like one of those medicines Mom made me swallow when I had a sore throat. 'Ugh,' I said.

'If you don't like it we'll order you something else.'

But I did like it. It wasn't as sickly as a Shirley Temple, nor was there one of those ugly paper parasols in my glass.

Our meal of barbecued spare ribs arrived. They turned out to be so messy it took us three finger bowls each and at least as many napkins to get through them. Stanley drank his Scotch and ordered two more, while I downed two more champagne cocktails – stopping once or twice to taste his J&B. I felt proud to be treated like a woman instead of ignored like a child.

'You look very grown up,' my father said. 'It scares me how beautiful you're going to be one day.' His saying that scared me too. Part of me loved the idea of growing up except that most grown-ups seemed stiff and boring and I didn't want to become one of those.

'I don't know if I want to grow up,' I replied. 'It might be better to stay a child. There are good things about being ignored the way kids are.'

'I don't think anybody is going to ignore you,' my father said. 'There's too much of you for anybody to ignore. You're going to be tall. You have a good strong body and a good voice. You carry a lot of energy. People are attracted to your light. Everybody's going to want more of it.'

'Is that why people are attracted to you?' I wondered.

He was gnawing on a spare rib. He stopped and sat there, with his hands covered in sauce, staring at me. Then he said, 'I think I did once, but I seem to have lost some of it along the way.'

'And Violet?'

'She is different than you or me. Your mother lives in her own world. She doesn't like mine much. When I try to talk to her about something she doesn't know about, she ignores me.'

'Do I ignore you?'

He shook his head and wiped his mouth, smearing the napkin with barbecue sauce. It looked like blood. The waiter arrived with more finger bowls. Stanley kept on staring at me.

'Stop staring at me,' I said.

'You're the one who's staring, not me.'

'I am not!'

'I always want to be better,' Stanley continued. 'A better father to you, a better friend, a better person. Then something gets hold of me.' His eyes began to water. 'You're smart, you cut through all the crap. I like the way you think. I admire your rebelliousness. It's in me too. But it's got all crumpled up somehow. Guess what?'

'What?'

'I'll bet you and I together could take over the whole world if we wanted to.'

I knew then that the Scotch had kicked in. It was making him say a lot of strange things. But they made me feel good anyway. It felt like I didn't have to be alone. I felt it was OK to be an outsider if he was an outsider *with* me.

When we finished our ribs the waiter asked if we wanted dessert. I ordered tapioca pudding. Stanley ordered two more J&Bs before drinking his coffee. 'You want a walk before we go to bed?' he asked.

'OK,' I said, not sure, after all the food and champagne, that I'd be able to walk at all.

The night was warm and sticky. Stanley put his arm around my shoulder. The top of my shoulder fitted perfectly underneath his armpit. I could feel the silkiness of his shirt against my cheek. I could smell his smell. We went down the steps from the veranda and walked along the sand. He wanted to talk. This time it was not about music. It was about him. His voice had a dreamy quality to it – like someone in a trance who has a hard time making words. He'd begin a sentence but there would be no verb in it. Or he'd start to say something, and the words would trail off before he finished.

He spoke about Stella and about what she made him do when he was a kid, and about Pop, his father. He told me he'd get 'the guilts' about lots of the things he did, but he couldn't stop doing them.

When we got back to our room it was sweltering. There was no wind off the sea to cool down the air. We pulled the sheets off the bed, dipped them in cold water, wrung them out hard and put them back on the bed so the evaporating water would cool us off. When we got into bed we were both naked so that the wet sheets could better do their cooling work. The sheets covered us completely, forming a barrier between us and the outside world.

That was a world which had nothing to do with us. We were hidden inside our secret tent. Instead of curling up back to back as we usually did, we met face to face. As I lay on my side with my head against his chest, he entered my body again. It hurt and I was scared.

Champagne, together with my being so tired, produced in me an anaesthetised state. Somewhere in a dark corner of my heart it felt as though what was happening had to be 'wrong'. But I couldn't figure it out. All I knew was that right here, right now – with this man, child, friend, father, stranger and fellow conspirator – I wanted to try my best to follow, wherever he was taking me.

When I look back on that time, it seems to me we were *both* children – responsible to no one, living a life unbounded by space and time. Children don't bother to think what price will have to be paid for such freedom. My father and I had our own unspoken pact – one that, over the years, would come to define the depth of our bond and its cost to our lives: 'cross your heart and hope to die'.

18

MANY MANSIONS

T HAT SUMMER MARKED the start of a different life for me, one in which I was forced to hold the secrets so tightly that they separated me from myself. Somewhere deep inside, the part of me which carried memory and pain went silent as death. Like an autistic child, it had divided itself off so completely from the rest of me that I didn't even know it was there. Nor did I have any idea then that the fear and rage, the grief and chaos locked inside this mute creature had begun to live its own life, and that, without warning, it would break through, wiping out any sense I once had that I could rely on myself.

At times I experienced physical pains. They would rise up in my chest over my heart. I'd lie in bed at night breathing so lightly that, had someone put a candle near my mouth, its flame would not have wavered. Often I would wake in terror. It was not so much that I felt afraid; it was more as if my body, independent of my emotions, registered so much terror – of what I did not consciously know – that my bowels would become loose and I would vomit. Unbidden, and without apparent cause, such experiences had begun to boil up and spill out of me.

Stanley too had been living in a continual state of confusion. Despite his blocking out of all conscious knowledge of the ongoing incest, he was haunted by his 'guilts'. They pursued him like harpies. He would wake from bad dreams, screaming. When I'd ask him what his dreams were about he would say, 'Nothing, nothing.'

I think he tried his best to resist touching me. Then – always drowning in a sea of alcohol – he would come to me, only to deny to himself the following day what had happened.

I now believe that my father had always been driven by his instincts and prey to his obsessions. He was a surprising combination of childlike innocence and indomitable will. You can hear this in his music. When the disarming combination of his disparate energies and personas came to the surface, any of those that did not fit with the way he wanted to be seen or how he wanted to think of himself would split off from conscious awareness, freeing him from any sense of responsibility. He would often 'lose time'. He could forget, with consummate ease, whatever was dangerous for his conscious personality to remember.

I remember when I first heard the biblical quote from John 14:2. It plunged me into a state of fear. Theologians say that Jesus is comforting his disciples, telling them that there were many dimensions to their saviour's divinity: 'In my Father's house are many mansions: if it were not so I would have told you.' The idea that Jesus' disciples could find comfort in such words still makes me shudder. In my own father's 'house' there were indeed many mansions but they were far from comforting.

Only decades later would I learn about the condition that has come to be known as dissociative identity disorder (DID). It used to be called the multiple personality phenomenon, in which the human psyche becomes fragmented as a result of severe or persistent traumatic experiences which are too much for the individual – especially a child – to integrate into what he knows about reality. People with DID are not mentally ill, even though in the past they were often treated as such. They are best described as ordinary people having a normal response to abnormal situations – events so disturbing that they often feel life-threatening. Such people lose the ability to respond adequately to what is happening to them. DID lies at the centre of what has come to be known as post-traumatic stress disorder (see Appendix).

Each one of us has our own mechanisms for survival. Like Stella, and, I suspect, many in her family before her, the way my father dealt with overwhelming pressure was by dissociation. Like shards of a broken mirror, broken then separated from each other, some parts of his psyche did not even touch each other. When faced with unbidden thoughts that frightened him, or that drove him to behave in ways that Stella's 'good boy' training did not allow, a different fragment of his fractured self would take over to think the thought or do the deed for him.

Whatever shard was most appropriate to the moment or to whatever challenge he faced would then come forward to help deal with it. Because this shard was separated from the rest of the whole, the everyday Stanley neither needed to know what had happened, nor did he have to take responsibility for it. But the cost of all this to him was enormous. He was forced to live his life against all odds. Given his sensitivity, his spirit and his life force, the pressures he must have endured – especially while growing up – would have been enough to split anyone into fragments.

When Carol Easton interviewed my father about his childhood for her biography *Straight Ahead*, she reported: 'Stanley's recollections of his early childhood are remarkable chiefly for their absence. Characteristically, he worried that such a blank masks a block.'

As Stanley got older and his addiction to alcohol grew worse, his mind became progressively more fragmented, like a mirror that was not only broken but had been shattered by the blow of a fist. Eventually it even destroyed his connection to what he loved most: music. Towards the end of his life he could not write a dozen bars of a melody that made sense.

Now summer was coming to an end. Audree, who for many years was intimately connected with the band first as a publicist and later as Stanley's manager, recalls that there were a few people in and around the band, including Bob Fitzpatrick (Fitz) and Gene Rolland, who observed that our relationship seemed 'unnatural'. As Audree had no clear proof and never saw Violet, now that she lived so far away, she kept her concerns to herself. Others commented that Stanley and I behaved more like a couple than father and daughter. But somehow they too seemed to have been drawn into the circle of silence that surrounded us.

In this new realm we had begun to inhabit, when Stanley and I argued our disputes were vehement. Our shared enthusiasm for anything from the taste of a good hamburger to a movie we liked was equally intense. Tears flowed easily. Laughter came with little provocation. So did grief and confusion. Every feeling, word and action between us seemed to be magnified. It was as though together we were living a rarefied life – a life we rode the way you surf a wave, hoping it will carry you back to shore. Yet in the dim reaches of consciousness lurked an unspoken fear: if, even for a moment, we were to stop and look at the wave we were riding, we might drown in the violence of the water that carried us.

A few days after we arrived in Chicago, the time came for me to return to Visalia to begin junior high school. Thanks to my family's fascination with recording events, Violet and Jimmy had shot a home movie both of my departure for the East two months earlier, and my return to California that September.

The footage begins as a small United Airlines plane pulls up to the gate at Visalia's airport. I climb the steps and wave goodbye. Then the movie cuts to shots of me arriving back in what could well have been the same aircraft. I run down the steps and across the tarmac to greet everyone. Seiko is there. So is my grandfather Pat. It is bizarre to watch. The girl who leaves and the one who comes back look like two different people. The one who leaves is composed and smiling – a bit like a young foal feeling its way. The one who returns is distracted and unfocused like a hyperactive racehorse. She keeps looking around, as though needing to protect herself from whatever or whoever might be coming at her.

'Tell us all about your trip,' my mother said in the car on the way home. 'What did you do? Where did you go? Was it fun?' Her voice sounded as if it was coming from down the end of a long corridor. It felt as though she were asking these questions of someone else, not me. 'Leslie?'

'What?'

'Tell us about your trip.'

'There's nothing to tell.'

'How is Stanley?'

'He's OK, I guess.'

'She's tired from the plane ride,' reasoned Jimmy.

'Of course. We can hear all about it later,' said Violet.

In the end we never talked about it at all. Not only did I not want to talk to anyone – even Seiko – about that summer, I could not have spoken about those months with my father even if I had tried. For, obedient to the secret agreement with my father and prey to the familial tendency to dissociation, I already remembered little about them. I was filled with confusion; frightened but not knowing why. Exhausted, yet unable to recover my energy, I felt as though the life force had gone out of me. No matter how long I slept, I didn't seem able to regain it.

I found it incredibly hard to settle into living once more in my mother's house. The life my father and I had shared was a life no one else could hope to understand. The few flashes of memory I had of our months together seemed like flakes in a snow globe. Every time I tried to pick up the globe to examine it, they swirled into a snowstorm, obscuring everything.

The hidden existence with my father had split me into at least two separate people. I was becoming more like him. Inexplicable things began to happen. I started to lose time. An hour or three or four would pass without my knowing it. Seeing a clock I would be surprised – sometimes frightened – to find the time had changed. When I went into the bathroom in my mother's house to brush my teeth, I had no idea what colour my toothbrush was. I would become so confused that I grabbed whichever was closest to hand.

Several times my mother chastised me for using her toothbrush, or Jimmy's. Yet it kept happening. Violet became furious. I had no way to explain how I could make such a stupid mistake. In desperation I took to carrying a toothbrush around in my school-bag and taking it out whenever I needed to brush my teeth, so I wouldn't make another mistake and enrage her further. After that, every time I left to go to Stanley, the same thing would happen all over again on my return.

Within two or three days of my return to Visalia, I started school. I had been a straight A student and I knew the best grades were expected of me. But I now developed a belief that my good grades had been an 'accident' I would never be able to repeat. I was plagued by the sense that it had not been me who was responsible for my previous successes, but someone else – someone who was no longer there. I remember working out that I had best pretend to be like her or somebody would notice that she had disappeared. If only I could prevent anyone around me from discovering she was missing, I might be able to fool the teachers into thinking she still existed and my good grades would continue.

This was desperately important since Seiko got straight As, as did both her sisters, Kikuko and Yoko. If suddenly I did not, I would lose my place as the Kawasakis' 'fourth daughter'.

This was how the *other* Leslie came to take over. She was nothing more than a facsimile of the girl who had once belonged within Seiko's family, who played football like a boy, and who felt OK about being who she was. At night when I was alone I came face to face with a terrible reality: this new Leslie was counterfeit – a cardboard cutout of a human being. I wondered how long it would take for other people to discover the sham.

In the end I don't think anybody ever did – at least not that year. I continued to get good grades. I even made some new 'friends' at school by behaving in the ways I thought people expected me to behave. I lived each day on high alert – a scared animal watching out for anything that might blow my cover.

The nightmares came flooding back. There was one especially frightening recurring dream: in it, I am running from something. I have no idea what. I dash into a house and barricade the door only to hear the sound of it cracking under the onslaught of what sounds like a monstrous beast chomping and clawing its way inside. I climb out through a window, race across mountains and fields then into a forest. Still it pursues me.

Again and again I dreamed the same dream. I would wake up drenched in sweat. I dared not speak of it to anyone. Everything about me had to remain a secret. I knew that.

In another nightmare, I am running over the flat roofs of Manhattan, leaping from one building to another, my relentless pursuer gaining on me. Exhausted by the effort it takes to save myself, this time I ask myself an obvious question: 'What am I running from?' I have, until now, been too terrified to find out. Racing across yet another rooftop, I turn to look behind. A hand comes up over the edge of the building, then a second hand, arms, a head. I freeze – terrified. The face is my own. The monster who has been pursuing me is myself.

I had begun to change. Repeated sex at the age of ten or eleven triggers cascades of hormones. The body tries to rise to the occasion by turning from child to woman as fast as it can. As I watched this happen, I developed bizarre fears. Although I knew, logically, such a notion was absurd, I imagined I would become pregnant if I sat on a bench next to a boy. I was pursued by feelings of shame. I sensed a mounting darkness threatening to drown me. I kept trying to fight it off before it could swallow up my life. I didn't realise it at the time, but I had taken on my shoulders all the blame, fear, anger and shame that belonged to my father. With help from the ever-accessible alcohol, pills and hard work, Stanley always fought hard to keep his demons at bay. Now, I was beginning to feel something like them start to fester in my stomach like rotten meat.

During the months my father and I were away from each other, I spent night after night waiting for him to call. I would go to bed as usual. As soon as I was sure Jimmy and Violet were asleep, I would drag my eiderdown and pillow down the hall to lie on the soft carpet in the living room next to the phone. He usually rang after a job, before he had become so blinded by alcohol that he was no longer coherent. After speaking to him, I would sneak back to my room and try to sleep.

I so identified with Stanley and his concern that it was as if I was *becoming* him. I wanted to take on as much of his pain as I could to relieve him of it. And I tried to grow up fast since that seemed to be what Stanley wanted – like Jennie in the movie. I would examine my budding breasts in the mirror as if they belonged to someone else. Was this the person I was to become? Was she someone my father wanted me to turn into? Or was all this a terrible mistake?

A few weeks before I left Visalia to join Stanley at Hollyridge for Christmas, my mother made a big announcement. She took the two of us – Jimmy and me – out for a Foster Freeze ice cream. Sitting in the car waiting for the kid in the white paper hat to deliver our tubs, she broke the news: 'I'm going to have a baby.'

I couldn't believe it. All my life I had wanted a brother or a sister but I never thought it would happen.

'I'm going to Los Angeles next week to see Dr McCarthy,' she continued.

'Why?'

'I want him to deliver the baby.'

'Los Angeles is such a long way,' protested Jimmy.

'I am not going to have some two-bit doctor in this one-horse town deliver my child!'

That was the end of the discussion.

Soon afterwards, my mother asked me the inevitable question: 'Leslie, what would you like for Christmas?'

Visions of black silk and handmade lace floated into my mind. 'I want a beautiful nightgown and *peignoir*,' I said.

A week before Christmas, as I was getting ready to leave for Hollyridge, she gave me my Christmas present. I opened the big pink box, tied with a gold ribbon, to discover a lovely blue nightgown and *peignoir* trimmed in beige lace. I was desperately disappointed because it did not seem 'grown up' enough. Also, I could see how beautiful and innocent it was. I felt unworthy of such a gift. Only black would have done.

I continually upbraided myself for not being good enough, for not knowing what was expected of me, for not being able to grow up fast enough to fulfil the role which had been thrust upon me. Meanwhile my body continued to change so fast it scared me. I grew four inches in as many months. My waist became slender. My hips were spreading. When I put on a blouse or a sweater, instead of lying smooth against a flat chest, it curved out, hinting at the shape of a young woman beneath.

'My God, Leslie, how you've grown,' my father said, when I got to Hollyridge. I didn't know how to reply. Did I apologise or should I feel proud? Maybe now, since I was becoming different, he would want nothing more to do with me.

Over the Christmas holidays we spent several days together in Catalina walking in the hills, swimming in the sea and sleeping. School, my worry over grades, my love for Seiko and her family were all forgotten now that I was back in the intensified world Stanley and I inhabited together.

Our room at Avalon had a balcony overlooking the sea. One night as we sat there together – me in a wrought iron chair, he on the tiled floor in front of me – he put his head in my lap and wept, talking about the music he wanted to write but feared he never would.

Some nights we had sex. Now at least the pain had gone from my body.

The mornings that followed were so different from the nights that it seemed as though two other people – not the pair of us – had lived through the events of the night. We bathed in sunlight, played endless games and made up funny stories. The days were filled with laughter, fights, dreams, fears and a shared sense of exhilaration. We were defying the world. We lived on the edge of ordinary reality, as instinctively as animals. We needed no words to communicate. Yet all the while, just beneath, a sense of ugliness was eating at me. It grew into a hungry beast, devouring everything in its path.

The morning my vacation came to an end, we set out together to drive from Hollywood to Visalia on the Ridge Route, California's historic US 99, now Interstate 5. This highway goes over the huge range of mountains separating the Los Angeles basin from the San Joaquin Valley. The sun shone brightly when we began our journey, so we put down the top of the Lincoln convertible. When we entered the mountains, the temperature dropped dramatically and it began to snow heavily.

'Are you cold?' Stanley asked me. 'Shall we put up the top?'

'Cold? No, I'm not cold. But if you're cold, go ahead.'

'No, I'm fine.'

'Me too.'

'Are you sure?'

'Absolutely.'

Neither of us was wearing a jacket. We drove for an hour like this while the open car filled with snow. Our teeth chattered. Yet we would not admit that we were freezing. Finally, my father burst out laughing. For the next five minutes we laughed ourselves silly at the way neither of us would give in and admit we were cold. Shivering uncontrollably, we put the top up.

19

RITES OF PASSAGE

BY THE TIME I returned to Visalia after Christmas, my mother looked pregnant. She let me put my hand on her belly. I felt the baby kicking. Something stirred inside me. I found it wondrous that a woman could carry a new life in her body. I couldn't get this out of my mind.

Nor could I settle back into school. I was continually haunted by a sense of dread. I did not know of what. It was like being lost in a fog or trapped in a force field. Separated from everything and everyone around me, I could not find myself. Only a year earlier, I had come to experience some confidence and a lack of self-consciousness which made it possible for me to relate freely to other kids, to my teachers, to Seiko and her family. I had felt safe enough to live spontaneously. All that had disappeared. Now I was the outsider – an intruder in a world to which I felt I had no right. I believed I was physically repulsive and I was ashamed.

All this coincided with my first flow of menstrual blood, about which, strangely enough, I had no sense of fear or shame. The blood that poured from my body felt like a badge of courage and a sign of impending womanhood. I was proud of it.

I remember the day it arrived. I had felt a warmth and stickiness between my legs but I ignored it, assuming it was nothing more than sweat collected on my thighs after PE. Later that day, in a trembling voice, a girl in my class whispered to me: 'You've a spot on the back of your skirt.'

'A spot? What is it?'

'The curse.' Lowering her voice still further, she added, 'You know, your "little friend".'

I pulled my pleated skirt around and looked down. There it was: blood – brilliant, red and flowing from my own womb – amazing. I suppose the thing I should have done was to go to the girls' lavatory and wash it out, but I had no inclination to do that. It was there, it was me. Through some ancient magic, I was becoming a woman and I loved it.

When school ended, as usual, I walked home to the house on Sunset Drive – a journey that took thirty minutes – in my bloodstained skirt. I opened the back door and found my mother in the kitchen, cooking.

'I'm menstruating,' I announced.

She responded as the psychology books had told her to: 'That's wonderful, Leslie. We must go and buy you some sanitary napkins.'

'Why? I can use yours, can't I?'

'No, you need to have your own. Change your clothes. We'll drive into town and buy some.'

My pride and enthusiasm evaporated when I heard her words. Violet was a beautiful woman. I longed to be like her. I had expected her to welcome me into her woman's world, sharing with me not only the secrets of female beauty but the magic of women's physical things – from sanitary towels to stockings and clothes; maybe even jewellery.

It never happened. She made it clear to me from that day forward that I was to touch nothing of hers. I was not even allowed to use her toothpaste, comb or hairbrush. Months later, when my body had grown to be the same size as hers, I would ask if I could wear a pencil-thin, blue and white check skirt she owned. She refused. When I finally mustered the courage to ask why, she replied, 'Because you ruin everything.'

My mother's persistent refusal to allow me access to any of what I looked upon as symbols of womanhood reinforced my own fears: it confirmed my ugliness. I was hideous – a monster masquerading as a girl – someone who should never be allowed to grow to womanhood.

I wanted to be good enough, smart enough, beautiful enough for my father to go on loving me too. I loved my father. He was the centre of my whole life. I wanted to bring to him the love I believed he had been forced to live without. It felt like my mother's rejection of my impending womanhood had placed a curse upon me which could last a lifetime.

At the age of eleven, it would never have occurred to me that her rejection of me might also have been a statement of disappointment with her own womanhood. Now, I believe it must have been. By this time too, the warm glow that had fuelled her first two years with Jimmy Foster, the sexual connection with him she had originally felt and her hopes of living a rich life with this man, were rapidly evaporating. When she compared Jimmy to Stanley – which she did often – Jimmy always came up wanting.

Uncertain about the child growing in her body, Violet was sick all through her pregnancy. Every month Jimmy would drive her to Los Angeles to see Dr McCarthy. I loved her being pregnant. To me she looked more beautiful than ever before. Then there was the baby – a *real* baby. I had wanted a brother or a sister all my life. It embarrassed me when my teachers guessed – as they invariably did – that I was an only child. I felt there was a real stigma to this and I wanted to belong to a family.

By the time Easter arrived at the end of the first week in April, Violet's birth date was imminent and another school vacation was looming. I flew to Chicago to be with Stanley who was playing at the Blue Note and recording a new album. My mother travelled on her own to Los Angeles to stay with her friend Nona and await the birth.

By the time my mother went into labour, I was on my way back to Visalia. Jimmy had left to join her at the Queen of Angels Hospital in Los Angeles. Mom met me at the airport with heartbreaking news:

the baby, a little girl, delivered on 21 April 1953, had been born with severe problems affecting her internal organs. They didn't know if she would live.

Only two surgeons in the United States had operated on similar cases. One of them happened to be in Los Angeles. My little sister entered the operating theatre at five hours old. She underwent an operation lasting seven hours. After surgery she was put into an incubator in the recovery room where she remained for two days.

My mother, who lay in a hospital bed regaining her strength, never touched her. At the end of five days, Jimmy drove Violet back to Visalia. The baby remained in her incubator in the hospital nursery for a further six weeks. Back in Visalia, Violet and Jimmy waited for news of her. My mother spent most of her days upbraiding herself for having given birth to a child who was 'not perfect'. 'What did I do to deserve this?' she kept saying.

'What are you going to name her?' I asked.

'You choose the name,' said my mother. So I did: Deborah Christi Foster. As it turned out, 'Deborah' got ignored in favour of 'Christi'. Violet said, 'I can scream "Christi" louder.' So Christi she remained.

After two or three weeks, we got the news that Christi was going to live. Excited about her coming home, I began to work out how best to feed her. My mother had a book lying by the side of her bed written by a woman named Adelle Davis. It was called *Let's Have Healthy Children*. I read every word, hoping to find secrets that would ensure my new sister stayed alive.

There was never any question of breast-feeding her. Received opinion at the time held that feeding a baby on 'formula' made from cow's milk was infinitely preferable to breast-feeding. After all, it could be 'scientifically' put together. Sugar and water with the odd additive were all that was needed.

Adelle Davis – the world's first serious nutritionist – had other ideas. Babies should be fed on 'tiger's milk', she said, not sugar and water. In preparation for Christi's homecoming, we bought a blender.

I busied myself learning how to whip up Adelle Davis's concoction from blackstrap molasses, brewer's yeast, cow's milk, powdered skim milk and vanilla essence.

I remember the day Jimmy and Violet went to bring her home. I was impatient for them to return. When Christi arrived, I took one look at her and decided this tiny creature was the most beautiful thing I had ever seen. In place of a bellybutton she had a big scar, but I didn't care. I had sterilised all her bottles and prepared her tiger's milk. I had begun weeks before to clear our cupboards of white sugar and flour, as well as anything else that carried the Adelle Davis 'curse' – pretty much all the junk I had been raised on. I dumped it into the garbage can. I announced that we would eat only whole-wheat bread and raw sugar. We would also drink the adult version of tiger's milk at least once a day. To me it tasted revolting, but Christi loved it.

Within three days I had successfully weaned Christi from standard hospital infant formula to feeding *à l'*Adelle. Looking at her tiny hands and feeling her beautiful soft skin as she fed aroused powerful protective feelings in me. Nothing, absolutely nothing, was going to take this baby away. I knew it with the conviction that, in years to come, I would have about my own children. For a time, my love for this little creature eclipsed even my love for Stanley. She became the most important person in my life.

LA BELLE ET LA BÊTE

IN AN EFFORT to stay connected to 'culture' while living in what she called 'this godforsaken town in the middle of nowhere', my mother decided we would join a film club which showed foreign films and offbeat American movies. The movies were screened once a week at a little cinema in Main Street called the Hyde. Like it or not, every Tuesday night my stepfather and I were dragged along to it. There we sat without popcorn in uncomfortable seats to watch movies like Vittorio De Sica's *The Bicycle Thief.* Because I loved movies so much, I was willing to watch just about anything – even without popcorn – so I usually managed to stay awake.

One Tuesday, the movie on show was Jean Cocteau's *La Belle et la Bête.* No film I had ever seen affected me so deeply or in so many ways. When I met the Beast on screen, I fell head over heels in love with him. At the end of the story, when he transformed into a bow-legged prince and floated up into a cloudy sky, I hated him. The prince – plastic and boring – was no match for the Beast in all his majestic complexity. I sensed in him the suffering I had witnessed in Stanley throughout my childhood. The Beast was powerful, yet he believed himself to be so ugly that nobody could love him. My father felt the same. To me, this Beast with his fangs and claws, his luminous eyes – one moment terrifying, the next brimming with tears – was wondrous. My empathy with him became all-consuming. How could anyone prefer a prince dressed in fluffy silk if they could have the Beast instead? Then there was the question of his enchantment. He had obviously been cursed just as my father had. I was certain it was the curse that periodically turned each of them – man and beast – into frightening beings and obscured their true nature.

One scene still makes me cry. Beauty is walking with Beast along the ramparts of the castle. His eyes are soft and gentle. He is deeply in love with her and he behaves with the grace of a king in her presence. All at once, a roe deer darts through the woods to the side of them. The Beast's eyes flare up in blood lust as his animal nature takes over. There is no way he can stop what is happening to him. I know this for sure. This knowing only makes me love him more. Like my father, Cocteau's Beast is a magnificent yet frightening being, trapped for ever in limbo between his animal body and the dazzling light of his spirit. His imperfections only made me love him more.

I was reminded of this when Stanley and I next met at Easter. I looked at him and, just beneath the surface of his charm and wonderful smile, I could see the shadow of the tortured Beast lurking. I had never before seen this so clearly. What, until this day, amazes me is how few others, who believed they knew my father, were conscious that the Beast was there.

Stanley and I were on the road together for almost three weeks that spring before Christi was born. We carried on with our usual activities – him leading a band, managing publicity and paying bills; me devouring books, going to museums and galleries when I could, and listening to music.

When we were alone, before alcohol soaked his brain and turned him into someone else, he talked a lot about money, music, promoters who didn't do their job and where he should go next. He would sit on the floor of our hotel room and put his head in my lap. Usually the conversations began with: 'Shortstuff, I don't know what to do.' Then he'd run through litanies of grief, mostly, I think, because he just needed to get it all out and his public persona would never allow him to express anxiety, confusion, weakness or uncertainty.

Stanley stored up things he wanted to talk to me about till we were alone together. I always listened with rapt attention. I felt proud that he trusted me so much he thought he could tell me anything. He often told me all about the women he met, none of whom were around for very long. He seemed never to connect with any of them very deeply. I had become his confessor, the one he trusted, the one he turned to when he needed help. He respected my opinions and I tried hard to live up to his expectations. I knew he loved me too since his face always lit up when I came into a room. I could tell as well by his anger when he didn't know where I was, and by his insistence that I be *with* him on the road even when, at times, I resisted it.

I noticed right away that he was taking too many uppers and drinking far too much alcohol just to keep going. The band's itineraries had been punishing that year. He often talked about ongoing hassles he had with the other guys. They played month after month of one-nighters. In an attempt to save money, my father told me how he had chartered a fleet of cars so his musicians could drive themselves – four to a car – from job to job.

One black night in the flatlands, Stanley took a curve too fast and ran off the road. The car wouldn't budge. He spent what was left of the night in Shoshone, Idaho, setting out through the snow at dawn, on foot, to find help. Soaked to the skin and trembling and feverish, somehow he made it to work that night. 'You know, Shortstuff, it's funny,' he said, 'I can't remember how I got there. I kept hitting one disaster after another,' he confessed.

During our weeks together that spring, the inevitable time of night would arrive when Stanley would pass the point of no return and become no longer accessible to me. In this state he sometimes reached for me in bed. Then this man-turned-automaton did whatever he had to do sexually. When this happened, I shut off from him and went elsewhere, disappeared into the ether, waiting for morning to come, hoping he would return to himself again.

In a world where protocols and regulations rule people's lives, living a forbidden life so close to someone whose blood and DNA you share can take on momentous proportions. You are breaking a dangerous taboo. Although you refuse to acknowledge this openly, somewhere in the vast ocean of the consciousness you are forced to live out the power and the terror of it. So long as you both remain true to what you are doing, and to each other, the bond between you can deepen in a way that transcends the sexual connection. When you share what you most love, hate, fear and long for, as well as a common ancestry, the affinity between you can become overpowering. You experience heaven and hell, not as philosophical notions but as immediate realities. One moment you live the life of the gods, the next you are plunged into terror or despair. Either way, you feel more alive than ever before. There is only one catch: turn against the bond you have forged, deny responsibility for what you are living, let fear of punishment and discovery invade that secret world, and the exhilaration will turn to horror.

21

CHANGING FOCUS

MY FATHER HAD always directed our relationship. It was he who decided what we did, when we had sex, what was allowed and what was not. In effect, he owned me. My attention, most of my concern and my deepest sense of purpose had been centred on him ever since the divorce. Now, the unfamiliar hormones surging through my body and the distractions of my new little sister began to undermine the single-minded focus that had once belonged to Stanley alone.

Christi needed me. Violet had not settled easily into motherhood. In effect, Christi was her first baby – certainly the first she attempted to look after herself. Mom, busy running Joan Crawford's or some other Hollywood luminary's household as well as playing guru to several more, was unavailable to step in and take over when things got tough. So by the end of the third week after Christi's arrival, I had taken on the lion's share of caring for her. There were several days when I stayed home from school to look after Christi because my mother seemed so anxious about it all. She became obsessed with the idea that something serious must be wrong with the baby. If Christi spit up after eating, she panicked. When Christi woke at night she burst into tears, unsure of how to help her. She and Jimmy ended up carrying the baby around each night until she would go back to sleep again. Before long, Christi was waking every hour. This meant that neither Jimmy nor Violet ever got a decent night's sleep.

As weeks passed, their anxiety increased. If I went for a swim in our pool, I was told to stop lest the noise of the water wake the baby.

Meanwhile, Christi, stuffed full of tiger's milk, was blossoming. Yet my mother was still afraid she might die. The four of us were living in an atmosphere of constant tension, arguments and frayed nerves. It became clear to me that I was an unwelcome guest in the house: someone whose presence only made everything worse.

Staying with Seiko's family for an extended period of time was no longer an option. Even though my psyche had blacked out memories of the illicit relationship with Stanley and the dramas Stella had involved me in, what was not erased was the amorphous sense of shame, guilt, self-blame and fear I carried everywhere with me. I felt myself unworthy to be in the presence of Seiko's family. I stayed away.

That left only boys, many of whom were lining up for my attention. I began to feel the power of being female for the first time. I wanted to flex these new muscles, but had no idea how to go about it. I sensed some kind of electricity that I aroused in boys and their presence aroused in me. This confused me a lot. I had no idea of this at the time, but my relationship with my father had programmed behaviour patterns into me, some of which would unconsciously rule my life for decades. The first was secrecy. Any connection with man or boy had to be kept secret. After all, love and secrecy went hand in hand, didn't they?

My first date, at the age of eleven, consisted of a trip to the movies with twins Dick and Donald Gibson. When we got to the box office they fought over who would buy my ticket. Inside the theatre they argued over who would pay for my popcorn. Dick and Donald were not identical. Dick was the good-looking twin – taller than his brother and more muscular, with golden skin, dark brows and full lips. Donald was the intelligent one who wore glasses and had a great sense of humour. I sat in the movie theatre between the two of them, secretly holding hands with both beneath the sides of my crinoline fluffed skirt. I don't think either of them ever knew.

It didn't take me long to make my choice: Dick. Although he was only two years older than me, he was already earning money. I found this appealing since I couldn't imagine that I would *ever* be able to earn money. A week or two after that first date I came home wearing a gold chain around my neck, on which hung a heavy gold ring with his initials on it. I wore it proudly over my sweaters.

Of course wearing Dick's ring meant that this particular romance could not be kept secret. That troubled me. It wouldn't do. I needed a *secret* relationship. Since Dick worked a lot, and I wanted to spend as much time as possible away from my mother's house, I cast around for other candidates. The next in line appeared, as if by magic: Jimmy Abercrombie, the son of a prominent lawyer. Jimmy was tall (an essential prerequisite since so was Stanley) not bad looking, shy, and – most important – someone I felt could keep a secret. So while Dick worked and my mother and stepfather worried over the next imagined Christi drama, I left the house several nights each week for clandestine meetings with Jimmy, who, conveniently, lived just on the other side of Mill Creek.

Neither Jimmy nor I had any idea what to do with each other when we met. After a few hesitant kisses fashioned after what I'd seen in movies, we would sit and talk past midnight, relishing the hidden nature of our connection and the exciting way we had been able to elude detection by our parents.

Summer came. I turned twelve. I had planned to spend far less time with Stanley than usual. The year had been a hard one for him. He had been publicly attacked by critics who not only didn't get the music he was playing but took a personal dislike to him. As a result, my father was particularly down on himself.

At 4 a.m. one morning, he rang in tears. I could tell he'd been drinking heavily. 'Everything I've ever written is crap,' he said. 'I can't write, I can't think, I'm like some guy leading an army of idiots into hell. I'm on a road to nowhere. I'm going crazy.'

Three years earlier, he had written 'Theme for Sunday', a lush tone poem I still find exceptionally beautiful. 'What about "Theme for Sunday"?' I said.

'Crap – nothing but crap,' he replied. He then went on to psycho-analyse the wife of one of his musicians, a promoter who had booked the tour, and some guy at the hotel. Our conversation lasted at least an hour and a half – a very long call for a man who worried about phone bills. Near the end of it, he told me he wanted me to join him on the road as soon as my summer vacation began. I looked at his itinerary. It was full of one-nighters early in the summer, mostly in the Midwest. One-nighters were boring since they gave us so little time to be alone together. Besides, there were boys in my life now – something I neglected to mention while we were on the phone together. Eventually we agreed that I would stay in Visalia until late July when he was due to play dates in New England, including a week at Steel Pier in Atlantic City, which would give us more time together.

So I remained in Visalia trying to find my feet as a budding adolescent in a provincial town where I understood none of the rules. Somewhere I had learned – maybe it was just one of those things that permeated the consciousness of every young girl in the 1950s – that there were said to be only two kinds of women: good women and bad women. I was pretty sure I was one of the bad kind, especially because I continued to be haunted by the sense that if anyone 'found out' about me I would be shunned.

That year I slept little and badly. I would leave for school early each morning and return late in an attempt to spend as much time as possible out of the house. I pursued my various romances.

Not until late July did I fly East to join Stanley. When I arrived he was not at the airport to meet me. I took a taxi to the hotel, found out his room number, and knocked at the door. The man who opened it not only looked haggard and grey, he seemed a stranger. He kept running his hands through his hair as though he were trying to make himself look presentable. 'Jesus Christ!' he said. 'What are you doing here? I thought you were coming tomorrow.'

Stanley was caught off guard, having got the dates wrong; and I suspect he was expecting a child, but found himself face to face with a creature resembling a young woman. I believe the changes in my body frightened him. Sometimes, they frightened me. Yet I also continued to find them fascinating. It felt as though I was taking part in some mysterious and magical metamorphosis through which every human being had passed since the beginning of time. I was reassured that it was a transformation over which I had no need to exert any control, since I could not have done so even if I wanted to.

The band played a few one-nighters then went on to Atlantic City where my father and I lay on the beach and ate delicious food. I drank champagne. He drank J&B. We slept together. I hung out in the ballroom on Steel Pier while he was working. That gave me a lot of time to read. Stanley never questioned me about books. But he liked me to read. So long as I had my nose in a book he knew where I was, he figured I was safe, and he didn't have to feel guilty about having left me to my own devices.

Deep into Nathaniel Hawthorne's *The Scarlet Letter*, I became fascinated by the character of Hester and the magnificent red satin 'A' for adulteress she had embroidered on the breast of her dresses. I knew adultery was supposed to be a horrible thing but I was certain Hester was secretly proud of that 'A'. 'I am what I am,' it said. 'If you don't like it you can go to hell.' She was an outcast, just as I felt myself to be. I envied her panache in the face of all the derision and hatred she had to endure.

When we left Atlantic City we headed north, playing amusement parks in New England. The band was booked to play the 'haunted ballroom' at Lake Compounce in Connecticut, where the rape (of which by then I had no conscious memory) had taken place. I did remember the town, though, and the roller coaster guy who told me all the bad things that were supposed to have happened there.

My father and I arrived in late afternoon, very hungry. We'd had nothing to eat since 2 a.m. We stopped at a diner before checking into the hotel. It had a fake pottery tomato on every table and more lining the counter. They were dripping with ketchup which, once red, had turned dark brown. We ordered spare ribs, one of my favourite foods. They arrived with heated cinnamon and raisin rolls smeared in white icing.

I began to shake.

'Shortstuff, what's wrong with you?' he asked.

'Nothing. I'm just cold.'

'You can't be cold. It's hot as hell in here. You must be hungry. Eat something.' He tore open one of the rolls and pasted a square of butter on it. The yellow stuff melted with the heat of the roll. It dripped down the side of his huge hand as he held it out to me. I shook my head.

'Come on, eat,' he urged.

'I'm going to wash my face.' I got up and made my way along the curved counter towards the ladies' room. When I got to the door, there was no handle. I couldn't figure out how to get it open. My belly tightened – an attempt to quell waves of fear surging through it, I think. 'Help,' I whimpered, 'help me.'

The waitress heard. She came out from behind the counter. 'What is it?' she said.

'The door, I can't open it.'

'Don't be silly,' she said, reaching out a brown-speckled hand with fingernails the same colour as the oxidised ketchup. 'Just push. See?'

I staggered into the tiny room and hooked the door behind me. I don't know how long I was in there. It must have been quite a while. The next thing I remember was Stanley's voice saying, 'Leslie, are you all right?' Then someone pounded on the door.

With difficulty I managed to unhook it. 'I'm OK,' I said. 'I'm just not hungry.'

Stanley made the waitress wrap up my meal in waxed paper. We got into the car and drove to the hotel. I think it was the same hotel we stayed at before, but I can't be sure.

By the time Stanley unlocked the door to our room my body was raging with fever and my skin was as dry as desert sand. I remember him tearing open the bedding, putting me down on the bed and covering me with everything he could find. He rang the housekeeper, demanding extra blankets. His voice was hard. The charm for which he was famous had evaporated. I heard him bark down the phone, 'Now! Now!' The last thing I remember is him sitting on the side of the bed, so close to me that I felt crushed by the weight of his body pinning my own beneath the covers. He laid one huge hand on my forehead, then everything went dark.

They told me later that my fever lasted three or four days. I slept mostly – in beds, in the car, in a dressing room somewhere while 'Artistry in Rhythm' blared so loud I thought my head would split open. And I dreamed. Fragments of memory came together to form pictures which didn't make sense, feelings I didn't want to feel and chaotic phrases that played over and over. Most seemed directed towards crushing me, cancelling my life, silencing my voice, blacking out my existence. They felt too dangerous. I knew they had to be kept hidden.

One day as the fever burned through me, travelling in the car between jobs, I started to get visions. A broken mirror. Its glass crushed by the blow of a fist so violent it left slivers in my flesh. I knew the broken mirror was me. That a thousand glass shards pierced my body. I felt they would go on making me bleed for ever. But I was supposed to bleed, wasn't I? I was supposed to be punished.

Later that week, the fever all burnt out, I took a plane out of New York to get back to Visalia. I was thin. The dark circles under my eyes had lent me the look of a recovering alcoholic. Stanley and the band flew off in the opposite direction. They were on their way to Europe on what would become the most exciting trip of my father's life.

When I returned from the East my mother said, 'You look terrible. Haven't you had any sleep?'

I told her I had been sick with one of my fevers.

She shook her head. 'You're thin and pale as parchment. The black circles under your eyes are so bad you look like a raccoon.'

'I'm sorry,' I said. 'I'm sorry.' My first day back, I slept for thirty-six hours. I let no one know I was home, not even Seiko. When I was allowed to swim, I swam laps in our pool – back and forth, back and forth – endlessly. The water felt safe to me, as though I were being held in the arms of someone who cared for me. In need of comfort, this was the only place I could find it.

It took me two weeks after returning to Visalia to get back my strength. Then I started eighth grade. But I had changed. I began to wear bright red lipstick. This shocked Seiko and worried my mother. I changed my hairstyle too. It had been long, tied back in a ponytail. Now I cut it short with heavy bangs and had it curled.

My mother spoke to Seiko's mother, saying she was concerned about me. She was of the opinion that Christi's birth had upset me – made me feel displaced. She could think of no other justification for my having become so distant and so changed. Seiko worried too, although she was quite sure that, whatever was going on, it had nothing to do with my little sister.

I not only looked different, I behaved differently. Where once I had been obsessed with excelling academically, now all I appeared to care about was how I looked and about boys. Seiko worried she was losing me as a friend, but was afraid to talk to me about how she felt. I sensed her concerns. I desperately missed the closeness between us and my previous sense of belonging to the Kawasaki family. I wanted to allay her fears but there was nothing I could do or say. I felt dirty and ashamed; unworthy of their company. I felt different in myself too, like another person. This scared me, so I tried as hard as I could to appear normal at school. By now, the sense I had that I was damaged, ugly – something to be hidden, someone who had no right to exist – had begun to take on monstrous proportions.

At the beginning of the fall semester, elections were held for class president, secretary and treasurer. The school was big, with hundreds of children in each class. I thought if I could get myself elected Class President, I might gain some self-esteem – I might not feel quite so ashamed to be whatever I felt myself becoming. With Seiko's help and a carefully planned strategy, I won by a landslide. But public confirmation of my popularity brought none of the rewards I was looking for.

By now I could see that the adolescent games I was playing with boys had no significance other than as a means to hide my confusion. Yet I had more admirers than ever. Photographs taken of me that year show a dazed person of indeterminate age – the shell of a girl lost in an unhappy world that doesn't make sense to her. Despite all this – or maybe because of it – I seemed to attract young men the way flowers attract bees.

This should have pleased me but mostly it made me uneasy since I didn't know what to do with them. I tried to keep my distance. I wore blouses – more like men's shirts really – buttoned up to the neck, keeping my body hidden from view. I developed an obsession with being as covered as possible at all times. My body scared me now; it didn't seem to belong to me. I thought of it – when I thought of it at all – as a foreign, dangerous thing over which I could exercise no control.

Sometimes at night, I would lie in bed with powerful sexual feelings surging through my body. It would feel like my flesh was on fire. Sometimes I had visions. I would close my eyes and see the face of the Beast from Cocteau's film gazing down at me, sad and lonely. That made me think of Stanley. I would wait for him to call me but his schedule on his European tour was so heavy that the calls became less frequent. I took to swimming in the pool late at night whenever the arousal in my body became so intense I couldn't sleep.

When Stanley returned to America at the end of September he was brimming with excitement. The tour round ten European countries had been a huge success. The critics loved the music. For the first time in Stanley's life, the reviews were free of the sarcasm and derision he had too often been forced to endure in the United States.

While he had been away, Stella had rung him to tell him that Pop had died, following a long battle with leukaemia. Grieving though he was, even this news could not crush Stanley's new-found spirit. He rang me from New York the day he arrived. 'It feels like I can conquer the world, Shortstuff,' he said. 'Nothing can stop me now.'

It felt strange talking to him. For one thing, he had called during the day. We almost never spoke except in the middle of the night. I could hear the excitement in his voice and I loved how happy he sounded. Yet there was a shrill, buzzy quality to the way he talked too – like someone on a roller coaster who has been speeding up and down so long he doesn't know how to get off.

The slowdown my father needed badly after Europe never came. He launched into a blockbuster US concert tour with Dizzy Gillespie and 'Bird' Charlie Parker. It bore the title 'A Festival of Modern American Jazz'. There were so many musicians they had to travel in two buses. While on the road between venues, one of the buses crashed into the back of the other. Several musicians were seriously injured. Ten passengers ended up in hospital.

The accident did as much damage to Stanley's confidence as it did to the cut-up bodies of the injured. He called me, riddled with anxiety. 'Shortstuff, I'm afraid the band's gonna fall apart,' he said. 'Guys can't blow with their mouths cut up. I've gotta find a whole new trombone section. Some of them are afraid even to get back on the bus.' He ended up having to replace half the band.

Part One of the Festival of Modern American Jazz tour finished at the end of November. It was followed by recording sessions and, inevitably, more one-nighters. Christmas that year found him playing in Detroit for a week at the Fox Theater. Violet decided we should spend Christmas with him there. Mom took a vacation from her work and came to Visalia to look after Christi. Jimmy, Violet and I flew to Michigan. It was a crazy time. In the few months since I had said goodbye to Stanley in New England, I had grown another couple of inches. My breasts were growing to match my height and I was wearing a bra. Again, I sensed the change in me made Stanley uncomfortable. I felt even more isolated. I was all alone, even in the presence of the person I loved most in the world.

My mother had her own agenda. By now she was certain that her marriage to Jimmy was more than unsatisfactory. She hated Visalia. She feared she was losing her looks and enthusiasm for life. She missed the glamour of show business and the glitz of Hollywood where life for her used to have the quality of a movie in which she starred. The movie in which she had been cast with Jimmy felt more like a *film noir* from which there was no escape. Most of all, she kept saying, she missed Stanley and the deep connections they had. I think this was the real impetus behind our going to Detroit for Christmas.

While we were there Violet talked to Stanley a lot about her life, her unhappiness, her frustration. I don't think he knew what to say or do. For the first time I could remember, he didn't seem to connect with her. We were there only five or six nights. It was hard on all of us. I was relieved to get back to Visalia.

Stanley went on to spend New Year's Eve in Chicago then he opened in Cincinnati, Ohio. From there on it was straight ahead towards Part Two of the Festival of Modern Jazz through January and February. On the last day of February the band played its final Festival concert at the Shrine Auditorium in Los Angeles. By then, my father was so exhausted his hands shook uncontrollably when he placed them on the keys of the piano. He knew he had to stop. The 24 March 1954 issue of *Down Beat* made the public announcement: 'Stan Kenton has broken up his band to take a long vacation on the West Coast . . . He says, "I'll do some writing while I'm at home, but first I want to see my family."'

22

THE WAGES OF ILLUSION

SPRING CAME LATE in 1954. I spent my Easter vacation at Hollyridge with Stanley. Mom had moved out, so now there was just the two of us. He was lonely and tired. His writing was not going well. In an attempt to create new sources of income, he had also been negotiating with Capitol Records to persuade them to form a jazz department with him as its head.

The house had a strange atmosphere about it, the way a room feels after there has been a wild party; even when the beer bottles and cigarette butts have been cleared away, a dingy aura of contamination remains. I wondered what had happened there. My father looked thin and haggard. It seemed he had aged years since our previous summer in New England – ever since Christmas in Detroit. I was glad to be back at my beloved Hollyridge, yet unsettled too. Even my own room seemed alien to me.

The night I arrived, we went to dinner at Trader Vic's in Beverly Hills, another of our private rituals. Since the divorce, every trip I made to Hollyridge included two or three intimate meals at Trader Vic's. My father loved the dark Polynesian atmosphere where he was unlikely to be recognised. We could sit and talk for hours without being disturbed. A special table was always booked for us. As soon as we arrived the *maître d'* would bring us delicious titbits to munch on. They were always different. This was a game he liked to play – he never fed us the same thing twice. With the hors-d'oeuvres came cocktails made from rum and fruit juice, or grog made with coconut milk, served in fresh coconuts with long straws.

I had not yet turned thirteen but by then I was five foot eight inches tall. I guess I looked more like a woman than a child. At least that's what Stanley and everybody else kept telling me. We sat at our table in the dark for two hours that night, hidden behind a fake palm tree and a reed partition from which hung a taxidermic blowfish, fish nets and glass floats.

Stanley seemed distracted. He talked about how he wanted to study music. He asked about Violet, about Seiko's parents, about what I had been doing since Christmas, but paid little attention to my answers and almost never looked me in the eye. Gradually, the atmosphere in the restaurant and the seductive food and drink brought about a shift in him. The lean, haggard worrier who had been sitting in front of me disappeared, to be replaced by the warm, intimate man.

'I have something for you,' he said. 'I want to give it to you but I'm afraid you might not like it.' He reached into the breast pocket of his jacket, brought out a little pouch made of white leather, took hold of my hand and laid it on my palm with gentle ceremony. This made me blush. I was longing to open it but I felt afraid. 'Go on,' he said. I pulled the strings of the little bag apart and looked inside. There, wrapped in black tissue, was an 18-carat gold half-hunter watch on a long chain. It was hallmarked 1875. Instead of numbers on its face, there were Roman numerals. On the back was engraved, 'For Leslie with all my love, Stanley – Happy Easter 1954'.

I put it round my neck immediately. The chain was so long the watch hung four or five inches below my waist. 'I love it,' I said. 'It's beautiful.'

'It's old,' he said. 'I met this guy who sells antique jewellery. When he showed it to me I knew I had to buy it for you. You don't care about it being old, do you?'

'No, I like it,' I said. 'But look, the chain's too long for me.'

'That's the way it's supposed to be,' he said. 'You're supposed to tuck it under your waistband or behind a belt when you go riding so it doesn't flop around.'

In my mind's eye, I saw an elegant young woman atop a shiny black horse. She was dressed in a red jacket, jodhpurs and slick black boots. Around her neck hung the shiny gold watch. The image was most definitely not of me. Whenever I rode – which by then was rarely – it was without a saddle in a pair of shabby jeans and a scruffy old shirt; no hat, no boots. Was it Violet he was seeing?

I wondered if my father knew me at all. I thought of the boys back in Visalia who pursued me. I was quite sure they didn't know me, which was not surprising since I had no idea who I was. They didn't matter. But Stanley did. What if he really didn't know who I was? Did *nobody* know me? Did I even *exist*?

That night when we got home, he said, 'Now that you're growing up you probably want to sleep in your own room, don't you?'

I didn't know how to respond. I had slept in his bed ever since my mother left. Holding back tears, trying to hide my confusion, I said, 'OK.' I got into bed and hugged my pillow, waiting for the warm feeling that always came when I was in my own room at Hollyridge – a sense that whatever happened, it would be all right because I was *home*.

I stayed in Los Angeles for just over a week that Easter. Stanley was in a continual state of conflict. I believe he tried his best to resist touching me. Then, as usual, drowning in a sea of alcohol, he would come to my bed, only to deny the next morning that he'd been there. Some nights he did leave me alone.

I became afraid because I never knew *who* would come through my door. I began to sleep on the side of the bed furthest from the door. This turned into a habit that would last another thirty years. Only decades later did I realise that I always did this, no matter where I was: at home, in a hotel, in someone else's house. The further you are from the door, the more time you have to prepare yourself for whatever is coming through it.

During this period Stanley's unpredictable behaviour grew worse than I had ever known it. I loved him. I couldn't help but love him, but I spent every day of that time in a state of alarm. The good times we used to have together playing on the beach, drinking freshly squeezed orange juice, combing Central Park for places where *Portrait of Jennie* had been shot, seemed to have disappeared down a long corridor leading to fear and chaos.

The gold watch he gave me that night at Trader Vic's remained on the table in my little dressing room. I never wore it. It was too shiny, too golden, too beautiful for me to hang round my neck. I knew it didn't belong to me. Maybe he didn't belong to me either.

Stanley had always said he knew I was his daughter because both he and I have the same crooked little fingers. I spent hours staring at my hands, wondering if he had been wrong about that as well.

I returned to Visalia and the final term at school, afraid I was losing hold of everything. My life felt like the script of a badly written sitcom which, if it were meant to be amusing, wasn't living up to its promise. Everything was flat, two-dimensional, rendered in shades of grey. My mother sensed this.

One morning while I was eating my breakfast, she asked, 'Do you like spending time with Stanley?'

'Of course I do,' I replied. 'We do lots of fun things together.'

'It seems like every time you come back from being with him you get more miserable. I'm not sure he's all that good for you. He can be very self-centred.'

'I know.'

'Maybe you should spend the summer here this year instead of going to Los Angeles.'

'But I promised him I would come. He's going to be at home alone all summer.'

'Think about it,' she said.

I didn't think about it. I was to spend the summer with my father. It had been decided and as far as I was concerned, that was the end of it.

Soon after school let out, near the end of June, I turned thirteen. Stanley came to Visalia and spent three days at my mother's house before driving the two of us back to Hollyridge for the summer. There was no children's party that year. Instead, he and I, one-year-old Christi, Jimmy, Violet and Mom ate cake in the back yard.

I had been given my first pair of high heels. They were snow white and very high. I was determined not to fall on my face in them. An 8mm movie of that day shows me plodding across the lawn. I must have figured the way not to fall down was to take giant steps with great boldness, since this was what I was doing in the movie. The same film displays Stanley's obsession with me. He behaves as if he doesn't want to take his hands off me. I appear uncertain how to handle his attentions. Now, as I look at the footage, I wonder that neither Violet nor Jimmy ever noticed that his behaviour towards me verged on the predatory.

Something strange happened that night. After dinner, Jimmy, Violet and Stanley had been sitting in the living room watching the sunset and drinking, as usual. Stanley began to talk about things like 'freedom' and 'power' and then his obsession with Dianetics. He had sent Violet a copy of L. Ron Hubbard's book the year before. She had not read more than a chapter or two before becoming bored with it.

Now she said, 'I don't trust the guy. I think he's a second-rate has-been science-fiction writer out to make a buck.'

'Yeah,' said Stanley. 'You're probably right. But this Dianetics thing is fantastic.'

'OK, what has it done for you?' my mother said.

He proceeded to go through a long list of people he had helped to 'clear' using the 'system'. 'Once we get clear, all the crap we've battled with since we were kids is gone,' he said. 'It's great, Violet. You gotta do it.'

There was a pause while Jimmy poured another drink. Then she repeated, 'What about you?'

'I'll tell you about me,' he began. 'It's gone – everything – all the crap. A guy named Bill came to the house twice a week. He cleared me of everything.'

'And?'

'I'm free, Violet. I have moved way beyond morality and all that crap. I'm the next Jesus Christ. Now I can do whatever I want and nobody can stop me!'

Hearing his words scared me. Despite her alcoholic cloud, they seemed to sober up my mother too. She got up, walked across the white carpet in her bare feet, put her hands on the arms of the chair Stanley was sitting in, leaned over and whispered something in his ear.

'I'm serious,' he said, pushing her away as though whatever she had told him had been something he didn't want to hear. 'I mean it, Violet. I am the next Jesus Christ. That's what it is to be free. I can do whatever I want. You just watch!'

She withdrew from him, returning to the sofa. Nothing more was said. Stanley's words and the intensity of conviction that accompanied them would come up again and again during dinner-table conversations for the rest of my mother's life. At the time, we had no way of knowing how destructive his belief in those words would be, both to him and to the lives of others.

23

POINT OF NO RETURN

DESPITE THE BOLDNESS of Stanley's claim to omnipotence and freedom from moral constraints, in 1954 he was running scared. Too many rumblings were taking place in and around him. Ever since he had fallen under the spell of Dianetics and its promise of mind control, he had been consoling himself with the assurance that he was on the verge of god-like living. He believed that Hubbard's system would allow him access to expanded creativity. Being cleared would make his life successful on every level. It would also take away the gnawing void in his gut which he'd carried with him as long as he could remember.

The year I spent the whole summer with him at Hollyridge – the year I turned thirteen – I had to stand by helpless, listening to his words and watching him sink into a cynical, bitter, resentful pit of despair as his disillusionment with Dianetics grew. Now, as I look back, I believe that what he was going through had something in common with members of a cult that predicts the world's going to end in three years. The three years come and go but nothing happens. Stanley had followed all the rules, been cleared by 'Bill', done his best to clear other people, and made contributions to L. Ron Hubbard's coffers. Given all this, he had been sure he would be 'saved'. But the promised breakthrough never arrived. Instead, without knowing it, he had climbed on a manic-depressive merry-go-round. It pushed him up, pulled him down and dragged him round and round, but it wouldn't let him off.

All sorts of contradictory forces kept crashing up against each other.

For a week or two he felt himself on the cusp of breaking through to the elite creative power which he had been longing for. He'd be in a state of high jubilation. 'This mind control stuff really works,' he'd say. 'I've got beyond morality, I really have, just like L.R.H. said I would. I'm becoming a god. I can *feel* it happening.' Then rumbling doubts would raise their ugly heads. 'Oh God, it doesn't work the way they promised me it would,' he'd say. 'I'm struggling with myself as much as ever. I'm short of money. I've written no music. Goddammit, Shortstuff, things are no different.'

When the breakthrough he'd been anticipating hadn't happened, he became afraid it never would. This did him major damage. The merry-go-round sped up. On Monday he'd say with great excitement that his breakthrough was just around the corner: 'I can feel it. Can't you feel it?' On Tuesday he would sink into despondency and depression again. The depression was by far the strongest force. It drained his body of the tremendous physical vitality he had always counted on. Up until now, when he had disbanded the orchestra because of exhaustion or confusion, he had always been able to bounce back. Now he felt just plain worn out. With each up and down on the carousel, he became more sure that the techniques he thought would free him were useless. Where once he'd been so elevated by what he believed Dianetics would do for his artistic genius, now he was in a state of shock, as though awakening from a bad dream. He felt below gutter level, beside himself with fear yet unable to tell anybody about it.

One night, a few days after I arrived at Hollyridge, it all came gushing out. We were in the living room listening to Wagner – one of the very few exceptions to his rejection of nineteenth-century music. He was drinking Scotch. Wagner was *not* one of my favourites so I was lying on my belly on the carpet in front of the speakers, half asleep.

He got up, came over to me and turned down the volume. I opened my eyes. 'Shortstuff,' he said, 'I want to talk to you.' He lay down beside me. I turned over, propped my head up on my elbow and got ready to listen.

'What do you want to talk about?' I asked.

'Lots of things. I don't know.'

'Like what?'

'I'm worried about money,' he began. He then went on to list more than a dozen things *wrong* with his life – things he felt he was powerless to change. 'Everything around me is crumbling,' he said. 'I've never questioned my ability to know what's *real* and what's not. But I can't tell any more.'

Not only were finances shaky, Stella was on the warpath. She'd been calling him every other day, telling him he needed to get his act together and get on with his career. It was time he made more money, she said; time he made more of himself and stopped messing around with all the 'foolish nonsense' Mom had involved him in.

Then there was Violet. Disillusioned with her marriage to Jimmy, ever since Christmas in Detroit she had been demanding more of a connection with Stanley – just when all this crumbling was happening. 'Your mother keeps coming at me the way she did when we were married,' he said. 'She keeps asking me to listen to her. I think she wants me to show up and rescue her from her life in Visalia,' he said. 'I can't do that, Shortstuff.'

More than twenty years later, when first Stanley and I finally spoke openly of our sexual relationship, he told me, 'Being with you that summer was like having a mirror held up to myself. It showed up all my weaknesses. I hated that.' My father seldom looked into his darker side. He did everything he could to avoid it. Whenever he got a glimpse of what he thought might be there, he would turn away and take another drink.

He went on to tell me, 'I always loved your fierceness. I loved the way you were true to yourself even when you were scared. That summer showed me what a phoney I'd become.'

Yet that was the summer he made me the scapegoat for his fears, his self-accusations and his sense of failure. Day by day my father's actions became more unpredictable. He started behaving like a caged animal, pacing up and down in a state of agitation.

'What's wrong with you?' he screamed at me one morning while I was on the patio reading a book.

'Wrong?'

'Yeah, why are you so nervy? Why the hell can't you sit still? Why do you always have to be going somewhere?'

'What are you talking about? I'm reading.' I continued, 'You say you want to write, Stanley. You spend twenty minutes in the music room, then charge out here ordering me to put my shoes on "'cause we're going out".'

'I hate you reading all the crap you do. Do something else. Christ, Shortstuff, I can't think. I can't write. I can't figure anything out.'

'Figure what out?'

'I don't know.'

'Then go away and let me read my book till you do.'

Despite his dissociation, at some level I believe he must have been terrified that someone might discover the nature of our relationship. This would have destroyed his life. Equally worrying may have been that, having opened himself up to me for three years and exposed himself in all his moral and psychological nakedness, he might have cracked open some kind of Pandora's Box. He had been inexorably drawn to my innocence. Now, he didn't know if he could even trust me. After all, he'd let me see so much of himself. Had he created a monster? Did I know too much? Was I now so wild and free that I'd become seriously dangerous to him? If I had opened my mouth it would have meant the downfall of everything.

It may have been these fears that were filling his dreams with grotesque figures from a Bruegel landscape during these months. In one dream, he told me, a giant, like Goya's *Saturn*, threatened to devour him head first.

What Stanley didn't realise was that I would never have betrayed the bond between us. How could I? The sexual part of our life was, by then, hidden even from myself by the dissociation which, I now believe, was carried in the genes of our bloodline. All I consciously knew was that our relationship was very different from any other I had ever seen and that I felt a lot of confusion about it. But the closeness between us was the very centre of my existence. Even if I had remembered the incest, I would never have told anyone about it. To betray him would have meant betraying myself and denying my very life.

The more frantic Stanley became, the more he accused me of things I didn't do and thoughts I didn't think. He began to take steps to cover himself. To his mother he would say, 'I'm concerned about Leslie, she's getting out of hand.' Hating me as she did, Stella not only accommodated his fears, she bumped them up. He spoke to Violet several times, saying similar things. Years later, when the incest became known in our family, my mother was able to recount, word for word, the things he'd said to her during those phone calls.

'I'm worried about Leslie,' he'd begin.

'Why?' she would ask.

'She's become a pathological liar.'

'What?'

'She's always lying.'

'Don't be ridiculous, Stanley! Leslie's never told a lie in her life.'

This particular ploy fell on deaf ears with my mother. Stanley knew well that, just as she said, I obsessively told the truth. I often got into trouble for it, since the truths I told were usually too blunt.

Stanley talked to other people about me too. One morning I heard him say on the phone, 'I'm afraid the kid is mentally ill. She needs help.' I have no idea who he was speaking to.

To my own face, he told me I was 'crazy'. He screamed at me that I was 'sick'. I think what he wanted was for the problems he thought I might create to go away. Finally, he convinced himself that if only he could get me 'fixed' then he might be able to find a way back into his life.

He kept coming into my room and waking me. One night, tortured by guilt, he would sit on the floor next to my bed, his tears staining the bedspread. I'd put my hand on his head and tell him it would be all right. The next night he'd rage at me about how 'sick' I was and I would cry. 'Stop it!' he would scream. 'Stop it!' He'd take hold of my arms just below the shoulders, yank me from my bed and shove me against the wall. He did this only when he was really frightened. His hands were so big and his arms so strong that he would lift me up so high my feet didn't touch the ground. Then he'd shake me and I'd begin to howl. He shook me the way a cat shakes a rabbit.

Obedient to his command, I always stopped crying. Then one night something broke inside me. I couldn't stop, no matter what he did to me, no matter how much he threatened. I could no longer absorb his confusion, his grief, his fear or his chaos. I knew I loved him, even when I hated him most. I would always love him. Yet even that didn't matter any more.

It was over. He had lost me. And he knew it. For three years we had been too close, too trusting, too open with each other for him not to have known this immediately. Beside himself with fury and frustration, he could tell he was powerless to change anything.

Dumping my body in a heap on the floor, he ran from the room, slamming the door. Despite his monumental will, this time the 'kid' could not be 'fixed'.

24

FROZEN

I HAD BEEN LIVING on a razor's edge, trying to adjust to Stanley's never-ending shifts in energy and emotions. That night he shook me I lost my ability to respond. Whatever broke inside me turned me into a traumatised animal.

I could have fought him but, by then, the sparring games we used to play had turned into terrifying contests of will which left me feeling I was being torn apart limb by limb. My second choice might have been to flee. But where could I run? Who could I turn to, given that not only was I living with secrets whose source I didn't remember, but I had also come to believe that I must be responsible for my father's miseries and everything that was happening around him?

Perhaps this was what he wanted me to believe. And, like most children of troubled parents, I was only too glad to become the fall guy, if that's what it took to release him from his anguish. After all, he was the man with whom I had shared more joy, more horror, more life, than anyone I had ever known. Trapped, with no way out, there was a third choice – a choice available to all threatened creatures, human or animal, although few are aware that it exists. I could freeze.

Biologists call the third possible reaction to trauma 'a freeze response'. Less common than fight or flight, it is an equally effective strategy for staying alive. One of the interesting things that happens to an animal that freezes and manages to get away is that, as soon as it reaches a safe place, it lies down and gives itself over to an uncontrollable trembling. This strange, balletic movement follows a predictable pattern, finally bringing the animal into a state of quietude, from which it is able to return to normal life. In humans, this restorative trembling is seldom allowed to take place. When it does not, alarm reactions eventually become the person's normal response to almost everything. Threats seem to come from everywhere. Psychologists have found that such people become so driven by the perceived danger that their perceptions become deadened in an attempt to protect themselves from having to feel at all.

I believe this is what happened to me the night I collapsed on the floor when Stanley shook me for the last time. The build-up of pressure over the three years of our incestuous relationship, the memory suppression that denied its existence, and the splits within my psyche created by it all, had become more than I could handle. I could no longer respond. My open-heartedness disappeared – not only towards Stanley, but towards everything. I withdrew to somewhere deep inside. As my feelings shut down, I began living in a state of suspended animation. I'd forget to eat. I slept little and I didn't care about anything.

Repeated trauma, especially at an early age, hardens a person. One day, far in the future, I would come to understand that, long before, Stella had been turned into such a hardened being. So had Stanley. In both of them, this led to the kind of relentless ambition that brooks no compassion for themselves or others, for they see it as a genuine drawback to accomplishing one's ends. Such hardening separates you from your heart and soul so you can end up living with a terrible loneliness which nothing can assuage. I know my father experienced this. He spoke about it all his life. So, I believe, did Stella. This may have been an important force in her having lived the double life she did.

There are other consequences too. When you can't allow yourself the luxury of trusting another human being, sex, instead of being a satisfying experience, can turn into something frustrating, difficult and unsatisfactory. You long to *feel* but cannot and you begin to tear at life in an attempt to grab pleasure wherever you can find it: in drugs, in alcohol, in meaningless copulation. When a human being lives his life in a frozen state, he has to dominate others before he feels safe enough to experience pleasure of any kind. Even then, pleasure often needs to be *ripped* from the body of another being.

During the years Mom lived at Hollyridge, Stella had stopped making late-night surprise visits there. Instead she would speak to Stanley on the telephone, and make the odd trip to see him when he performed nearby. By the summer of 1954, Mom had long departed and he was not performing. After he'd repeatedly told Stella over the phone that he was 'having trouble with Leslie', she began to visit Hollyridge again.

One evening, she arrived unannounced, laden with bags. Stanley was out. I had no idea where he was, but by then I didn't care. I was lying in the music room underneath the piano, reading Dostoevsky's *Notes from Underground*. I felt a kinship with the narrator's self-loathing, his torment and his paranoia, which his body turned into an agonising toothache and liver pain. Like me, this guy seemed to be paralysed with inertia – trapped by an inability to do anything to make his life better. I also related to his sense of shame and ugliness. I had just come to the point in the book when Dostoevsky describes how fearful the narrator is that Liza, the prostitute, might invade his privacy, when Stella invaded mine.

I heard a key turn in the lock of the front door. I thought it was Stanley. I knew he was unlikely to come into the music room at that hour and, since the door to the hall was shut, I kept on reading. I could hear footsteps overhead. Two doors opened and closed. That didn't sound like Stanley. He almost never shut doors upstairs. With book in hand, I opened the door to the hall just in time to be greeted by Stella coming down the stairs, on her way to the kitchen.

'There you are,' she said. 'I hear you've been having a rough time. Stanley asked me to come. He thinks I might be able to help.' She laid a hand on my shoulder and smiled. I recoiled from her touch with all the will left to me – which wasn't much. 'I've brought you something to make you feel better,' she continued.

'I feel all right.'

'You look terrible.'

'I'm OK.'

She took the book from my hand, laid it on the telephone table and ushered me into the kitchen. She took a water glass from the cupboard and removed an envelope from one of her bags. From this, she scooped out what looked like dried leaves and tossed them into the glass. Then she filled it half full of water. Opening the refrigerator door, she found a bottle of maple syrup, added that to the mixture and stirred. 'Drink this,' she said. 'It'll help you. Then we're going to meet some friends and get you some healing.'

When I think back to that evening, I find it hard to understand why I actually did what she told me to do. But I drank the mixture. It was viscous and full of particles, some of which had not dissolved. It was also sickly sweet. 'Good girl,' Stella said. 'Now, let's go.'

It was ten or eleven o'clock at night. She made me put on my coat – despite my protests that I was not cold – and led me down the front steps. We got into her car and drove down the hill. By the time we reached the canyon, I felt pleasantly calm. A strange thought came to me: maybe I'd been wrong about Stella. Maybe she really did want to help me. I could feel my face going numb and tingling. This feeling spread through my body, and down my hands and legs. I dozed off.

I don't know where she took me. It could have been Manhattan Beach or Redondo, or even Venice, but when she helped me from the car, we were standing in the street of a beach town lined with old wooden houses, none big or well-kept. I could feel the night air on my cheeks. It smelt salty, like the ocean.

We had parked directly in front of a building which looked like a deserted church. Wooden steps with rickety railings led up to a double wooden door. I held on to one to keep my balance. I got a big splinter in my right hand. I was surprised to find that it didn't hurt.

I heard Stella's voice say, 'Do be careful, Leslie. We don't want you to fall.' I looked up. The sky was brilliant with stars. Then there was darkness.

I don't remember how I got back to Hollyridge. Stella could not have taken me back on her own. I was five foot nine inches tall by then, and weighed 130 pounds. She would never have managed it.

I didn't wake up until early evening the next day when Stanley came into my bedroom. 'You must be exhausted, Shortstuff,' he said, leaning over me. 'You've slept the whole day.' He looked at me more kindly than he had for a long time.

'I did?'

'You sure did. I was starting to worry. I thought I'd better get you up or you might not sleep tonight.'

'I could sleep for ever.'

He lays a hand on my forehead. 'You're hot. You're not going to get one of those fevers again, are you?'

I shake my head.

'Are you hungry?' he asks.

I nod.

'Take a shower. I'll go down and make us something to eat. You're not gonna go back to sleep, are you?'

I shake my head again.

'I've been missing you,' Stanley says.

He walks out of the room, leaving the door to the landing open.

I find it incredibly difficult to get up. I pull myself to a sitting position, put my legs over the side of my bed and stare down at my feet. My body is naked. I notice there is blood on the insides of both my thighs. I wonder if I got my period in the night. But this blood is dried.

Everything looks so far away. I see a coat lying on a chair. I try to remember putting it there. I pull myself up, holding on to the door at the right of my bed. I begin to walk with deliberation – like an animal in a slow-motion movie. My legs feel like they're made of rubber bands. It is only six or seven steps from the side of the bed, through to my dressing room, into the bathroom. I take one step at a time, bracing myself against the closet door on the right and the dressing table on the left. I see my reflection in the mirror. I feel guilty. It is like I am seeing some other person's body whose privacy I have invaded. She has scratches on the side of her arm. After much deliberation I conclude she must have caught it on a nail. I make my way across the bathroom. It is no more than a yard from my dressing room door but it seems a mile. I turn on the shower. Holding on to the sliding glass doors, I climb into the tub.

Hot water pours down my chest and over my body. I stand still, letting it warm me. The heat feels clean and comforting. The sun is almost gone and the room is filled with a pinkish golden light. I decide the light and the water must be friends, come to make me stronger.

I don't know how long I stood in the shower. I didn't want to leave it. I kept hearing the words 'forget, forget, forgotten'. I didn't know why. The words made me shiver so I turned the heat up as high as my skin could bear.

By the next morning, those words were gone. Others had taken their place: *No matter what they do to you, you will never be harmed.* They were strangely comforting. It would be more than fifteen years before some of the memories deliberately buried that night would begin to return.

25

FOUR WOMEN AND A MAN

STANLEY MADE DINNER. He had grilled lamb chops under the broiler – the kind with the little crunchy tails – and cooked frozen string beans. The lamb chops tasted wonderful. Eating them reminded me I was alive. We sat together at the dining-room table for a long time that night. At least it felt like a long time to me. My body was weak and shaky. I'm sure he noticed this, because he kept looking at me as though he were waiting for reassurance of some kind. I was the last person in the world to be able to reassure anyone about anything. He didn't ask me about the night before. But he did lean over several times, lay his hand on mine and ask: 'How do you feel, Shortstuff?'

'I don't know.'

'You wanna sleep more?'

'I guess so.'

'Stay here with me for a while.'

'OK.'

'You wanna go to the movies?'

'No.'

'We'll go tomorrow then?'

'Yeah.'

'Get some rest.'

When, finally, I got up from the table and started upstairs, I was still woozy and off balance. I tripped on my way up the stairs and fell against the door chimes that hung in a recess on the wall. I heard Stanley's voice say something. I couldn't hear what. He sounded far away. I got to the landing, entered my room, just made it to the edge of the bed, fell into it with all my clothes on and passed out. When I woke late next morning, I was alone in the house.

A few nights later, we went to the movies. Yet we were like two strangers. He didn't even grab my knee to tickle me as he always had. In the days that followed, we would connect for just a few minutes while sharing a French dip sandwich at Felipe's or while watching a Mexican fiesta in Olivera Street. We even laughed a little. But mostly we lived like shadow figures cut from tissue paper. We wafted by each other but we never met.

For a couple of weeks Stella didn't make any of her visits to Hollyridge. She did call Stanley on the phone, though. She always seemed to know when he was at home, since she never rang when I was alone. I knew when it was her because he would carry the phone into the music room and shut the door.

Then came a night I never want to remember. Stanley was gone – I didn't know to where or when, even if, he would come back. I had come to feel scared at night in our house at the top of the mountain when I was there alone. Hollyridge seemed full of dark shadows. I turned the lights on all over the house and I left the radio playing in the living room. When finally I fell asleep, I dreamed a long complicated dream which became a nightmare that would haunt me for years to come.

I didn't know then but the dream was both a premonition of things yet to come and a metaphor for the way my mind had become split into shards.

In it, I'm in bed in a dingy hotel room. To the right of me, in a room I can only enter by going out into the hall, a woman sleeps. On the other side of me, through a door adjoining my room, another woman sleeps. Both of them look just like me.

I leave my room to hunt for something. I wander down a corridor, turn right, pass a broken elevator on the left and come to another room. Its door is ajar. I can see a woman and a man inside. There is a double bed and a sash window in need of repair. A soiled and torn net curtain hangs over it. The window is open. When the wind blows the curtain, this fills the room with dust.

The woman lies on the bed naked. Her eyes are sunken and black. Her body is emaciated, like a survivor from Auschwitz. Her body's surrounded by grey, blood-spattered sheets. They seem to be moving slowly round her like waves.

I notice her chest is rising and falling in rhythm with the moving bedclothes. She weeps. The haggard man stands across the room next to the open window. He seems afraid. He's naked except for a towel round his waist. A psychopath, he has been both enchanting and torturing the woman. 'One day I'll kill her,' he says. I don't believe him. I think what he likes best is torturing her. If he killed her, the torture would end.

The woman stirs, opens her eyes. She lifts an arm – reaches out to him. It's the limb of a skeleton covered in loose skin. The woman smiles faintly. I see she's in love with him. I see she's in danger. I know she doesn't want me to interfere with them. 'Please go,' she whispers.

I leave the room, shutting the door behind me. I run down the corridor, burst through the door to my room, leap into the bed, cover my head with a pillow and fall sleep. I wake up to terrible screams. Oh God, he's torturing her again. I think I must call the police and stop it. Then I remember that what they're doing is none of my business. I try to go back to sleep. More screams. I get out of bed and go to the connecting door. I want to speak to the woman in the next room. I want to get someone to share responsibility for what I am going to do. I open the door.

She is deep in sleep. Why does she look so like me? I see she loves the warmth of her bed. I know her. I like it when she's in my body. She likes curling up, drinking hot chocolate and picking flowers. Her golden hair blazes across the pillow. She hates disturbance so she sleeps, dreaming of other times and places. I take hold of her shoulders and shake her. 'Wake up,' I say, 'wake up.' She gets out of bed and walks to the window, looks out on the morning and smiles.

She's not going to help me so I leave her and go out into the hall. I bang on the door of the room to the right. A woman opens it. She too looks like me.

'What do you want?' she snaps.

'There's a woman screaming. The man's she's with is hurting her – maybe killing her. We need to help.'

'You help her.'

'What?'

'Let her scream.'

I woke up from this dream in a fury, afraid, dripping with sweat. I leapt from the bed in a frenzy, desperate to find Stanley. I headed through the dressing room into the bathroom. The other door from the bathroom opened directly into his bedroom. I barged through it. His bed had not been slept in. I called out, 'Stanley, Stanley, Stanley!' No one answered. I heard the radio playing in the living room. He would have turned it off if he'd come home. I sat down on the edge of his bed with my head in my hands.

I don't know how long I sat there but it was long enough for the sweat on my body to dry. I got up, I went back to the bathroom, switched on the light and opened the medicine cabinet. As always, it was full of bottles of pills, lined up on glass shelves. I opened three or four and poured their contents into the basin. I filled a glass with water, grabbed a fistful of pills and swallowed them. I did this three times since I couldn't get them all down at once. I had no thoughts about what I was doing or why. I felt nothing. I went back to my room and got back into bed.

When I woke I was lying in a hospital bed with a tube shoved down my throat. There was an ugly sucking sound. It seemed to be coming from me. There were people I didn't know, talking in loud voices. My head throbbed. My ears were ringing with horrible sounds – many horrible sounds. The air in the room didn't look like air at all – more like water. The blue colour of the curtains and the yellow walls were so intense I couldn't stand to look at them. I closed my eyes.

I don't think I was in the hospital for more than a few hours before Stella came to take me home. I knew it was her even before she came into the room. I heard her say in an irritated voice, 'I don't care. I am taking her with me right now, whether you like it or not!'

When we were in the car she scolded me. She said Stanley had come home only minutes after I'd swallowed the pills. She said I was a wicked girl to have done something so horrible to my father. She said I was lucky to be alive. As soon as he saw the pills in the bathroom sink he called her. She was the one who rang for an ambulance, she said. Without her I would be dead now. I should be grateful. She was at the hospital to meet the ambulance when it arrived. Stanley was not there. 'We can't afford nasty publicity just because you do decide to do such a stupid thing,' she snapped. My head was still ringing and throbbing. It was hard for me to listen to her.

I still have no idea what possessed me to take all the pills. God knows what I took – probably everything from aspirin to amphetamines and barbiturates. I remember feeling indifferent to whether I lived or died when Stella brought me home. But there was one thing I learned from that night: the thought of committing suicide by swallowing pills disappears for ever once someone pumps your stomach.

For many years afterwards I experienced a constriction in my throat and a heaviness in my stomach that I could never figure out the cause for. They would show up when I felt very tired or sad. This stopped happening once my memories of that night began to surface. After that the symptoms never returned.

26

CRACK IN THE SOUL

STELLA HAD DECIDED that Stanley's life was crumbling. She could see that he was in the midst of an acute crisis. If she could handle it for him as quickly and quietly as possible, this would bring her two rewards: firstly, he would be eternally grateful. Secondly, all her decades of waiting would not have been wasted, and if she could fix his problem – namely me – she would be firmly back at the helm of his life. It was the chance she had waited for. What she didn't take into account, however, was the greater love my father had for me, or his own integrity of spirit, even at the darkest times in his life.

Because I had always disliked my grandmother and I made no secret of it, she rarely had access to me alone while I was very young. So she had never been able to program me as she had Stanley. The older I became, the more fiercely independent I grew. On one level, I think Stella admired me for this. She told me, 'Your strength is my strength, Leslie' – the only time she said anything to me that was even vaguely complimentary. I think she hated me for it too.

Certainly she looked upon me as a serious threat to her goals for Stanley. She had spent a large part of her life honing Stanley to become the man she wanted him to be. First Violet had interfered with her plans by marrying him, then I had by being born. I was too volatile, too unpredictable. Unless she stepped in and took over, I might become unstoppable – and that might not just postpone or weaken Stanley's success, it could deliver a death blow to it. And if I ruined his career she would not, at her age, be able to hone another child. All the goals in her life could be lost. The time for her to take action had arrived.

'It's time to face facts. Leslie's unhinged!' Stella kept saying things like this to my father, usually when I was in a nearby room so I could hear every word. 'She swallowed all those pills, didn't she? We've got to get her under control.'

During the third week of July, my father had to fly East to emcee the first Newport Jazz Festival. I didn't know when he was coming back, but Stella came to stay two nights before he left. The last thing I heard him say to her as he got into the car to go to the airport was, 'I know Leslie needs help, but where are we going to get it?'

'Leave Leslie to me, Stanley,' Stella assured him. 'You don't need to worry about a thing.'

Hollywood has always been – still is – a place where, if you know the right people, as Stella did, and have money, you can get anything done 'to help a friend with a problem'. The connections between government, the underworld and the entertainment industry are strong in this city. And the way such things are handled is, above all, discreet. First there are telephone calls. Usually no more than four or five are necessary. As soon as a phone call strikes pay dirt, you are given the name of someone who can 'take care of things' for you; then you're quoted a price for the job.

At an agreed time, a car arrives, as it did for me. It's driven by someone who does not know you. The driver has his instructions. He has no idea why you are being taken to the destination he has been given. You are passed from one hand to another only on a 'need to know' basis. The *problem* gets solved and you are returned to where you're supposed to be, with no one the wiser.

Stanley was the friend with the problem. Stella was the handler. I was the problem.

As soon as Stanley left Hollyridge, Stella worked on convincing me that I was in a dangerous state: 'If something isn't done to help you, Leslie, you're gonna end up in an insane asylum. You don't want that, do you?' She kept saying to me, 'All this has to be kept secret or everyone will know you're mentally ill.' If I protested that I was not mentally ill, she would shake her head and turn away. Later she would come back at me with, 'How can you be so ungrateful?' She kept telling me how much trouble I had caused Stanley: 'Don't you see he's beside himself with worry?' She kept saying, 'He has more important things to do than deal with your foolishness.'

Two days later, a car arrived in the evening to pick me up and take me to a place where, Stella said, 'They can make you better.' By then, my grandmother had worn me down and filled me with guilt. I went willingly, just to get away. There were three men in the car. One was dressed in a chauffeur's uniform. The other two wore suits.

Stella had packed a small bag for me. 'You won't need more than this,' she said. 'They'll give you everything else. And for heaven's sake don't take a lot of books with you. You need to rest and recover.' She handed the overnight bag to one of the men as we were going down the steps to get into the limousine. None of them spoke. The whole trip was made in silence. We drove down the hill and along Los Feliz Boulevard. We passed Griffith Park then headed into the San Fernando Valley. After that I lost track.

Stella had given me three pills just before we left Hollyridge, 'to help you feel calmer on your journey'. Her methods always included stuffing me with one or more of the new neuroleptic pharmaceuticals that were just beginning to come on to the market. Somehow, she always remained up to date with the latest mind-blunting drugs.

It was nearly dark when we arrived at our destination. The place looked like a huge complex with lots of low buildings resembling wooden cottages, but much longer. Some had two storeys and were surrounded by lawns, hedges and fir trees. One building was smaller than the rest. It had a square tower, with a cross on top and a pointed roof and a portico made of what looked like stucco covered by a tile roof. The place looked as though it had been put together piece by piece over a long time. The buildings didn't match each other very well.

The car stopped in front of a long building with a veranda

stretching the entire length of it. One of the men helped me from the car. We entered the lobby. It had a tiled floor and a few indoor plants. A woman, dressed in white, sat behind a high counter on one side. Leaving me standing in the doorway, the man went up to her and said, 'I'm delivering Miss Leslie. I believe you're expecting her.' The woman nodded and took my bag.

'Come this way, please,' she said, taking hold of my arm. I followed her down a long corridor with lots of doors leading off it. She opened a door and switched on the light. 'This'll be your room while you're with us,' she said. 'You have your own toilet and shower. It's important to get as much rest as you can while you're here.

'Are you hungry?' she asked. I told her I wasn't. 'Good,' she said. 'Let's get you to bed, then.'

I started to open the bag Stella had packed for me to find my pyjamas. 'No, dear,' she said. 'You won't be needing those while you're here.' She opened a tall cupboard and took out a starched hospital gown like the one they had made me wear when I had my collarbone set at the Queen of Angels.

'Is this a hospital?' I wondered.

'Good gracious, no,' she replied. 'It's a *sanatorium*. It used to be a place people with tuberculosis came to rest and get better. Now we use it for other purposes. We help people like you get well.'

I climbed into bed. The woman handed me a paper cup with two pills in it and a glass of water. 'Take these.'

I noticed there was no light next to my bed. 'I want to read,' I said.

'Not tonight, we can talk about that tomorrow,' she said, before leaving me and closing the door carefully behind her.

Later – I don't know how much later, but it was dark still – a man came into my room and stuck a needle into the back of my hand. It was connected to a tube that went up to a bottle hanging upside down over the bed.

In all the time I was there I never remember being able to take a shower or read a book. Tomorrow never came.

*

Deep memory – the kind that resonates throughout life triggering joy or grief – bears no resemblance to the kind of memory involved in summoning up timetables, recalling telephone numbers, or regurgitating poems learned by rote in school. It's forged from a collection of sense impressions: touch, smell, taste, sound and feelings. Fear, heat, pain and pleasure become encoded in our brain and body. Over time they coalesce to form pictures, beliefs, thoughts and themes that play over and over throughout our lives.

Some of my memories are so clear that, when they arise, it seems they are happening in the present. Others drift in and out of consciousness so I can never hold on to them or anchor them in a specific time or place. My memories of my incarceration in that strange place have this amorphous quality.

There I am now. It's daylight. Through the window of my room I see expanses of lawn and huge dark fir trees. They are beautiful. Strange that somebody has put bars on the window since the view is so nice that nobody would want to leave.

Men and women keep coming and going. They are dressed in white. None of them asks my name. In the mornings, even when I tell them I am hungry, they always refuse to give me any food. When I ask why, someone explains, 'We don't want you to vomit.'

My bed is on wheels. It's like a cart on stilts. These people in white push me in it. Sometimes they push me outside. I know when they take me outside because then the light is too bright. I don't like bright light. It hurts my eyes.

They push my bed along the corridor to the door of a different kind of room. There is an old woman already there lying in front of the door on a bed just like mine. They leave me in the hall. They push her bed through the door. I hear her crying. I guess she doesn't like the room. When they push her back out to the hall, her eyes are all red and she is snorting and twitching.

Now they push my bed through the door. People lift me off it and lay me on a narrow table. They strap my chest down, then my arms and legs. 'No,' I say, 'no!'

'It's so you don't fall off the table,' a voice says.

'Where am I? What am I doing here?' I demand to know.

The woman shoves a piece of wood wrapped with rubber in my mouth. It feels slick against my tongue. 'Shhhh,' she says. 'Bite down.' When I don't open my mouth fast enough, she grabs my jaw and pulls it open. Someone presses cold things against my temples, then straps them to my head.

This room – which they wheel me into once or twice a day – is large with huge windows. They have no bars. The room is always empty except for some people, a wooden slab with leather straps attached to it that they make me lie on and a black box covered with dials and switches with black wires hanging off it.

'Watch me,' says a lady in a hat with blue stripes. She always stands by my head. I look up. Explosion. Blinding light. It tears through my body, ripping, searing, blue-white. I'm on fire, wiped out, obliterated.

In that room they fill my body with 'electro-convulsive therapy', ECT, sometimes more than once a day – for two or three weeks. Even now, as I write these words, I shudder at the notion that slapping electrodes on somebody's head, strapping their arms, legs and chest to a table, shoving a gag in their mouth and shooting bone-crunching high voltage into their body could ever be considered 'therapy'.

I wake up. It feels like I'm smothering. There's a huge patch of emptiness somewhere inside. A chunk of my brain has been ripped out. It's gone. There's pressure on my chest. My head aches, and my legs, and my back. My body keeps going into spasms. Tears pour from my eyes from some grief I can't even remember. When I try to smile I discover I can't because my face has gone stiff. All my movements are clumsy and slow. I must have done something really bad to deserve this.

*

In the beginning I was in such a state of shock from what was happening at the sanatorium that I became almost comatose. I hated waking up each morning. My hair was filthy. My body felt sticky and itchy. I only remembered waking and going to sleep – but nothing in between.

One day I fought them. Spewing with rage and violence, I struck out against them when they came for me. I wanted to kill them when they lifted me from my bed to put me on the table, but I had no weapon. When I woke up I kept on screaming. I wouldn't do anything they told me to. I believe my fury lasted for several days but I can't be sure. 'Hit her with all we've got,' I would hear them say. 'What she needs is a good spanking' and then, 'OK, let's give her the works.'

Another memory surfaces: now I'm in a strange room. There's no way out. It is all white with no windows. The walls here are softer than the sofa in our living room at home and there are mattresses on the floor. They thread my arms through the sleeves of a canvas shirt. Its sleeves are so long they wrap all the way round me and tie. I can move my legs but I can't move the rest of me. I don't scream any more. There's no point since no one hears me. I don't know how long I've been in here or why they put me in this room. They must hate me as much as I hate them.

Sometimes I leave my body. It's easy. I float just above the girl all wrapped in canvas below who looks like me. I see that she's unhappy but I don't know why. Up here, everything's fine. Up here, I'm the Emperor of Ice-Cream and I can make any flavour I want.

When they open the door I see the white people walking up and down the halls again. They look like doctors and nurses except that this place doesn't smell like a hospital.

I see a broken mirror. The broken mirror is me. Dagger-shaped pieces of glass pierce my flesh. They make me bleed and go on bleeding. I guess I'm supposed to bleed. I'm supposed to be punished. Maybe if I take on the role of punisher, then they won't have to go on punishing me.

*

In the name of 'curing depression', or killing off inconvenient memories, they burn your brain. So violent is the assault on your body and psyche from ECT that you lose consciousness. In the mid 1950s, it was given without anaesthetic. It still is today in many countries. This is based on the belief that the more suffering you cause the patient, the more effective you can be in exorcising the 'devils' that possess him. In my case, ECT not only wiped out memories, it shattered my central nervous system, separated my spirit from my body and reduced me to a shell of a human being.

I would be thirty-five years old before fragmented memories of the weeks spent in this sanatorium began to make sense. I am still not sure where it all took place. Over the intervening years I experienced a number of dreams about electrocution. In many of them I heard the words 'olive view'. I was never able to figure out what connection olives could possibly have with ECT. Then, by accident – except that I no longer believe in accidents – I discovered there had been a sanatorium in the San Fernando Valley at the foot of the San Gabriel Mountains named 'Olive View'.

It was founded in October 1920 as a tuberculosis sanatorium for Los Angeles County. Once TB was curable by antibiotics, Olive View metamorphosed into an acute care hospital with a facility for carrying out 'experimental medical procedures'. The first open heart surgery in the San Fernando Valley took place at Olive View.

Gradually, Olive View became affiliated with UCLA. In 1970, UCLA opened a newly constructed hospital, adding to the existing facilities. Two months later, the new building was destroyed completely by the famous Sylmar earthquake which was 6.5 on the Richter Scale.

In the course of my research for this book, I interviewed two people who had been given ECT at Olive View. They were part of the now infamous MKULTRA mind-control programme initiated in the early 1950s by the Office of Scientific Intelligence. Could I have somehow been slipped into this programme? Stella certainly had connections with important military people who could have arranged it. It may also be that the words 'olive view' which echoed in my dreams are nothing more than a strange coincidence. I will never know.

They brought me back to Hollyridge in another limousine, with a big bottle of pills 'to help you relax'. This time there was a man with a black chauffeur's hat and a woman wearing old-fashioned reddish brown lace-up leather shoes with Cuban heels. I remembered my mother hating Cuban heels.

It was dark. The woman had a key to the house. I wondered who gave it to her. She took me inside. 'Which room is yours?' she asked.

We went upstairs. 'It's been a long day,' she said, pulling back the covers of my bed. She peeled off my clothes and pulled a pyjama top over my head. It was my own pyjama top. 'Now get some sleep,' she said.

I climbed into bed. I had never been so obedient in my whole life. I was like a ghost in someone else's body. The woman handed me two tablets, white with a blue stamp on them. She put the bottle of pills on the stand at the side of my bed.

'Where's Stanley?' I said.

'Who's Stanley?' she asked.

I drifted into darkness.

27

GRUNION HUNTING

WHAT HAPPENED IN the first few days after they brought me back to Hollyridge still remains a black hole in my mind. The next thing I can remember is Stanley driving me to a beach house in Malibu and leaving me there. The house was small, made of wood and weathered by the sea. It smelt like iodine. A boy named Michael – three years older than me – was there with his mother, Virginia Wicks.

More than fifty years would pass before I spoke to Virginia Wicks again. A mutual friend told me she was still alive and gave me her telephone number. When I called her, Virginia recounted the time we spent together at the beach house. 'You were so sad,' she said. 'It seemed like all the light had gone from you. Michael and I were really worried.' She said that she had known nothing about what had happened to me.

Virginia is now in her eighties. She's done public relations for jazz festivals, Nat King Cole, Ella Fitzgerald, Rock Hudson and many others, including Stan Kenton. When I asked her what I was like during the years she worked for Stanley, she said, 'You were slender like your father and you looked a lot like him too. You were quiet but so interesting when you spoke – more like an adult than a child. I admired your intelligence and maturity. You were interested in everything. That is, until those days at the beach.'

Unlike many memories, which only returned piecemeal in decades to come, I have always remembered the days I spent at the beach that summer with Virginia and Michael. It's as though they happened yesterday. Those days mark the beginning of my struggle to piece together the facsimile of a new person out of the pieces that were left.

I go back there now: I remember how these people call me 'Leslie'. That's as good a name as any, I guess. It seems like somebody's switched off the sun. The world's gone grey – house, sand, sea, sky. Michael and his mother look familiar. They are kind to me. I don't know why, but I'm grateful. I don't know what I'm doing here.

Virginia hands me plates, knives, forks and spoons. She asks me to set the table. I hold them in my hands. I know each utensil has a proper place but I can't work out what goes where. I wonder if they will punish me if I get it wrong. Virginia's beautiful face stares at me from across the room. I must pretend I know what I'm doing so she won't realise I'm lost. I pick up a knife. It shines so bright I can see my face in it. The light hurts my head. I put it down. I pick up a fork. Maybe this is a game? Maybe it's like singing. I hold the fork in my hand. I remember the lady with the long hair in the movie *Hamlet*. What was her name? Ophelia. That's it. She floats down the river and the water carries her to her death.

I wonder if I can sing like Ophelia. I begin to hum as I rearrange the plates, the forks, the napkins and the knives. Nothing looks right. Never mind. It'll come to me. It doesn't come so I abandon the task. I look towards Michael. He smiles and finishes setting the table for me.

'Wanna go grunion hunting?' he asks.

'What's that?'

'They're fish. They run at full moon. They come in on a breaker and try to bury themselves in the sand before the water goes away. The trick is to dig them up before they disappear.'

'Before they disappear?'

'Yeah.'

I wonder if I'm a grunion. When the tide goes out, maybe I'll disappear too.

Bedtime. Virginia says I need to brush my teeth now. The bathroom is small. It smells of wet salt and tin cans. I rub my thumb over the bristles of each and I choose the only dry brush. It must be mine, I tell myself. After I finish, I take a towel and dry off the bristles so if I got it wrong, no one will notice.

Someone has put pyjamas out on a bed. They must be mine since they're too small for Michael or Virginia. I put them on. I slip in between crunchy sheets. It feels like I'm getting into a refrigerator. I wonder if this place is safe from fishermen and grunion hunters.

Virginia not only worked for Stanley, she was an intimate friend of Mom's. 'Yvonne was always so good to me,' she says. They even lived together while Virginia was pregnant with her daughter, Christina. Virginia was also a dedicated follower of L. Ron Hubbard. She told me that Mom, Stanley and she used to visit Hubbard on his ship anchored nearby.

Virginia also told me that, before the time we spent together in the beach house, Stanley used to bring me to her often. He would arrive unexpectedly for dinner. Then he would leave me with her overnight or for a few days, she said. I even spent a week once driving up the coast with her on a vacation. I remember none of this. She told me, 'When Stanley dropped you off to stay with me, he always said, "It's good for Leslie to spend time with you."'

I have always remembered her son Michael with affection, and have often thought back to the days we spent together on the beach. I had looked up to him then. Even though he was only a few years older than me, he seemed so grown up. I sensed his concern and warmth towards me, and I was grateful for it.

After making contact with them both after all these years, I asked Michael too what he remembered of that time in Malibu. Since then we have spent several hours on the telephone talking. He told me about other times we spent together at Hollyridge and Pacific Palisades.

There was some confusion in Virginia's mind over the dates I came to stay with her and Michael. She seemed to think it may have been earlier than I remember it. When I told Michael I was concerned that my recollection of when we were together differed from hers, he said, 'I would go with your gut feeling. I remember those days well.'

28

ON THE RUN

Aᴌᴌ ʜɪꜱ ʟɪꜰᴇ Stanley had relied on fixes. Stella had convinced him that getting his life back on track depended on getting me *fixed*. Then he'd be able to 'leave all the crap behind' and get on with his life. Most of what follows I only came to know fifteen or twenty years later as we began to speak together about that summer.

Stella had promised she would take care of whatever 'adjustments' were needed and he had given me over to her, knowing she would keep her promise. He didn't want to hear what her plan was, but he felt confident she would piece together the right story afterwards, which he could pass on to Violet and to others. Of course, it needed to be a truth which he could also tell himself and feel OK about.

When he took off for the Newport Jazz Festival in July, he was feeling more confident than he had for a long time – expecting to return and find everything handled. Leslie would be all right again and everything would get better.

The reality that confronted him when he got back to Hollyridge was not what he had anticipated. Years later he told me, 'When I saw you I felt sick. The fire that always burned so bright in you had gone out. It was like you were dead – an empty shell. Except, when people die, they stop moving. They stop breathing. Your body still worked in a minimal way. It wasn't grey or pockmarked or anything. But it was flatter, greyer, duller. Your eyes wouldn't focus. You kept looking in all different directions. Your hair looked different too. It was thinner or something.

'When I saw you it scared me more than anything in my life. I just wanted to go back. I kept wishing there'd be anguish in your face, or hatred or fear – anything at all. But there was nothing.'

Towards the end of that summer I heard Stanley arguing with Stella. It was impossible not to hear them since they were shouting.

'What have you done to her?'

'Only what needed doing, Stanley. Calm down.'

'Calm down? What does that mean? You always hated her. Now you've destroyed her.'

'I did no such thing,' Stella snapped.

'Take a look at her.'

'I only did what you asked me to do.'

'I never said to turn her into a vegetable. What are you? Some kind of a monster?'

'Stop it. I don't deserve to be treated like this after all I've done for you. You get me to clean up your garbage, then you hate me for it.'

Stanley was insistent. 'Tell me what you did to her.'

'You want to know, Stanley? You really want to know?'

I assume he didn't want to know since their fight ended abruptly. If he had forced Stella to tell him, she would have rubbed his nose in everything he had been fighting so hard to avoid. That night he sent her away. Their relationship was never quite the same again.

Stanley was still on a downward spiral and was hideously angry. He had already given up the pills after they pumped my stomach. The collection in the bathroom cabinet had vanished, to be replaced by a tube of Alka-Seltzer and a bottle of aspirin. Even the pill pouch he had carried with him on the road was gone. But alcohol was a different matter. It was not only a way of getting through the night for him. He used alcohol as a way of *decompressing* – as an attempt to create space inside himself, in the hope of making his day-to-day life manageable. 'I always feel so damned pressured,' he'd say. 'I need a drink.'

We spent the remaining time together at Hollyridge before I had to return to school. He refused to talk to anybody. He didn't answer the phone. The mailbox bulged with uncollected letters. I retreated into my books, rereading some I knew I'd read already but of which I had no memory. We lived together in silence like two people lost in a fog.

Years later he told what had been going on for him: 'I got into an awful darkness where I questioned everything. I didn't know what to do. If I'd owned up to the wrong decisions I'd made I would've had to admit that everything was wrong: house, wife, kid, music – all of it. I couldn't do that. I kept thinking, "Thank God I can go back on the road." At least I knew how to do that.'

Stan Kenton's prestige was not in the least diminished by what was going on in Stanley Kenton's private life. That was the year he got elected to *Down Beat's* Jazz Hall of Fame – celebrating a lifetime's achievements in jazz. He was only the third musician to have received the honour.

Yet money was still scarce. Big touring bands had become less and less viable financially. They were being replaced by small house bands that stayed in one place. Theatres had already turned their back on stage shows. Radio networks had stopped doing remote broadcasts. Even the 'bread and butter' one-nighter circuits in the South and Midwest were becoming a thing of the past. The benchmark for success in the music business had shifted away from touring towards selling hit records. In spite of his celebrity and drive, all my father's future projects seemed doomed to financial failure.

Meanwhile, back at my mother's house I was now living in a state of constant fear – fear of the dark, fear that I'd been damned, fear that I was a hideous being that carried a deadly plague which anyone I let close to me might catch. Haunted by my own spectres of shame, grief and confusion, I was struggling to remember even simple day-to-day things. I had no sense of identity.

Before then, I had always been good at mathematics; a year or two ahead of the rest of my class. Now, I could not work out the simplest equation. I couldn't even remember telephone numbers. I stopped playing cards since I couldn't remember which ones had already been played.

My one object in life became to appear as 'normal' as possible. I hoped this might make me acceptable to everybody. The words 'don't let anyone find out about me, or they'll send me away' had turned into a haunting litany that played over and over in my brain. I had no idea where these words had come from or what they meant. They would plague me for years to come.

I got up each morning, dressed myself, made sure I ate enough at breakfast that my mother wouldn't hound me, and left the house. I walked the streets until it was an acceptable time to arrive at school. Sometimes, late at night, when everyone was asleep, I would get up, steal clothes from my mother's dressing room, put them on, go out and walk up and down the highway for hours. In the mid-1950s this was perhaps not such a dangerous thing to do but it was certainly stupid. I don't know why I kept doing it. I seemed to be looking for a place where I belonged. Maybe I was hoping to meet someone who could tell me where it was.

In recent years Seiko and I have had many conversations about the times we spent together as children. She says every time she looked at me that following year, she was sure she was losing her best friend. What was worse, she was equally sure there was nothing she could do about it. She recalls: 'You'd changed so much. You still did your school work, but you weren't interested in academic things any more. I had to stand by helplessly, watching our friendship go down the tubes. You weren't the same person. The changes were like night and day.'

I could see that my mother was concerned about me as well, especially after all the phone calls Stanley had made to her over the summer saying how 'concerned' he'd been; how I'd become a pathological liar and how I was mentally unbalanced. At first, she had dismissed his assertions, treating them as nothing more than his perennial tendency to project his own states and problems on to other people. Often in the past, she had been forced to put up with his accusing her too of being crazy – usually during periods when he had been under a lot of pressure. But now Violet was too preoccupied by her own worries, including the early onset of menopause and her continuing dissatisfaction with her life, to pay much attention to me.

Soon after I returned to Visalia I came down with another of my blazing fevers. My mother called Mom. Mom dropped everything to look after me. My fever was so high that, despite her competence and her nursing skills, even she was at a loss over what to do. I became delirious. I spoke a lot of strange words which frightened her. She couldn't understand them. She feared I would get pneumonia. She was right; I did. Determined to care for me, several times a day Mom rubbed my body with alcohol, changed my bed and force-fed me on home-made chicken broth and her famous milk toast. Thanks more to her will than the magic of milk toast, I survived. When the fever cleared I was able to go back to school, somewhat the worse for wear. Yet the fire seemed to have burnt something from my body. All I know is, afterwards I found it easier to pretend to be 'normal'.

I knew I had to get away. But how? Where could I go? I visited the town library and rummaged through magazines searching for advertisements and listings about private boarding-schools. I wrote to three schools in California I liked the look of, requesting brochures, information and application forms.

On the grounds that my current school wasn't challenging enough for me, I persuaded Violet and Stanley to send me to Castilleja, an all girls school in Palo Alto with an extremely tough curriculum. The school accepted my application, so it was all arranged. After Christmas vacation, my mother drove me there and dropped me off.

Thrown in with all sorts of privileged girls among whom I was quite sure I didn't belong, I was terrified at first. I hoped being at Castilleja would give me the time I needed to work out the kind of human being I wanted to be and develop the skills needed to achieve this. I knew I had to reinvent myself to survive. I needed to be accepted. It was do or die.

Castilleja was tough, but I soon found my feet. I made friends and I devoted myself to my studies. I dived greedily into my books. Once a month, as part of our 'cultural development' we girls were packaged in best dresses, shoes and crinolines and ushered off to view paintings, hear opera, or take part in something else which the school considered an essential part of our 'intellectual, artistic and social development'. Soon after I arrived, I learned that the trip of the month was going to be to the San Francisco Opera House where we would be forced to listen to Beethoven's Fifth Symphony, conducted by some Englishman named Sir Thomas Beecham.

Schooled by Stanley to believe that any music written before the twentieth century was 'irrelevant to now and therefore a total waste of time', I had taken on his beliefs as though they were my own. All the way to San Francisco I blabbered on about what a stupid idea it was for us to be spending time listening to 'that old stuff'. When we arrived, I was still seething with disapproval at having been press-ganged into being there at all.

Then the music begins. No more than three minutes pass before my mouth drops open. I am scared to breathe, afraid that the sound of my breath will prevent my immersing myself in this wonderful sound. Incredible. Magnificent. Beethoven. In the presence of this music something occurs that has never happened to me before. His music cuts through my fear, my rage and my confusion. It fills the hollowness inside me with something so stark, so real, so vital, I can't begin to describe it. It and I become one. So long as it is playing, I am no longer alone.

For the first time, words come to me – words which will return again and again in the years that follow: 'If such things exist, I want to go on living.'

Thanks to that experience I would come away from Castilleja with a great gift. It opened up a world of music that had been hidden from me until then. It gave me spiritual nourishment and encouraged me to seek my own values in the world.

*

One morning, six weeks or so after getting to Castilleja, I woke up paralysed from the waist down, unable to walk. The headmistress – a tiny but powerful woman, Miss Margarita Espinoza – came to my room and did everything possible to force me to stand. Despite vehement threats about what would happen to me if I didn't, I could not. I was also getting terrible pains in my abdomen. Yet I didn't seem to be sick in any explainable way.

Having failed to get me to walk, the furious Miss Espinoza called my mother. She picked me up and drove me back to Visalia, where she took me to see Karl Weiss, MD. By that time I could walk, but only with a lot of help. The pains in my abdomen had grown worse.

At first Dr Weiss suggested I might have appendicitis. But the diagnosis didn't check out. The pains lasted five or six days, then slowly disappeared. He never did figure out what was wrong with me. I now believe they were my body's cry for help – an unconscious attempt to tell someone about what had happened between Stanley and me. With memories burnt out, physical pain and paralysis were the only way it had of crying out for help.

No one even considered examining me internally, of course. After all, I was only thirteen years old. If they had, they would have discovered I was not a virgin.

PART THREE

GRACE

29

DOUBLE HELIX

As I LOOK back on the summer of 1954 and all that came after, I am drawn once more to the image of a double helix. I see two souls – Stanley's and mine – wound together in a vortex of energy. One strand of the helix – the dark one – is forged from lies, denial, rage and grief. The other is luminous – shaped from shared joys, excitement, wonder and a childlike loyalty. These two strands could not be more different. Yet neither would have existed without the other. So inexorably did this double helix bind my father and me together that nothing could break us apart. That is, until the double helix could be seen, honoured and accepted equally for the pain it caused as much as the gifts it gave us.

Love? Yes, there was love, in all its many forms – from tenderness and joy to obsession and desperation. It was love that created the vortex. Despite the horror incest causes, no betrayal of innocence will ever be a match for love.

Incest. The very sound of the word instils fear and guilty fascination. Incest remains the greatest taboo in our culture. Both torture and murder are forced to take a back seat to it. For generations it remained a thing unspoken, although it has always featured in works of art and literature. From the plays of the ancient Greek tragedian Sophocles to the novels of American writer Toni Morrison and films such as Polanski's *Chinatown*, stories of incest have intrigued us. More recently it has received clamorous public attention and become the focus of serious investigation.

The one thing on which we nearly all agree is that when incest happens somebody should be blamed for the evil that's been perpetrated. In virtually every incest story – whether in folklore, plays, literature or film – there is a punishment attached to it.

Brother–sister incest seems to be easier to accept. It is parent–child incest that sticks in our throats. This is not without reason. In recent years psychology has taken a close look at parent–child incest and charted many of its devastating consequences. Thanks to all the recent studies, when it comes to the destructive consequences of father–daughter incest – now believed to be the most frequently reported kind – they are easy to list. They range from ongoing anxiety and sleep disturbances, to substance abuse, chronic pain and eating disorders. Even deeper damage is done to victims by the loss of self-esteem, the rage, dissociation, helplessness and feelings of worthlessness that incest causes. The fear that results from an incestuous experience often turns into terror. Victims become perfectionists to mask their feelings of worthlessness. They feel sad, depressed, suicidal. Almost every victim ends up with a sense that she is hollow – an experience of emptiness which can last a lifetime. I know these findings are, on the whole, accurate. I have experienced many of them myself.

Psychologists also report that women subjected to incest in childhood frequently wear baggy, dull-coloured clothes in an attempt to appear larger and, at the same time, to camouflage their bodies because they feel too vulnerable to the outside world. I did this. I never allowed myself to wear a sleeveless blouse or a pair of shorts. On the few occasions when I put them on, I felt dangerously exposed and quickly took them off again.

Most often, I believe, it is obsession that ignites incest, then feeds its flames. Stanley was certainly obsessed with me, almost from the very beginning. When I was in my late twenties the memories of my incestuous relations with Stanley would return, as I will explain in more detail soon. When I shared these memories with my mother, she was understandably shocked. At the same time, she said, 'I'm not surprised. Even when you were a tiny girl, Stanley felt drawn to you. When he'd see you naked after a bath it provoked what he called "unnatural feelings"– *sexual* feelings. He spoke to me a lot about them because they scared him. "Don't be ridiculous, Stanley," I told him. "You can't possibly have sexual feelings for a child."'

Yet the connections between each parent and child are unique. Although all incest victims share the grief and damage that incest creates, the relationship between parent and child can be far more complex and difficult to fathom than many experts realise. Just as each of us is a unique human being, so is each person's experience of incest unique.

Almost all the research done on incest focuses entirely on the suffering of the victim while damage to the perpetrator is virtually ignored. Perhaps this is because most of us still divide the world into good and bad. We need to point a finger at somebody we can damn. Dismissing the validity of another human being can make us feel better about ourselves. 'I would never do such a thing,' we say. The taboo of incest may be another reason why researchers almost completely avoid studying the effects on the perpetrator.

Stanley's loneliness was vast. The incestuous relationship with me was in no small part a desperate attempt to alleviate it. Unable to take adult responsibility, he did his best to possess me, to absorb my soul and keep it in bondage. The worst of it all is, I am quite sure he had no idea he was doing this.

It is my observation that father–daughter incest occurs most often when a man has become separated from his heart; if you like, from the *female* side of his nature. Such men – Stanley among them – never come to experience themselves as whole human beings. They are always searching for the *feeling* part of themselves outside – usually in women. Inevitably this causes trouble. None of us can find outside ourselves what, ultimately, must be found within. These men fear drowning in a sea of isolation so they turn to one-night stands, children, prostitutes, in an attempt to alleviate the emptiness they feel. They often become the kind of men who will sit in a bar and over a few drinks tell you, 'Women. Can't live with 'em, can't live without 'em.' Stanley felt this emptiness. 'He relied on prostitutes to alleviate impotence. When he lost Violet, he lost connection with himself,' Audree says.

In studying incest, the powerful connections it creates and its consequences, psychologists seldom appear to take account of the fact that the participants in father–daughter or mother–son unions share the same genes and come from the same bloodline. The consequences of an ongoing union between people who are physiologically and energetically bonded by blood and DNA can be central to what they experience. It can also persist long after their sexual union has ended.

Such biological connections are powerful. They can be too strong – DNA too closely matched. You may share the same fascinations, as Stanley and I did. You may be plagued by similar fears or ambitions, frustrations or longings. If so, your bodies, your feelings, your lives can become so tightly woven together that not even rage, shame, guilt, fear and denial can unravel the helix. That is what happened with my father. At times he and I would even share the same thoughts.

Stanley once said to me: 'There is something strange about you. It's like you're an *unbounded* being. You always make me feel that I exist more inside *you* than I do in my own body.' When intrinsic biological and emotional bonds between you have been strong to begin with and when there are so many things you share in common, as he and I did, the awesome realm that we so often lived in together still remained: the joy, the playfulness, the wonderment and the intense desire to spend time alone together. Such experiences formed the luminous side of that double helix.

Reading *Wuthering Heights* by Emily Brontë marked the moment at which I finally started to begin to understand the complexities of my relationship with my father. When I came across the passage where Cathy explains to Nelly the nature of her ties to Heathcliff, I realised that I *knew* the reality of what Emily Brontë was writing about: I was still living it.

> . . . he's more myself than I am. Whatever our souls are made of, his and mine are the same [. . .] My great miseries in this world have been Heathcliff's miseries, and I watched and felt each from the beginning: my great thought in living is himself. If all else perished and *he* remained, I should still continue to be; and if all else remained, and he were annihilated, the universe would turn to a mighty stranger: I should not seem a part of it [. . .] My love for Heathcliff resembles the eternal rocks beneath: a source of little visible delight, but necessary. Nelly, I *am* Heathcliff! He's always, always in my mind: not as a pleasure, any more than I am always a pleasure to myself, but as my own being.

The words 'a source of little visible delight, but necessary' haunted me. They could have been my own.

Although the relationship between Heathcliff and Cathy was not incestuous in a literal sense, it shares many of the qualities that my relationship with Stanley had – qualities I associate with two things: strong biological connections and childlike bonds. Children can make deadly serious commitments to each other, the strength of which adults often underestimate. These are sometimes so strong that you feel the two of you are one being. Again, as Stanley put it, 'I exist more inside *you* than I do in my own body.'

Such intense connections take both of you into what feels like a different Universe with a whole new set of rules. So long as each of you remains true to the rules and the secret bond, you continue to live in this heightened, rarefied state of being: colours are brighter, feelings of every kind are more intense and everything feels vibrant with life. In this state the outside world doesn't exist, only the richness of the intimacy between you. It is far beyond anything you've ever known – powerful, simple and enticing. But betray the loyalty, the secrecy that this union demands of you, and the Universe created by it splits wide open.

Literary critics have written volumes in an attempt to explain Heathcliff's abominable behaviour towards Cathy when she betrays him by marrying into the superficial world of the Lintons. I have always been surprised by how so many fail to understand it. I was *living* the grief, the rage, the horror that follows a betrayal of such bonds. I believe it is the most primordial wound possible to inflict on another human being. Only years later would I come to recognise the difference between the effect of Cathy's betrayal of Heathcliff and Stanley's betrayal of me: Heathcliff directed all his rage, grief and pain towards the outside world, including Cathy. Still a child, I had no choice but to turn mine against myself.

Through Stanley's treatment of me, I experienced the betrayal of my very *being*. This was the dark strand of the double helix with all its destructive power. Meanwhile, the luminous strand went on binding Stanley and me together like children with a desire to celebrate just being alive and created a bond between us which, despite the pain and horror, never broke.

I believe my father saw in me a brightness, an innocence, a hopefulness and an energy which he was so out of touch with in himself. All the fixes he tried, from psychiatry and Dianetics to alcohol and sex, could not help him get them back. He made the same mistake we all do at times, but in a larger way. He convinced himself that, if only he could get close enough to me, own me, draw me into him, he would be able to retrieve the qualities he felt he lacked.

In a sense he was right since, for a time, he did. But what he didn't understand was that, when he and I lived in that inexpressible world of joy, deep feeling and aliveness, this was not because he took these qualities from me. It was because at the core of the double helix was simple love. It was this love that made it possible for him to reconnect – if only for a time and often at great expense to his life and mine – with those marvellous qualities within himself.

For a time, I became a tuning fork for the feeling side of my father's nature. Whenever I was away – not only from him but from myself – he was thrown back on the only connection to feeling he believed he had: alcohol. Ironically, it was alcohol that became the mechanism for hiding from himself and negating all feeling. With the alcohol flowing freely, he headed back on the road once more, beating himself senseless as he always did just to keep going. Meanwhile, hidden within the darkness of his unknowing, the double helix kept on spinning.

30

BID FOR REDEMPTION

IN THE SPRING of 1955 my father started flooding my life with letters. He had never written to me before. Stanley found it hard to write to anyone. He lacked confidence in what he called his 'poor penmanship' and his bad spelling.

Every card and telegram he had ever sent me had been signed, 'Stanley'. Now he begins to sign his letters 'Dad', 'Your father', or 'Your father, Stanley'.

Today, more than fifty years later, I sit at my desk sifting through a huge pile of his correspondence. I am moved by the depth of love and concern he expresses for me. I am saddened by the chasm between his dreams for a new life and his terrible dissociation. Full of hope for the future, the letters have been written by a man passionate to put right any wrongs he has committed. Yet there is a terrible irony here: the part of my father's psyche filled with remorse is completely split off from the part which holds the knowledge of what he has done. Lost memories are submerged in the darkest parts of his psyche as though they belong to a completely separate being.

I am fascinated by the way, in his letters, my father seems to be trying to practise a kind of psychological alchemy. For instance, he reports on the world as being more the way he wants to see it than the way it really is. It is as though the conscious part of his psyche is trying to work sympathetic magic: by seeing only what he chooses to see, he may be able to bring his hoped-for reality into being. And that includes me.

Some of his letters contain information about his work, where he is, and what he is worried about. Others are replete with fatherly thoughts and advice – neither of which he had ever offered before.

Written on a TWA flight to Los Angeles and posted on 13 May 1955 in Beverly Hills, his letter tells me:

> I am at the moment flying from Amarillo Texas to Hollywood for two days. I was not able to finish the album Christy and I are making so I'm taking advantage of the two days open for the band to come back and finish it . . . I enjoyed seeing you so much. Honey you look wonderful! You also seemed very free from any serious problems which shows what wonderful progress you are making. Even though I'm going to be away for a while, I want you to know that you are part of my thoughts every day. I want you to learn and to grow and to develop your love for everyone. Honey you have so much to give and so much inside you for others to enjoy. I'm very proud to be your father and I also want to make you more proud of me. This I promise.
>
> I love you. Your Dad

Despite his denial that he has had anything to do with 'Leslie's problems', he is trying to behave like he believes fathers are supposed to behave towards their children. He often writes about things he knows he and I have always shared: a movie he has seen, a musical theme he is in love with, the passion we have for the elements – wind, rain, sea and storms.

He speaks of the love he has for me, of the pride he takes in me. He celebrates the future he envisages with me.

In another letter, sent 31 May from Huntington, West Virginia, he writes:

> My first words are 'I love you' and my second remark is that I just received the finest letter you've ever written me. What an exciting experience. Thank you! My third expression is to tell you how proud I am of you; your being so happy lately, your lack of problems, your

nomination for student body secretary and class president . . . Finally your love for me. What a wonderful person you are going to be!

If I don't achieve real success in the next period of my life I shall consider it personal defeat. We are moving closer to New York and the big challenge.

Soon you will be fourteen. My God, things are moving forward, aren't they? You know you looked so grown up the last time I saw you. Remember? I told you about your face and your eyes . . . It's beginning to look as though many people are aware of your strength and love. Here is my

Love . . . Your Dad

At this time Stanley was looking for a new singer. Two songwriters introduced him to eighteen-year-old Ann Richards, playing him a demo of her voice. He liked its sound and hired her. Soon she began touring with the band.

When I first met Ann, while spending my Easter vacation with Stanley in Los Angeles, I had no idea that, within months, she would become my father's lover and soon after his wife. Ann was uneducated, impressionable and well-meaning. She liked me and she always wanted to hang out with me. Because we were close in age, she wanted to look upon me as a younger sister – a confidante – with whom she could share everything, from her concern over what kind of a haircut she should get and what shoes she should buy to go with her new dress, to how she should handle the troubles she was having with her singing or with her relationship with Stanley. It became obvious to me that she had fallen head over heels in love with 'Stan Kenton', but had no idea who 'Stanley Kenton' was or what she was getting herself into.

Ann liked movies but they were very different movies from the ones Stanley and I took to. Just before we met she had been to see Judy Garland in *A Star is Born*. She identified strongly with the character. 'When I saw that movie,' she said, her eyes shining, 'I knew that if only I hung around LA long enough the same thing was gonna happen to me. Just look at me. Now it has.' The developing relationship with my father inspired in Ann the highest level of hope for her future. In Stanley she saw her ticket to everything she had been waiting for. Her vision was surrounded by a fog of illusory glamour. She looked upon him as her saviour.

Following that vacation, I didn't see Ann again until the late summer of 1955. I flew back East to spend time with Stanley, only to find that the three of us were sleeping together in the same hotel room every night. We spent every day together in the car travelling from job to job, but we were probably as far from the Three Musketeers as you could get.

Ann was still intent on making me her younger sister. The one thing I needed less than 'an older sister' was being been thrown into this bizarre *ménage à trois* with no previous warning and no explanation. I did my best to appear friendly and accept it all. But I could never figure out what Stanley was doing with Ann. Apart from her singing, virtually everything of interest to her was of no concern to either him or me. During the long hours, driving from job to job, he did do his best to entertain both of us but, invariably, interactions between the three of us turned into conversations between him and me, and Ann didn't appear to understand most of what we talked about.

Ann longed for Stanley's protection: she wanted a father figure who would take care of her. She was a hopeless romantic. While we were on the road together, there was much talk of marriage. 'Should we, shouldn't we?' they wondered. I was given the role of the neutral party each of them consulted privately. Stanley had convinced himself that Violet had been the problem in his previous marriage. Even though he would always love her and he himself was – in his own words – 'not perfect', he insisted that it was Violet who had wrecked their marriage, although 'naturally' he would accept some of the responsibility for its failure.

I believe my father thought that if he married Ann it would show that he was a good enough man to make a marriage work. It would make clear to the world that it hadn't been his fault that his marriage to Violet failed. With Ann, he could build another life – a fresh new one. Unconsciously, I suspect, he was hoping to transfer his obsession with me to Ann. He wanted to remove any 'unhealthy' connection to me, and turn me into a proper daughter.

I did not return to Castilleja that autumn. Instead I transferred to Chadwick, a coeducational boarding-school in Palos Verdes near Los Angeles. By the time I had gone back to school Ann was regularly writing me long chatty letters telling me things like, 'My ponytail's getting so long. When I see you at Xmas you will be amazed', or describing a dress she bought 'with three tiers of lace' which 'looks like a $100 dress, but I only paid $45'. On 23 September from the Hotel Wolverine, Detroit, I received a letter from her which was touching in its naïvety and sad in what it revealed about her lack of self-esteem. She had already been coached by Stanley to believe that any problems in their relationship were always her fault – never his:

Now I'll tell you something about us. We are having a few problems. Things that are basically my fault, but I think they are caused by an incomplete understanding of everything. And inexperience causes me to create certain problems. I've learned to understand lots of things and to adjust to an extent but I've still got improving and growing to do and it does take time. Thank God for Stanley's patience. And, as you know, Stanley is rather apprehensive towards marriage, more so than most men because he has certain fears and qualms from his first failure. So naturally, when I create problems and try his patience or anger him he begins to doubt how good or healthy our relationship is and then he shows reticence to accept a life with me forever. And I naturally realise that most things are my fault and begin to hate myself for certain lacks that I have not yet been able to compensate for. So you see, this makes him angrier and he wants to put off marriage until we know what we are doing. When that will be who knows. I am so sure that I can conquer my certain sicknesses and weaknesses but it will take time and reassurance from the man I love. Without his support it would be useless because he's the one I am growing for. And actually myself for I'm trying to become what I should be someday. But it all takes time. I just thought you should know what's going on. Don't worry about anything. Things always work out with time. All for now.

Love,

Ann

Determined to start his 'new life', Stanley saw Ann as someone young enough to be moulded into the wife who would love him for himself, support him in everything he wanted to do and cause him no headaches. They would make a home together, have more children – to whom he would be a good father – and make a wonderful life.

Stanley continued to use me as a sounding board, sharing his concerns and upsets over his relationship with Ann. I kept getting phone calls from him as well as letters. The struggles he and I had had the year before were now replaced by his struggles with Ann. His letters are full of worries and possible solutions, as well as soul-searching about whether or not he should get into this marriage.

On 18 October 1955, they finally got married at the courthouse in Milwaukee, Wisconsin. The day following the ceremony, Ann called me, sobbing. 'It was terrible, Leslie,' she said. 'I had a bad cold. I couldn't sing that night so I was waiting in the hotel room for Stanley to come home after work. I was wearing the beautiful white baby doll pyjamas I wrote you about – the ones I bought special for our wedding night.

'Without even telling me, Stanley brought a lot of guys from the band back to the hotel room with him. I was so embarrassed. He paid no attention to me at all. Then he started playing the new June Christy album. He kept going on and on about what a great singer she is. We had a violent argument and I threw the record out the window. He went to get a hamburger at the White Tower and slammed the door so hard it made the walls shake. When he got back we just went on screaming at each other. The house detective banged on the door and threatened to throw us out if we didn't shut up. It was horrible.'

On 21 October 1955 – three days after the wedding – Stanley sent me this letter, written on stationery from the Bliss Hotel in Tulsa, Oklahoma:

My dear Leslie,

I went to bed about three, slept a couple of hours then woke up and couldn't get back to sleep. Maybe if I get a letter off to you it will help me relax.

I'm feeling much better and am almost recovered from my attack of 'whatever it was'. However, Ann is ill now with a cold and sore throat. She hasn't sung for three days now and has been trying to stay in bed. This whole scene was caused by too much emotional stress together with lack of sleep on both our parts. Believe me, Honey, this thing has not been taken lightly on either of our parts. I myself have worried about this marriage until I thought I was going simple. All of my life I've been so aware of what those around me thought about my doings. Maybe because my music has always been allowed such privileges I've felt so much obligation to present myself to society as conforming with society's concept of common sense. My attempts at reasoning ran like this:

> Am I trying to prove that I'm still attractive enough physically to attract a young girl? Is it a daughter fixation? Do I want to subject myself to ridicule, in search of punishment? Has my ego run out of challenges and am I taking on another challenge? Is Ann suffering from a father fixation? Is she in love with me or Stan Kenton? Is she desperate for security? Is she so career conscious that I'm being used?

These and a thousand other things entered my mind until I believed I was going out of my mind. I know what a task it is to separate emotions from objective thinking so I've learned many tricks to achieve this. I worked every one I know.

The one big thing that helped me to make up my mind was my memory of my life the last four or five years. I don't want to sound melodramatic but I've been a pretty lost and lonesome guy. Music has always meant so much to me. I've been able to supplant many things with it but still there has been big, hollow, lonesome holes.

These somehow can only be filled by having a love that demands of you and at the same time gives. Constant giving and gaining affection in a personal way is fuel for living.

You might say, yes, but why does it have to be some person so young. At my age the chances of meeting a woman suited for me in my age bracket are practically non-existent. Anyone old enough for me that isn't married or hasn't been married, is usually a crackpot and you've seen a few of the disgusting examples that have been around. Then there are those that have some brains and are worthy but would marry again to gain a meal ticket for themselves and their usual children. It seemed the only thing for me and my career was to find someone like Ann.

Believe me, Honey, it is not her youth that appeals to me so much because ever since I've gotten gray I've had the most charming and beautiful young girls around. It is much more than that. She is very much in tune with what I am trying to do in music. She is most sensitive to my emotions which includes not only my pleasant attributes but my agonies, and there are many. She has seen me under emotional strain that has made me terribly abusive and ugly. Circumstances that would have scared anyone else away. I've grown up a lot the last few years but I still occasionally become ridiculous. I have tremendous strength and it sometimes gets going in the wrong way on a one way street.

Darling, I know I have you. I also know that you have much to gain in your life ahead and you already are aware of some sort of moral obligation to me that is over-balanced and out of proportions.

After your mother and I separated and especially when she married Jimmy and finally with the birth of Chris, you and I started to cling emotionally closer. It has been a sort of minority kind of clinging together. This thing with Ann has been the last straw. Now you really feel lost. There have been some things about our relationship that have not been healthy and they were caused by me, not you! If you and I struggle to admit it, I believe we have been headed towards one of those daughter father relationships that would prevent you from ever falling honestly in love with anyone because of your feeling so obligated to me. This could have caused you and I to want to be together for the rest of my life, with you probably looking out and taking care of me until such time as it would be too late to build a life of your own.

Now all of this seems painful, but growth is that way. Shortstuff, I want to be your father in a strong, healthy, inspiring manner. I am terribly concerned over you and your future. I want you to know that I am security – morally, spiritually and materially.

Please don't become alarmed about this marriage unduly. I know your concern for me. Both Ann and I want you to be with us every chance you get. This is sincere.

I am going to try to sleep now a couple of hours before my appointments start. Please excuse any misspelled words. I couldn't find my little dictionary I use for reference. You and your letters make me a little self-conscious these days.

I love you,

Your father, Stanley

After their wedding, Ann's first disappointment was when she woke up to the realisation that the marriage was not going to be a ticket to the life she had been expecting. The disillusionment, begun on her wedding night, was followed by an accumulation of other negative experiences which began to make her feel trapped, ignored, overwhelmed. Was she at a dead end? She started to worry about what she'd got herself into. Meanwhile, Stanley kept on planning a bright new future for the three of us.

In December, after seven months on the road doing one-nighters, he brought Ann home to Hollyridge. She was pregnant. Without consulting her, he had invited my mother, Jimmy and Christi to spend Christmas with us there. Ann had never even visited Hollyridge before. She was shocked to find herself face to face with my mother, in this house that Violet had lived in and decorated – a house in which nothing had been altered since her departure.

The profound connections between Violet and Stanley quickly became obvious to Ann. While Jimmy had learned to live with this emotional intimacy and to manage it behind the scenes, Ann was devastated to find that here, once again, she was being made the outsider. It was a role she began to suspect she might have got herself landed with for ever.

After Christmas the band played at Zardi's in Los Angeles for a couple of weeks, then Stanley and Ann headed back on the road while I returned to Chadwick. My year there was full of new people. A good number of them were sons and daughters of directors, producers, actors and others in the entertainment industry in Los Angeles, and a majority were Jewish. I soon realised that the Jews were allowed to celebrate Jewish holidays with days off from school, while the Christians were given the standard holidays off. I was neither Christian nor Jewish but I managed to take both sets of holidays by pretending to be one or the other on the appropriate days. I became quite a rebel at Chadwick, doing all sorts of forbidden things, like letting chickens loose in the girls' dorm and keeping a bottle of Scotch, in a Breck shampoo bottle, on the dresser in my room, but I never got caught.

At Chadwick, the school work was easier than it had been at Castilleja. This meant I had more time to read the stuff I wanted to read. I immersed myself in Dostoevsky that year, reading *The Brothers*

Karamazov, *The Idiot* and – my favourite – *Crime and Punishment*.
I developed a serious infatuation with Raskolnikov, and became much
taken with the idea that one could commit a murder just for the sake
of doing it, even hatching plots against my roommate when she
annoyed me. Once I was certain I could carry out my plan and get
away with it, I decided I didn't have to do it for real, so shelved the
project. My roommate never knew.

That year I also developed a crush on a boy three years older than
me. John was six foot four inches tall and often treated me badly, as
Stanley had done. He used to kick me under the table at mealtimes
because my table manners did not come up to his specifications.
John was the first person I had sex with apart from my father. It took
place lying on a sheet he carried in the back of his car, which he had
spread on the sand at the beach one night. We had both been
drinking – just like I did with Stanley. I don't remember much about
the experience except that I questioned John at length afterwards to
find out how much blood was left on the sheet when I lost my
virginity. He insisted that there had been none at all. Neither of us
could understand why.

Later that year we had sex a second time, this time at Hollyridge.
Stanley and Ann were on the road and the house was empty. It took
place in Stanley's bed and it turned into a real fiasco. On one of her
midnight visits to check on Hollyridge, Stella showed up. There was
a small balcony off Stanley's bedroom, overlooking the back yard; the
same one Seiko and I had used for our Rapunzel play. When we heard
her arrive, John leapt out of bed, grabbed his clothes and jumped off
the balcony, landing on the lawn. I was left to deal with my grandmother. It was perfectly obvious to Stella what had been going on and
she scolded me vehemently, but I don't think she ever told Stanley.
Maybe she didn't dare.

John had invited me to the Senior Prom. The closer it came to the
date, the more he complained to the senior girls that he wished he
were going with one of them instead of me. When I heard this,

something inside me turned vicious. I was determined to use all the wiles available to me to get back at him for the insult.

That year, for the first time in my life, people had been telling me that I was good-looking. They kept saying – and writing – complimentary things about me. So I decided I would turn myself into a *femme fatale*, make John fall in love with me, and then discard him. To my surprise my scheme worked. He fell head over heels for me. After school broke up for the summer I returned briefly to my mother's house in Visalia. Within a week John had followed me there, laden with gifts, swearing lasting devotion. He stayed for three days in the guest house. I was barely civil to him. This only seemed to further inflame his passion for me, but I stuck to my guns and had nothing more to do with him.

While at Chadwick I saw Stanley and Ann a few times when they were back in California. Each time Stanley was supposed to pick me up for a weekend he would arrive late. This embarrassed me. He knew that all the kids had to leave the school by noon. I'd be left there alone with some poor teacher who had been forced to stay with me until he got there. Sometimes he didn't arrive until ten o'clock at night. Once it was past midnight. Another time he never got there at all.

Yet his letters kept arriving. He kept affirming his determination to get off the road and stay home permanently. He continued to share his worries and his hopes. He wrote to me often during his gruelling tour of Europe that spring. As usual the trip was plagued by flat tyres, band members who got in trouble and had to be replaced, and poorly scheduled itineraries.

Ann had gone on the European tour with him. She was miserable since she never saw him. Because she was pregnant, she couldn't travel to many of the concerts – impossible on a bus with bad suspension over pothole-filled roads. When he'd come back to where she was staying he would always be drunk. She finally left him over there and returned to Los Angeles.

When the European tour finished by the third week in May, Ann flew East to join him on the road again. Back in New York, Stanley was still trying to work out how he could get off the road permanently and create that new life, complete with wife, baby and me. Together, he saw us becoming the perfect family. In a letter sent from the Park Sheraton Hotel in New York on 23 May 1956, he confides:

As you know from my past letters, I've been doing a great amount of planning for the future. I'm through being away from home, other than for short periods from September on. I've got to establish some routine to our home life in order to safeguard the future. I don't know how long Ann is going to stay on the road with me but we are going to try to make it home together; that is if she continues to feel well and the road doesn't become too rough.

We're planning on your being with us at home this fall and I want us to be together until such time you feel it is necessary for you to leave for some particular schooling that will take you away, such as the university or whatever special schooling you decide to want. I would like you to enquire (or maybe you know already) about schools you can attend so we can help decide on things for September. I want you to stay in a private school but also I want you to live at home. Things will work out well this way now that we are establishing some home life. I am so anxious to redecorate and fix up Hollyridge so it is pleasant for us all. I have spoken to your mother about this and she informed me that this is what you want also. This makes me happier yet.

I am feeling fine and very ambitious. There are so many things I want to do when we get home. I hope I have one half the desire when I get there as I have now.

Shortstuff, I'm insisting that you write me more often than in these past weeks. Regardless of how much you think you've written, I still have received only one letter. I've got a right to yell! I'm going to try to call you the last of the week.

Ann sends her best,

Love,

Stanley

From the time of the European tour onwards, for the rest of his life, all the 'Dad' and 'Your father' signatures are gone. He has reverted to signing his letters, cards and telegrams 'Stanley'.

31

FLEAS IN ORGANZA

BY THE AUTUMN of 1956 Stanley believed his dreams of the perfect home and family were about to come true. Ann, my father and I moved into Hollyridge together. Decorators had been at work transforming the house into something as far away as possible from what it looked like when Violet lived there. Ann was heavy with child. I had left Chadwick in June, at the end of my sophomore year, to begin my junior year at Marlborough School – the most exclusive school for girls in Los Angeles – because Stanley was adamant that I leave boarding-school to live with him. That suited me fine since I was still on the run. Unknown to myself, I was living according to a painfully inadequate formula for survival which both Stanley and I had been following blindly: 'Keep moving and the darkness might not catch up with you.'

My father had worked a few dates in California before settling down to do a two-week stint at Zardi's in Hollywood. On 10 September Ann's baby was born – a girl who they named Dana Lynn.

Seven weeks later, tens of thousands of Hungarians rose up to demand an end to Soviet rule while the Soviet airforce bombed Budapest. A thousand tanks entered the city as part of a massive dawn offensive. When I heard this on the news I could not stop crying. I kept seeing, in my mind's eye, thousands of people, wanting only freedom, who were going to be slaughtered. Stanley sat on my bed for hours that night, holding my hand and stroking my head. This is the only time I ever remember him comforting me. He kept telling me something strange, though: 'You're not crying about the Hungarian revolution, Shortstuff, but something else.' I never figured out what 'else' he thought had provoked my tears.

As part of the redecoration programme at Hollyridge, builders had closed in the little balcony off Stanley's bedroom to make a small room for Dana. I remember watching Ann with her new baby at the breast and thinking what a wonderful bond there can be between a mother and child. Dana's birth seemed to anchor Ann in a reality in which she felt safe and satisfied. For a while she was happy being a new mother.

Stanley did everything he could to provide his wife with what he thought would make her happy. He bought her a pink Thunderbird. He organised a psychotherapist for her to 'help her work out her problems'. He continually asked me to support her. I think this was because he didn't know how to do it himself.

In 1950, as part of Violet's 'cultural programme' to make living in Visalia more bearable she, Jimmy and I had gone to see *The Men*, a Fred Zinnemann movie staring a completely unknown actor: Brando. It tells the story of a wounded World War Two veteran and his struggle to return to civilian life. I had sat in the smoke-filled Hyde Theater dumbfounded by the depth and breadth of this actor's genius. I had seen a lot of movies and a lot of actors but I had never come across anything like Brando. That night, I decided I would become an actor. I longed to touch the depths of feeling he did, with the honesty and inventiveness he showed. I never told anyone about my decision because, in Visalia, there was no opportunity for me to begin learning the craft. Now all that had changed. Now I was back living in Hollywood. I told Stanley I wanted to learn acting. I didn't know where or how, but I knew I had to start now. There was no way I was going to wait until my high school education was finished. Marlon Brando came to my rescue.

Marlon was a fan of Stanley's music. That Christmas he arrived at Hollyridge with a present for him: a beautiful tie. It came with a little card saying only 'Love, Marlon'. Brando was the obvious person for me to ask where I should go to take acting classes. He said that, since I was still in school during the day, there was only one person in Hollywood I should work with: Sam Gilman. A charismatic character actor who, after a long career in the theatre, appeared on screen in the 1950s and 1960s in films like *One-Eyed Jacks*, Sam held evening classes for working actors twice a week. You had to pass an interview and an audition to get in.

I was determined that Sam would accept me, although I had no idea how to carry out an interview or do an audition, and I was scared to death of both. I went to see him. He welcomed me into his class – in no small part I suspect because, although he was a talented teacher, he was attracted to the fifteen-year-old nubile creature I'd turned into.

I loved the work I did with Sam: every moment of it, no matter how difficult it became. And it was often very difficult. Sam demanded that I give everything – that every word I spoke, every improvisation, every gesture and every exercise be free of false emotion or pretension of any kind. He said I must never *act*.

The passion for acting took over my life. I'd show up at school and sit through my classes half-present, thinking about the scene I was going to do that evening. Most of my classes at Marlborough bored me anyway. I particularly hated chemistry. ECT's lasting effect on my brain rendered me unable to figure out the simplest mathematical equation. In any case, it seemed stupid that we were supposed to carry out experiments which other people had done a thousand times before and which we already knew the outcome of. To me, *experiment* meant going to the edge of what you think you can manage then pushing the boundaries deep into unknown territory.

Since only acting gave me that, I immersed myself in it. I sensed that in acting I might have found a home – a place where I belonged. I didn't know it then, but acting was important to me also because it gave me access to fragments of me that had become split off from my conscious awareness. Without realising what I was doing, I had begun to call on some of these fragments, expressing what they contained when playing some of the characters I took on. I must, at some level, have sensed that acting might help bring together in me those fragments that had become lost somewhere in the dark.

One of the parts I played was Annabella in John Ford's 'Tis Pity She's a Whore, about brother–sister incest. I received a lot of praise for my performance. 'You got to the guts of her, Leslie,' Sam said. 'You really did.'

Stanley wholeheartedly supported my desire to act. Actually, I think he would probably have supported my joining the Salvation Army, so keen was he to create a harmonious family. What with school, rehearsals and acting classes, my time and attention was so taken up that I never did become the emotional coach for Ann he hoped I would. I'd come home in the afternoon, change my clothes and be off again to rehearse. The three of us often met at dinner; seldom a happy experience for Ann since, inevitably, conversations at the table turned into dialogues between Stanley and me.

Stanley had started studying composition, harmony and counterpoint with a wonderful teacher named Paul Held, an Austrian in his eighties. Not only did Paul inspire him, but Stanley found in him another father figure. Over dinner, Stanley would talk about what Paul had taught him and what he was trying to do with it. His enthusiasm excited and inspired me. I would question him at length about it all. Then I'd tell him about the latest scene I was doing for class, or a character from a play I was reading that I wanted to act. In the midst of all this, Ann languished, unable to understand why she was being left out, and we remained unconscious of how painful all this was for her.

Stanley had begun to write again – music that was exciting, mysterious, lyrical. I'd go into the music room while he was working and sit on the floor to listen. He never let anybody but me in there. Sometimes he would come looking for me when he was about to start. 'Shortstuff,' he'd say, 'I'm going to do some work. You wanna come?'

The music room was small, just large enough to take a grand piano and a bench. There was nothing else in the room except bookshelves built into two walls. My father seemed really happy when he was in that room working. In that room, at the piano, I'd watch him get caught up in a stillness I had seen in him only fleetingly before – when he'd been trying to work out how to do something or while we were lying on a remote beach.

While he worked I'd lie on the floor reading. 'Shortstuff,' he'd say, 'what do you think of this?' Then he'd play a portion of a melody. 'Does it work or not?' To my ears, he had never written such wonderful stuff – at least not since 'Concerto to End All Concertos' many years before.

One day I came into the room unannounced. Instead of speaking to me as usual he went on playing. When he finished he looked up at me and smiled. 'That's incredible,' I said. 'How come I've never heard it before?'

'I've been keeping it a secret.' He smiled. 'It's called "A Letter to Leslie".'

In spite of the horrors both of us had lived through – horrors which would, in time, surface to claim their due – I believe that at that time the connection between us had deepened and it was becoming something altogether different. Maybe, now that sex between us belonged to the forgotten past, we were beginning to experience a new kind of freedom: the freedom to be together and let things be whatever they were.

The music room was Stanley's sanctuary. Ann left him alone when he was in there. There were no knocks at the door to say somebody wanted him on the phone or ask, 'When are we going to the grocery store?' He spent progressively longer hours there writing and studying. He never drank while he was working. But when he did drink, normally later in the evening, he would still turn into somebody else – usually someone so unpleasant that Ann and I gave him a wide berth.

As painful for Ann as being excluded from our conversations was the way Stanley seemed always to blame her when anything went wrong – never me. In my junior year I was too young to drive a car. Sam Gilman volunteered to bring me home after my acting classes. Sometimes they didn't finish until close on midnight. He'd ask if I wanted to get a hamburger and we'd sit and talk for hours about acting, so I wouldn't get back until 2 a.m.

This infuriated Ann. 'No fifteen-year-old girl should be out until two in the morning,' she kept telling Stanley. 'Don't you think you should say something to Leslie?'

His reply was always the same: 'Why? I trust her.' He would never take a stand against me.

More than once I heard Ann say, 'She's a neurotic, high-strung girl. You've gotta do something.' Stanley would just shrug his shoulders or laugh.

One morning, getting ready for school, I came into the kitchen to find Ann's face all red on one side. She was crying.

'What is it?' I said. 'What happened?'

'He . . . he hit me,' she sobbed.

'What?'

'Stanley hit me for saying you shouldn't stay out too late.'

I took a bag of frozen carrots from the freezer, wrapped them in a dish towel and pressed them against her cheek. She kept on crying. When I got home that afternoon, Stanley was in the music room at the piano.

'Is Ann all right?' I asked him.

'Yeah, she's fine.'

'She says you hit her.'

'Yeah, I shouldn't have done that.' He shrugged.

'Why did you?'

'She keeps bitching about you coming home late. She thinks you have a "thing" with Sam Gilman. I lost my temper.'

Ann's insinuation made me laugh out loud. Stanley laughed with me as though it were a relief to him. Her instincts had been half right. Sam had tried to kiss me three or four times when he brought me home. Although I loved working with him, Sam was Stanley's age. He seemed like an old man to me – physically revolting.

That day marked the beginning of the physical abuse Stanley visited upon Ann. I don't know all the reasons why. I don't think it was always to do with me. The violence may well have been an expression of his disappointment and frustration. He could see that his dream was turning sour and he was powerless to stop this.

Ann began to blame me for her miseries. 'Living with you is like living with a black widow spider,' she screamed at me one afternoon.

I was standing in the kitchen making myself a tuna sandwich. I said nothing.

'Or . . . or . . . a tarantula,' she snapped. 'He takes your side, never mine. He never listens to what I say.'

Stanley heard the commotion. He opened the door to the music room and came into the kitchen.

'It's true,' she told him. 'You don't give a damn about me!'

He moved to comfort her, putting his arms around her. 'Ann, I love you. You know I do.' She laid her head against his chest. 'Maybe we need to get more help,' he said.

When the 'more help' materialised, it came in two guises: a more high-powered psychotherapist-cum-marriage counsellor than Ann's previous therapist, ostensibly for both of them, but in practice – at least according to Ann – every time Stanley did go with her to a session he would come away insisting that the problems were hers, not his.

The second took the form of selling Hollyridge and buying a big, expensive house in Beverly Hills. That was near the end of my junior year at Marlborough. Stanley bought the house on North Alta Drive, between Sunset Boulevard and Santa Monica. It boasted seven bathrooms and seven television sets. When we got there, Stanley's childlike persona suggested we flush all the toilets at once 'just to see what happens'.

Despite all its bedrooms, dressing rooms, the maid's room and bathrooms, the house on North Alta Drive had no music room. My father's piano sat ignored in a corner of the large living room which, despite its lavish furnishings, always looked and smelt like a mausoleum. He had stopped writing music completely after a big scene that took place between him and Ann at Hollyridge just before we left. She'd gone into the music room when he wasn't there and rifled through the music he was working on which he always kept in piles on top of the piano. She found the score to 'A Letter to Leslie', tore it up and burned it in the fireplace, along with everything else he had been working on for almost a year.

Despite the big house and all the marriage counselling, things between the two of them were not improving. Having to pay for an expensive house was just the excuse Stanley needed to send him back on the road. Ann was preoccupied with her own affairs and pregnant again. Nobody cared where I was or what I did. I could have been missing for a week – it would probably not even have been noticed. I didn't want to go on living like a ghost in a sepulchre. I rang my mother's best friend, Nona, and asked, 'Can I come to live with you until I graduate from high school?'

Nona agreed straight away. I packed a bag with school uniforms and books, got into my father's Lincoln convertible and drove myself to Long Beach, where she lived in a two-bedroom condominium with her husband John Cooper and the second of her sons, Craig, a rebellious boy two or three years older than me, whose large room I shared. Living with Nona and her family was a great blessing, even though Craig liked to play his radio till one in the morning, listening to the worst music I had ever heard. Not only did Nona care what time I left home, what time I got back, where I was and what I was doing, she was the kind of mother I had always hoped for. She collected my dirty clothes when I forgot to put them in the laundry basket; she made dinner every night; sometimes she even got up early to make sure I had toast and eggs before leaving for school. She cared for me.

She was also a very smart woman with a lot of integrity, a lot of political savvy and a firm commitment to social service. Being around her opened me up to a great big world out there which neither of my parents cared much about. I was in heaven.

On 16 January 1958, Ann gave birth to her second child, a boy they named Lance. Stanley was delighted to have a son, but he was having to borrow more and more money each month to keep going. He had bought the Rendezvous Ballroom in Balboa to use as a home for his orchestra, but the plan was proving to be an expensive failure. By the end of three months at the Rendezvous, he was $150,000 in debt. This scheme, in which he had invested so much hope and money, was obviously going down the drain. One night in the middle of February, after the job, Stanley got into his Porsche to drive from the ballroom back to the house he rented nearby. He had been drinking heavily. He passed out and ploughed into a parked car on Balboa Boulevard. He was going so fast that the impact turned the Porsche over. The police didn't arrest him. He always said this was because they were grateful for what he had been trying to do to help the town.

A few hours after the crash, in the early hours of the morning, he called me to tell me about it. 'Shortstuff,' he said, 'I've been in an accident. I didn't want you to hear it on the news.'

'Are you all right?'

'Yeah. I was lucky. I got a knock on the head and a deep cut but no broken bones.'

'And the Porsche?'

'I think it can be fixed.'

I knew how important that car was to him – he loved it like a baby. He and I used to drive it up over lonely mountain roads together on moonless nights playing a dangerous game that we loved. We'd turn off the headlights then, driving along these twisting roads in the dark, see which of us would chicken out first and turn them back on.

Two days after the accident Stanley called me again to say, 'You know that knock on the head? Well, it's sobered me up. You and Ann are right. I gotta to give up drinking and I'm gonna do it.'

After the accident he started ringing me at Nona's often. Usually it would be after a job; sometimes not long before I would have to get up to start my drive to school. As always, he talked about everything from his cold-turkey symptoms from giving up alcohol – chills and fears and things crawling under his skin – to how difficult his relationship with Ann was becoming. At first her spirits had been lifted by his going on the wagon, but it was not enough to make up for the anger and resentment she had built up against him ever since their wedding night. Even my no longer being at home hadn't helped things. 'I'm sick of listening to her bitch,' Stanley grumbled. 'She doesn't seem to understand anything. To hell with her.'

The Rendezvous project would last a little over three months. When it ended, Stanley hung around Los Angeles trying to figure out what to do next. 'I haven't had a drink for nine weeks,' he told me one night. 'But, I gotta say, it's hard being with Ann too much when I don't drink. I can never think of anything to say to her.'

Sometimes I came out of school to find him waiting for me in the car park at Marlborough. 'You wanna get a Monte Cristo sandwich?' he'd ask. Then we'd go to the Brown Derby in Hollywood or to a drive-in where we could sit and talk. He was always surprised when I rang Nona to tell her I wouldn't be back for dinner. I don't think my father ever considered having to answer to anyone. He didn't understand that I actually liked the way Nona worried about me if I was late.

In June I was to graduate from high school. By then I had spent two years at Marlborough which for me epitomised a world to which I did not belong, as girls in pastel golf dresses went about preparing to take their place in privileged society where all is gentle, in good taste and – above all – opulent.

Graduation from Marlborough was a grand affair which went on for a couple of days. Included in the festivities was a swim with parents, the formal ceremony and a father–daughter tea dance. Stanley came to all three. I was proud of him. Having to make the most cursory visit to any school always terrified him. He said he never knew how to behave.

The formal graduation ceremony was full of fleas. Each of us was dressed in an identical full-length white dress made from layers of organza. After the ceremony we were photographed on the front lawn, smiling and full of self-congratulatory *noblesse oblige*. Amidst the smiles I suddenly became aware that my legs were itching. I looked down to discover that hundreds of fleas had invaded the layers of my organza dress. The tiny black specks of their bodies were visible beneath the fine white cloth. White organza invaded by tiny insects spoke volumes to me, not only about my time at Marlborough, but about the way Stanley's dream of domestic bliss had become undermined by virulent enemies from deep within himself. Unknown to him, they were at work, destroying his life.

There was one part of the graduation events I loved: the father–daughter tea dance. Even though my father could barely dance, he and I whirled around the floor faking it and having a great time. I looked around at the fathers and felt sorry for the other girls. None of the other fathers had the energy and spirit of Stanley, nor his awkward honesty. That day, all the fun we had was helped by the fact that, for the first time in my life, my father had not had a drink for three months.

When it was over Stanley and I drove up to Griffith Park to look out over the city. I felt happy. I began to sing. Suddenly, he turned to me and said, 'I never realised you have such a beautiful voice, Shortstuff.'

I felt that something fundamental was changing between us. I was no longer a mere appendage – an outgrowth of him, driven by his will. Stanley was beginning to see me as a separate being with her own loves and talents. This was my real graduation. What a gift.

32

BLACK SHOE WEDDING

A FTER GRADUATION, STANLEY went back on the road and off the wagon. I flew to New York with my mother to board RMS Queen Elizabeth on her way to Europe. The trip was a graduation present from Stanley. It came packaged with a brand new Austin Healey. My mother was to chaperon me.

By then she, Jimmy and Christi had moved from Visalia to another no-face town in the San Joaquin Valley, called Modesto. They had hired a woman to take care of Christi while Violet was away. We were scheduled to pick up my car in London then drive through France, Italy and Switzerland for several weeks. On my return to America I was to join Stanley on the road until my university classes began.

The trip was an incredible experience. Everywhere we went we bumped into helpful strangers who told us the best architecture to see, the most delicious little restaurants to eat in, the finest sculpture and paintings. I enjoyed seeing my mother's joy as she discovered an exciting new world in Europe that fed her passion for beauty.

It was strange spending so much time with Violet. I had been away from her for many years, during which Stanley had become the focus of my life. She seemed far less sure of herself now than she had been when I was a child. She was frightened when I drove us along the twisting roads above the Mediterranean in France and Italy. I suppose this was understandable. At the age of seventeen, I was a fast driver. But there was more to it than that. Ever since Violet and Stanley had split up, my mother had been living a life of terrible isolation. She had become so separated from the outside world that I think it scared her. When we were approaching Alassio on the Italian Riviera she began to cry, afraid that the car would go over the cliff. I got angry and growled at her.

That night when we got to the hotel I felt so bad about my outburst that I drew a small figure – a dwarf beast with spindly legs, a body like a frog and fangs for teeth. Underneath it I wrote, 'Please forgive me for being such a beast.' After her death I was moved to tears when, going through the materials I inherited from her estate, I discovered she had kept this little note all her life.

For me the most important event on the European trip happened in Florence. The morning after we got there my mother announced we were going to the Accademia di Belle Arti Firenze. I had hardly slept. All I wanted was to be left alone to stay in bed. I dragged myself up, pulled a T-shirt over my head, stepped into a pair of trousers, stuffed a baguette smeared with butter in my mouth and staggered on to the street. It was a bright morning. I cursed the sun, hoping it would go away. I had a splitting headache.

I was still only half awake when we arrived at the Accademia. We entered the room at the end of which stands Michelangelo's *David*. My exhaustion vanished. Although the room in which he stood was not long, it felt to me as if it went on for ever and, like the night I first heard Beethoven's music, I stopped breathing.

Light falling from the rotunda penetrated the surface of the marble, bringing him to life. David's hand – his right hand, huge and covered with veins – was the most magnificent thing I had ever seen. His face shone with a spiritual force I would never have imagined possible. His very presence demanded that I surrender every thought and feeling so I could just be present with him in that moment. I walked round and round, looking up. Those now-familiar words rose up inside me again: 'If such things exist, I want to go on living.'

I don't think I ever really recovered from that first encounter with Michelangelo. From that morning onwards I sought out his sculpture, his paintings, his architecture wherever I went. What drew me to his works was not only the titanic energy in all he created but his way of bringing the fire of spirit into physical form. A numinous force emanated from everything he made. It was so powerful I could not help but be changed by it.

When we returned to New York, Violet flew back to California while I joined Stanley on the road in Worcester, Massachusetts. It was good to be with Stanley again – just the two of us – but he was now drinking heavily and the dates he'd been playing had been poorly attended.

He questioned me about the European trip: where did I go, who did I meet, what did I love? I couldn't stop talking about Rome. I told him I never slept while we were there – how I wandered through the city at night, spellbound by its illuminated fountains and buildings. I told him about Venice and how mysterious I found it, about Michelangelo's painting of *The Damned* on the wall of the Sistine Chapel and how everything he painted there was a perfect fusion of mind, body and spirit.

My father listened more intently than he ever had. Some things I spoke about brought tears to his eyes. Stanley reminded me of a tired, hungry animal wanting to be fed. Apart from when he was on stage leading the band and he came alive for a few hours, the only 'food' that had been available to him had been Scotch and it was poor nourishment. Even he could see the alcohol was destroying him, yet he seemed powerless to stop it.

That night in Worcester a reporter named Dan Smith came to interview Stanley. Dan and I spent a couple of hours after the interview, chatting. He was much older than me – seven years feels like another generation to a seventeen-year-old – but he spoke about things that interested me, books mostly. Over the next few months Dan would write me endless letters. He even came to see me in California for a few days before I entered university. We were to become firm friends.

Having caught up with Stanley at the end of the summer, I went to college in September. While at Marlborough I had applied to two colleges: Stanford University in Palo Alto, California, which epitomised upper-middle-class aspirations, and Sarah Lawrence in New York, an independent liberal arts college – at that time for women only – which emphasised the humanities, performing arts and writing. I was accepted at both schools. While I knew in my heart that I wanted to go to Sarah Lawrence, the adults in my life insisted that Stanford was where I 'belonged'.

Still running from the shame, guilt and low self-esteem which kept disrupting my life, I opted for Stanford. I deeply regret that I didn't have the courage to follow my own convictions instead of going along with other people's values. Had I chosen Sarah Lawrence I would have had the great mythologist Joseph Campbell and the dancer Martha Graham as my teachers, and I could have continued the dance training I had begun all those years earlier with Bolm. The only thing I learned from my mistake was something which has, since then, become a principle of my life: trust what you want on the gut level. If the rest of the world thinks you're wrong let them go their way. Never follow them, even if you are in a minority of one.

Some of my courses were exciting and I loved biology, logic, Shakespeare, philosophy and speech and drama, but Stanford was not an easy place for me to be. I felt the distance between my inner life and my outer personality growing wider. This frightened me. Attention from young men worried me too. I went on several dates but all of them felt superficial – without meaning.

I didn't sleep at night. My sleepless nights gave way to days when I would sleep through my classes. Some of my papers were handed in so late that my grades were affected. It's a near miracle that I didn't fail all my courses that first year.

I kept to myself mostly, hounded by the thought that I must tell no one what was happening in me lest 'they' put me in an institution. I still had no memory of either the incest or the summer of 1954. Sooner or later, every part of the psyche that is shut off from you begins to rebel and demands to be heard. I felt terribly alone at Stanford and I often thought of suicide.

Often I wanted to die but thought I had no reason to feel this way. I would stay up three or four nights in a row, then get in my car and drive for hours, ending up at the edge of the Pacific Ocean in Russian River Country. I'd run into the water, swim out dangerously far and ask it to take me. But the force for life inside me – over which I could exercise no control – was too strong. Besides, water had always been my natural medium and I was a strong swimmer. Then I'd find myself back on the beach again. Still alone.

Something happened while at Stanford for which I have always been grateful, since it changed my relationship to alcohol for ever. One night I was on a date with a young man named Jim. We ate dinner and drank a lot of cocktails before setting out in his car to go to a party at a country club some way from the university. Jim was weaving all over the road. We got stopped by the police who made us walk in a straight line, stand on one foot and do a lot of other silly things to find out how drunk we were. Jim failed all the tests. I passed them with flying colours, carrying out every one as though I were stone cold sober. At first I thought this strange since he and I had drunk the same amount, but then I remembered I had inherited Stanley's genes. With a lot of heavy drinkers, until the alcoholism becomes deeply ingrained, they are able to drink massive amounts of booze yet still appear sober. This made me realise that I, like my father, was constitutionally susceptible to the same addiction he had.

The police were great. They asked where we were going. They said I was to drive and that they would lead us to the country club provided we promised to take a taxi back to the university when the party was over. I remember clearly arriving there, dancing and singing a couple of jazz numbers with the band. I even remember the black dress I was wearing that night.

At my hall of residence we were required to return by midnight. Two nights each term we could sign out until 2.30 a.m. – which I had done that evening, knowing it was likely to be a late party. If we did not return by then we could be expelled from the university. The next morning I woke in a state of panic. I was certain I had stayed out all night and was going to be thrown out for breaking curfew. Yet there I was, lying in my own bed. I had no idea how I got there. Everything after ten o'clock the night before was a complete blank. This frightened me so much that from the age of seventeen onwards I seldom drank more than a glass or two of wine and even then only occasionally. I give thanks for that blackout. It made me aware of just how vulnerable I am when it comes to addictive behaviour. If that night had not happened, I might well have followed in Stanley's footsteps and allowed alcohol to destroy my life.

The first year at university I became involved emotionally, then sexually, with a young man named Peter Dau. Three years older than I was, he was majoring in philosophy and doing a pre-med degree so he could go to medical school the year after graduation. Peter was smart, passionate about philosophy, and the son of a well-to-do landowner in the San Joaquin Valley. He had a mother whom I adored and a father who adored me. From the moment we met, Peter's father, Bud, told Peter he wanted him to marry me. A few months later, Bud died. His death affected Peter deeply. It seemed to intensify his attachment to me as well. We became lovers and, in April 1959, as I was nearing the end of my freshman year, I became pregnant.

I knew the night we made love that I was pregnant. I can't explain how. I have been pregnant four times in my life and I have known every time the moment it occurred. Because this was my first pregnancy I didn't have the same confidence in that knowing that I would come to have later, so I said nothing to Peter or anyone else until term was over and I had returned to my father's house at North Alta Drive in Beverly Hills for the summer holidays.

I wanted a job for the summer, and got one at Capitol Records. The work was fun. I turned it into a race against time. The faster I could get it done the more fun it became. This meant that I'd finish my work by eleven in the morning. When I asked for more there was none so I would settle down to read my latest book. They said I wasn't allowed to read – that I had to be working, even when there was nothing for me to do. What they were really saying was I was supposed to *pretend* to be working. Since I was incapable of doing this I quit. This was not only my first job, it would turn out to be the only office job I've ever had. It lasted a mere three days and it set me on the path to being self-employed for ever.

Back in Beverly Hills, Ann was away from home most of the time now. Lance and Dana were often left with Margaret, the live-in maid. She would take them out to dinner on her American Express card, so I fell back on my usual meal plan – tuna sandwiches for breakfast and steak for dinner. The trouble was, every time I ate a tuna sandwich I vomited. This confirmed for me what I knew already: that I was suffering from morning sickness. Ever since then, tuna sandwiches have served as the most reliable pregnancy test available to me.

I rang Dr McCarthy, who had delivered me when I was born, and told him I was pregnant. I thought he should take a look at me to make sure everything was all right. By then it was late May or early June and he was able to confirm my pregnancy by internal exam. 'You couldn't be better designed to give birth to a baby – your hips, your pelvic basin – the whole lot,' he said. Then he asked, 'What's your last name now?'

I replied, 'It's Kenton. I'm not married.'

The next step was to ring Stanley and tell him; then, of course, Peter. 'I'm pregnant,' I said to my father over the telephone. There was an unexpected irony about the day I had chosen to ring him. That night the band was playing a one-nighter at Lake Compounce in Bristol, Connecticut.

He questioned me about who the father was and how I felt about being pregnant. Then he asked, 'What are you going to do?' This was years before abortion was made legal in the United States.

'I'm going to have the baby, of course.'

'You can't do that unless you get married or you give the baby up for adoption after the birth.'

'Then I'll get married,' I told him. 'Nothing's going to take this child away from me.'

'Then what?'

'Then I'll go back to Stanford and finish my degree.'

'Can you do that?' he asked.

'Why not? Women have babies and still go to university.'

'If you say so.'

'I'll take care of the arrangements for the wedding,' I assured him. 'We'll make it at the end of August. We'll have it in the garden. I'll do everything – invitations, minister, music, champagne, flowers – the lot. You'll need to cancel a couple of dates and fly home.'

'OK.'

That was the end of our conversation. Because Stanley had so much sway over me, I did not question what he insisted were the only two choices open to me. Although I was fond of Peter and his immediate family, I had no desire to get married. But the alternative of giving up the baby for adoption I did not consider for one moment. Nor was abortion an option, even if it had been legal. I was impressed that Stanley knew me well enough that he'd had the sense not even to raise the issue. It had never occurred to me there was a third alternative. If, at that time, even one person had suggested I tell my father to get stuffed, have the baby on my own and finish school, I would have done it. But I was still only seventeen years old and very much under his control. This was a pity. Had I done this, it would have saved Peter, his family and myself a lot of heartache.

Peter was good about our getting married, especially given his father's insistence that we should. I set about making the arrangements. The wedding would be all in white. Seiko and Peter's sister, Sissy, would be maids of honour – also in white. Christi would be the flower girl.

The garden would be decorated with white lilies, white freesias, white roses and white satin ribbons.

I ordered wedding invitations and sent them out. I made a mistake in the spelling of my father's middle name, 'Newcomb'. I had spelled it without the 'b'. Stella went wild when she received her invitation. She screamed at me down the phone that every invitation must be retracted, printed again and re-sent. I ignored her.

I was surprisingly sanguine in the way I methodically carried out all the arrangements. In the late 1950s, being pregnant and unmarried was still considered a shocking state of affairs. I was aware of this. I treated the wedding preparations – all the while vomiting from morning sickness – as something that had to be done to prepare for the birth of the child now growing in my body. I wanted this more than anything I had ever wanted in my life.

When the wedding day arrived on 25 August it could not have been more perfect. Stanley cancelled three dates to fly home from the East and host the celebrations. The weather was ideal, the guests were happy, the music was terrific and everybody was delighted, except Stella, who was still furious about the invitations. The fact that we served only champagne succeeded in preventing anyone from getting drunk. Many guests wrote to me afterwards to say that it had been the most delightful wedding they had ever experienced.

Violet looked magnificent in a stunning grey organza dress and matching hat. I think she loved being back in the world of glamour again. She more than lived up to her reputation for beauty.

Mom was in top form. From the moment she arrived everybody understood that she was now the person in charge. I was happy to hand over all responsibility to her after having carried it myself for the previous two months. Stella, with her keen eye and reptilian sensibility, picked up on this immediately. Two or three times I saw her glaring in Mom's direction as Mom busied herself making sure everything ran smoothly.

There was only one thing out of kilter: with all the care I had taken that the preparations be just right, I had never bothered to buy a pair of white satin shoes to go with the dress. I didn't realise this until I was getting ready in my dressing room, which overlooked the garden where the ceremony was about to take place. I remember quite clearly sitting down at the dressing table, looking at my reflection in the big mirror with its theatrical lights, and asking the image in front of me, 'Why?' There was not a moment's hesitation before the answer came: 'You are renouncing your own life. You don't want to marry anyone. The black shoes are a symbol of the sacrifice you've chosen to make so you can keep this child. Are you sure you want to do this?' It took me seconds to decide. If this was the price that had to be paid I would pay it, no matter what the consequences.

33

EPIPHANY TIMES TWO

I REMAINED UNSURE OF Stanley's attitude to my marriage. I suspected he was relieved to get rid of me. With the miseries he was trying to handle in his relationship with Ann, his struggles to keep the band going and all the money pressures, my marrying Peter had freed him from having to worry about me at least. Yet his behaviour concerning me and my life was strange. It would only become stranger in the years to come.

At the wedding Stanley had taken Peter aside to give him some man-to-man advice about 'how to handle Leslie'. 'You gotta use a firm hand with her,' he said to him. 'Keep her in line. Show her who's boss.'

'It was weird,' Peter told me afterwards. 'He went on and on. I wasn't sure what to make of it. He seemed so forceful.' When Peter told me this it made me sad.

After the wedding, Peter and I went to stay with his mother in a dream house she and her husband had been building before he died. It was a beautiful house in the country and Elva was a woman for whom I developed a deep affection. She treated me with real acceptance and generosity of spirit. She made me feel a welcome member of the family.

We stayed with Elva until we were to return to Stanford that fall: Peter to complete his senior year before going on to medical school and I to begin my sophomore year.

Despite the severe morning sickness I adored being pregnant. My purpose in life seemed clear: I was to do everything possible to care for this creature growing inside me so it could be born into the world strong and happy. Being pregnant felt more real to me than anything in my life ever had. I sensed I belonged to the earth – that I was fulfilling the most important function I could imagine: bringing new life into being. I dedicated myself to making my marriage as good as it could possibly be. I respected Peter and loved him, but more like a brother than a lover or a husband. I thought this was the only kind of love possible. You choose to love someone and you devote yourself to fulfilling that intention. I had chosen to get married for the sake of my child and I would do my best to make it work.

It was not an easy task. Peter had an interfering aunt who lectured me on how to behave towards my new husband and on how to become socially 'acceptable'. Living with Peter was equally challenging. We had a lot in common intellectually. He was a philosophy major and I was fascinated to learn about Kant, Plato and the rest. But he seemed to have a fascination with Hitler and the Nazis, which I found disturbing.

Peter also loved dove-hunting. He would go out with a gun and return with his hunting jacket pockets jammed full of tiny birds covered in blood. I hated Peter's bloody jacket and hated his killing the birds, yet I was powerless to stop it. Disagreements about this and a number of other things meant that, soon after the wedding, a deep loneliness rose up within me.

This had two effects. Because I had no one to talk to about how I felt, I began to write. I bought a notebook and started to record everything arising from inside me, censoring none of it. I just let words pour out, hoping it would ease my pain, at least enough for me to go on appearing 'normal'. Those weeks started a practice which I would continue for thirty years, eventually filling ten feet of bookshelves with notebooks in which hundreds of thousands of words were recorded and few of them ever read. These are some of the entries I made at the time:

August 31 – 4 am:
Awaken in anxiety wanting to kill myself. I know the evil is within me but what do I do about it? I am so frightened and so alone. If there is any good in the universe, please bring me some help!

September 12:
Full of self-loathing, I see myself as an undisciplined, self-indulgent slob – a junky who wants to drink or eat herself into oblivion taking a certain sadistic defeat in my own destruction . . . What am I doing? Is it a self-punishment? For what? Why am I involved in this futile internal struggle that will ultimately burn me out? I know it does no good to hate myself and yet I can't stop doing it.

September 20:
A frightening fatigue is taking hold of me – maybe I need to give in to it. Perhaps it is meant to be. It drags me into a terrible dark place. I want to sleep all the time. I feel there's a demon within me full of greed and hatred and selfishness. I think it wants to destroy me. No wonder I try to push it away.

October 4 – 3 am:
I'm frozen with fear that I can't be a good enough wife to Peter. He wants to make love to me but I don't desire him. When I go through the motions, it feels like I am letting myself be raped. I know I'm wrong to feel this way but I can't help it.

Peter and I returned to Stanford to begin the next year's work. It was a relief to be studying again. We moved into a small two-bedroom bungalow only five minutes' drive from campus. I dived into homemaking even though I could still only prepare two dishes: steak, and tuna sandwiches.

I rang Nona to ask for her recipe for tuna casserole – a rather revolting mixture of tuna, tinned Campbell's mushroom soup and crushed potato chips. But I figured it would be simple to make and I thought Peter might like it. I set about cooking our first meal together. Nona had neglected to tell me how much salt to put into it so I guessed a heaped tablespoon would probably do it. I baked the thing in the oven and proudly presented it to Peter. He took the first bite. 'It's delicious, Leslie,' he said.

I dipped my fork into it, had one taste and scraped the rest into the garbage. 'What do you mean?' I said. 'It's disgusting!'

'Not at all,' he said, trying to make me feel better. 'But, you know, I think it might be just a bit salty.'

Not to be defeated, I decided to cook a roast for dinner the next night. We had been given lots of wedding presents, some of them quite useful. Unfortunately a roasting pan was not among them so I used a cookie sheet. The roast released all its liquid fat, which spilled over the cookie sheet and covered the oven, which caught fire. The house filled with so much smoke it's a wonder somebody didn't call the fire department. Peter put out the fire. But the roast turned out to be delicious.

The next homemaking challenge I faced had to do with the house itself. I couldn't figure out why it seemed so dirty. It was certainly clean when we moved in. In fact every house I had ever lived in had been spotless. I'd never had to do anything to keep it that way. This time I called Mom for help. She explained to me that I needed to *clean* the place and then she told me what kind of brushes, rags and other paraphernalia were necessary to get the job done.

Back in classes, my grades improved out of all recognition. I am certain this was because my pregnancy made me feel more safe and solid. I had returned to Stanford with a certain trepidation over the fact that I'd become pregnant when unmarried. Like Hester, in my beloved *Scarlet Letter*, I expected to be ostracised for my sin. I had prepared myself to behave as brazenly as possible if I sensed the slightest hint of disapproval from any quarter. After all, this was the late 1950s, when self-righteous disdain for young women such as me was widespread. What greeted me was so far removed from what I expected that, at first, I found it hard to believe.

During my freshman year I had never really got to know the girls in my dorm. Yet now they decided to throw a huge baby shower for me. Dozens of girls came. I didn't even know the names of many of them. Each one presented me with a useful, often beautiful, gift for the baby. These young women were so generous and so enthusiastic about my pregnancy and the forthcoming birth that, overwhelmed, I burst into tears. I had never felt this kind of acceptance. And it had come from people who looked upon me as a friend even though I had remained completely unaware of this. It felt almost like a promise that giving birth to my first child would be full of joy.

At Christmas vacation Peter and I returned to his mother's house in Fresno. After the holidays Peter went back to Stanford while I headed for Beverly Hills to wait out my time until the birth. The plan had been for me to take the second term off, have the baby and then return to school at the beginning of the third term, after Easter. Peter and I decided that we would take the same upper division philosophy courses which he needed to complete his degree. This would mean that one of us would go to class and take notes while the other looked after the baby.

I arrived at North Alta Drive just as Stanley returned from many months on the road. He had said he wanted to be around when the baby was to be born. Ann was not there. In 1959 she had recorded her second album for Capitol, *The Many Moods of Ann Richards*. Now she was spending as much time as possible on the road to promote it. Margaret was still looking after Dana, then three, and Lance, almost two. I moved back into my room. I remember thinking how lovely it was to go into my dressing room and find my clothes, including my beautiful satin wedding dress, still hanging all fresh and clean in the cedar-lined wardrobe. At last I was in a place where, for a few weeks, I didn't have to worry about cleaning the house.

Stanley and I had had little contact since the wedding. It was good to be with him again. Apart from daily visits to his office and a couple of hours each day he spent trying to get to know his younger children again, we spent two or three weeks together while he was not working. In the evenings we would go out to the rumpus room, listen to music and sit at the bar. We would talk until I became so sleepy I had to go inside to bed. There was a familiar ease between us, as though we had never been apart.

Branton was born at the Queen of Angels Hospital on 16 January 1960. It was the same day that Stanley's son Lance had been born two years earlier. It was also a day before my father was to start work again at the Crescendo in Hollywood. While I was in labour he paced the floor. When it was all over he came into my room, his arms full of a mixture of white roses and white daisies, my favourite flowers.

Inspired by the example of Ann, I had made up my mind that I was going to nurse my child, no matter what. But I had no idea how to go about it or what was expected of me; nor did anyone think to explain this to me. When my baby was brought to me, all trussed up in a soft white blanket, I held this tiny creature in my arms and stared at him in stark wonder. Then, twenty minutes later, the nurse came and took him away again. At three-hourly intervals he reappeared for twenty minutes at a time. The nurse would slip him into my bed and there he lay until she showed up to take him back to the nursery.

The third or fourth time she brought him to me, he began to cry. I nestled him, rocked him, and spoke gently to him but he wouldn't stop. So I rang for help.

'My baby's crying,' I said. 'What should I do?'

'Have you burped him?'

'Burped him?'

'Yes, burped him,' the nurse repeated.

'What does that mean?'

'You have fed him, haven't you?' she asked, incredulously.

'Fed him? Nobody told me I'm supposed to feed him! I thought my milk wasn't supposed to come in for two or three days.'

'Jesus, Mary and Joseph!' Clucking like a hen, the nurse unfastened my hospital gown and put him to my breast. His tiny mouth opened. He reached for me as if he had known for ever what to do. He began to suck with such force it took my breath away.

I started to laugh. I couldn't help myself. It seemed incredible that such a tiny creature had such power and determination. He too had a purpose. It was raw, insistent and real. With every fibre of his being, this child was drawing life from me. He would not be denied.

Tears of joy ran shamelessly down my cheeks as he sucked. There, in the midst of all that clinical green and white, I discovered the most important thing I would ever learn. It would change my life for ever: Love *exists*.

And it's all so simple. Love has nothing to do with gushy proclamations, or the self-interested demands made in its name. Love is solid, real and strong – a meeting of two beings. The age, the sex, the species doesn't matter. That day two creatures – he and I – met. We touched each other in raw honesty. There was nothing romantic or solemn about it. No obligations, no duties, no fancy games. And you didn't have to read a manual on baby care to have it happen. Somewhere in body and spirit he and I were friends.

When the clucking nurse came to take him away, I lay in bed wondering if I could build a life predicated on my discovery. If love exists, could I create a home, a place, a way of being, that would make it possible for my child, myself, and others, to grow into the fullness of who they really are? On that day this became the goal of my life. This was the first epiphany.

A few days later Peter arrived to meet his son and take us back to Palo Alto. The three of us settled into an unfamiliar way of life known as *family*. Peter adored Branton. He took to fatherhood with ease. He went to his lectures while I gave myself over wholeheartedly to my bovine existence. Each morning Branton would awaken in his crib and we would hear him gurgling and laughing for half an hour. Then

I would go to nurse him. The three of us lived a peaceful, rich, quiet existence for two and a half months. Then, when the time came for me to return to school, I made one of the biggest mistakes of my life.

Our paediatrician told me there was no way I could go back to classes and continue to breast-feed. He insisted we put Branton on a bottle. He recommended a formula and told me to begin by giving Branton a bottle once a day, then twice a day and so on until he had been completely changed over from breast to bottle. I did as I was told but Branton refused to drink from a bottle at all – even if I left the house and Peter fed him. Days passed. We were getting nowhere. I rang the doctor in desperation and asked what to do. 'Stop feeding him altogether for a day, then he will take the bottle. Don't worry – you'll see,' he said. Branton did not take anything at all for forty-eight hours. I lived in fear that he might die. When, at last, he took the bottle he would never again touch the breast.

I am convinced that the trauma I created, by not ignoring our well-meaning paediatrician's advice and continuing to breast-feed until Branton was himself ready to give up the breast, cost my first-born son dearly. The trust between us, which until then had been absolute, must have been shaken badly – especially because he was so young. Only years afterwards, while reconnecting with my lost memories, would I come to understand just how devastating the breach of trust between a mother and her child can be.

Apart from my struggles while trying to wean Branton, my life had never been happier. I was looking forward to going back to school and excited about the classes I was going to take. Had someone told me what was going to happen next in my life, I would never have believed them. For love comes when you least expect it.

I remember it vividly: it is 8 a.m., my first day back at school. I walk into a cold auditorium for a course on botany. It is given by Dr Page, a tiny white-haired man with such a passion for his subject that when he paces the stage announcing: 'Here we have the most exciting example of root hairs,' I am covered with goose bumps and get carried away with his enthusiasm. I want to take notes. I discover I have no pen. There is a young man in the row in front of me, just to my left. Maybe he has one I can borrow. I tap him on the shoulder. He reaches into the top pocket of his shirt and hands me the shortest pencil I have ever seen. I look into his eyes and fall head over heels in love for the first time in my life.

Dick Givens was three years older than me and a year ahead of me at Stanford. Through knowing him I would discover I could not only have love for a child, I could also love a man.

I had never fallen in love before. Of course I'd read about it in books. But I'd always assumed the stuff Jane Austen, D. H. Lawrence and Dostoevsky wrote about love was more literary fantasy than reality. I was committed to building a life with my husband, Peter, and my son Branton. His birth had brought us closer together. Now we shared a goal: being good parents to our son. I had come to have greater acceptance of our marriage and to feel good about our future. Sooner or later, I believed, I would come to love Peter the way he wanted to be loved. It would be OK in the end. But meeting Dick turned my world upside down.

I had never experienced anything like this. The feelings I had for Dick overwhelmed me. At first, both of us behaved as though nothing serious had taken place between us. We walked together, studied, talked. I told him about Branton and Peter, how rich motherhood had made my life. He told me how he'd transferred from back East to Stanford, about things he liked to do, about his former girlfriend and his early life. I wanted him to meet Peter and Branton. He came to babysit for Branton a few times while Peter and I went to a movie or out to dinner.

Our friendship grew until I could no longer ignore the truth: that we were deeply in love. I had had no idea I was capable of feeling such emotions, of experiencing such intense physical sensations, or of abandoning myself so completely to another human being. Our affair lasted three months. The end of the year arrived. Peter was graduating. He had decided he wanted to go East to medical school and applied to New York Medical College Flower and Fifth Avenue in Manhattan.

I was faced with a terrible decision. Do I leave Peter? Do Branton and I stay at Stanford with Dick? Or do I leave Stanford and Dick to go to New York with Peter? The formless guilt I had been carrying around inside me since I was ten years old had become magnified a hundredfold by my having betrayed my marriage. Fear and shame took on monumental proportions. What kind of woman was I? How could I lie? How could I let Peter down – Peter who always told me how much he needed me and worried about how he would survive the pressures of medical school? He would tell me again and again how grateful he was that Branton and I were going to be with him.

I had nowhere to go for guidance so I turned to Stanley. 'I have fallen in love,' I told him over the phone.

'Fallen in love? But how? I mean who?'

I told him everything I could tell. I told him about the decision I had to make, how frightened I was, how guilty I felt, how deeply I loved Dick. I was half expecting him to be happy for me. Instead he behaved as though it was he I was betraying, not Peter. He accused me of being heartless, of disregarding all he had done for me, of being a 'loose woman' unfit to be his daughter.

His words wounded me badly. These accusations were the same I had been levelling at myself for weeks. The way he'd said all this had a violently possessive feel to it as well. I could tell he was quite beside himself. It was as though I had stuck a knife through his heart. Our conversation threw me into a state of chaos. All the thinking I had done in an attempt to do the right thing was instantly rendered useless. Between the lines I could hear my father telling me that I was worthless, that what I felt was meaningless, that my love for Dick was nothing but a schoolgirl crush. He was telling me Dick had to be obliterated from my mind and from my life.

Another twenty years would come to pass before I understood that Stanley had behaved equably about my marrying Peter because he had never felt that Peter was a threat to the bond between us. So long as I remained with Peter, my father knew he would never lose me. For me to tell him I was in love with another man was the worst kind of betrayal. I belonged to *him*. I always had and always would. How could I possibly be in love with someone else?

Just as I'd made the decision with my head to go to Stanford University instead of following my heart to Sarah Lawrence, now – silenced by my guilt and shame – I made a second decision. I would be a 'good girl' and do 'the right thing', denying what my heart told me and, in the process, wiping out every trace of the fragile trust in myself that had been slowly building since Branton's birth. I would leave Dick and go to New York. I would walk away from love and do my duty.

Peter's plane left for New York a day before mine. Dick and I had never spent a night together. Now we would have twenty-four hours together in San Francisco before I had to leave. We walked through Golden Gate Park. I had been there many times before on my own – visiting the Japanese garden, lying on the grass in the sun, looking at the paintings in the museum. But I'd never paid much attention to what was around me except in the vague way I always appreciated being amidst the trees, grass and flowers. Today was different.

Dick and I wandered aimlessly, aware that, in a few hours, we would probably never see each other again. It felt like death was sitting on my shoulder. I loved this man with such intensity that I could hardly bear the fire that burned in my flesh when he touched my face, nor the surges of bliss that flooded my heart and body when we made love. With no warning suddenly the world changed. For reasons I will never understand, my consciousness – my awareness of the ordinary world – became transfigured, luminous. I had never experienced anything like it.

As I walk with him, the structures of ordinary reality crack wide open. We come out of a wood, cross the road and step on to the kerb. Old men are bowling on the green. Absorbed in their game, they pay no attention to us. Without warning the trees, the grass, the small knoll behind the men that rises to a copse above, turn into a wondrous but terrifying Universe. Space expands in all directions as though a million tiny holes are piercing the fabric of reality. Each emits brilliant light. The air, the grass, the sidewalk, the bodies of the men, the clouds above us, the trees around us – everything trembles with a radiance. It breaks over me in great waves, simultaneously wiping me out as though it is even bringing me to birth in a new form. I understand nothing of what's happening. In the presence of this overwhelming beauty, I sense I have tumbled into a deep mystery.

Discovering love with my son, Branton, had been my first epiphany. That day brought my second. The intensity of the love I felt for Dick had triggered it. But this experience was far greater than either of us. It seemed to me that day that I was being invited to live a different kind of life: deeper, richer, larger and more connected with all living things. It was my first experience of something overwhelming which, instead of being terrifying, carried with it a sense of exhilaration. It brought me incredible hope. That was the day I became certain that the Universe is a place far greater than I had ever imagined.

Given that this invitation had come to me while I was so in love with Dick, I asked myself why I had made the decision to leave him. Was I insane?

At that time, I had no understanding of the unconscious programming that still ran so much of my life. It had trained me to walk away from whatever felt most valuable to me. It had made me believe I had no right to it. It taught me that nothing I instinctively felt was to be relied on. It would be many years before this would change significantly. But that day was the beginning for me.

The next morning I got on the plane.

34

NEW YORK, NEW YORK

BRANTON WAS EIGHT months old when Peter began his medical training in the fall of 1960. We were living in a tiny one-bedroom apartment at East 88th Street and East End Avenue, just across from Gracie Mansion, the mayor's house, where Robert F. Wagner – famous for establishing the right to collective bargaining for city employees and barring discrimination based on race, creed or colour – reigned supreme. From our front window I watched in fascination as groups of men in expensive overcoats and dark hats arrived there in black stretch limos at all hours of the day and night, looking suspiciously like up-market gangsters from a *film noir*.

Motherhood had come naturally to me, but marriage was not so easy. Having walked away from a man I loved to do my duty as a wife, I became more distant from my marriage as the months passed. This was not Peter's fault. He was a good father to Branton and he loved me. I still loved him too, but as a friend. I was never cut out to be his wife, no matter how great an effort I made to succeed at the task.

The first few months in New York, I did nothing but keep house, cook and care for my son. I was revolted by the foods you were supposed to feed to babies: biscuits made from white flour and sugar, revolting jars full of spinach and overcooked meats to which manufacturers added sugar. I determined that my son was not going to eat them. This was the kind of junk I had been raised on, and it played no small part in my being continually sick as a kid.

I bought a miniature dachshund as a companion for Branton and we named her Gretchen. When Branton was teething I went in search of something hard he could bite on which had no sugar it. I opted for dog biscuits. After carefully reading the packages I went for the brand Tuffy and I used to share. Branton and Gretchen would sit on the floor together while he fed her a dog biscuit after taking one for himself. I found it interesting that, just like Tuffy more than ten years before, neither of them liked the black ones.

Branton, Gretchen and I walked everywhere, sometimes covering sixty or seventy blocks at a time. I bought a little yacht which we sailed at the boat pond in Central Park. Together we explored the whole of Harlem, ignoring warnings that this was 'dangerous'. We never had the slightest trouble from anyone – nothing but smiles and adoration for Branton and the dog, who was unusual not only because of her small size but also her colouring, a deep blue-black.

Everywhere we went we made friends. I came to love New Yorkers. Unlike people on the West Coast who often pretend to be cheerful even when they are miserable, New Yorkers say what they feel and think in no uncertain terms. When I'd get into a taxi and the driver snapped at me I would conclude he was probably angry with his wife that morning and that his state had little to do with me. Often as not he would tell me what was happening to him without even being asked. At the same time, I had never known people to be so helpful to each other when somebody was in trouble.

Living on the Upper East Side, between First Avenue and East End, placed us smack in the middle of German Town where half of the store owners spoke nothing but German. Because Branton and I were both blond with blue eyes and we walked around with a German dog, they assumed we were German too. One person after another would stop us in the street and blurt out with great enthusiasm, *Ist das ein Dachshund? Er ist so schön.* ('Is that a dachshund? He's lovely.') I understood not a word of German but I'd heard this so often that I learned to reply, *Danke, das ist sehr nett.* ('Thank you, that's very sweet of you.')

One day, in search of someone to alter one of Peter's jackets,

Branton, Gretchen and I wandered into a small tailor's shop on First Avenue, three blocks from the apartment. It had a little counter, a pot-bellied, wood-burning stove and piles of newspapers going back forty years. They were stacked everywhere. The shop was owned by an eighty-year-old Armenian named Mr Aznavorian.

He took one look at Branton, called him 'Little, Little', and reached down to grab both his hands. Before I could get to the reason I had come into the shop, he turned to me and asked, 'You like Armenian Goulash?'

I had never heard of Armenian Goulash. 'I – I have no idea,' I spluttered.

'Good, you come back tomorrow,' he said. 'I make it for you. The best.'

We did come back the next day. On his tiny pot-bellied stove sat the oldest, blackest pot I'd ever seen. It looked like something a witch from a Russian fairy tale would brew her magic potions in. Sitting on a pile of dusty newspapers, with Branton and Gretchen next to me, we watched the pot simmer and give forth the most powerful aroma of fragrant herbs I had ever smelt.

While we ate, Mr Aznavorian told me about his life. That day marked the beginning of a wonderful friendship that developed with this old man over many bowls of Armenian Goulash – lamb so tender it melted in my mouth, in a rich wine sauce with zucchini, onions, garlic and eggplant, served over rice or couscous.

When, a year later, Mr Aznavorian decided to retire his little pot-bellied stove in favour of a new model, he gave it to me because I liked it so much. I took it home, scrubbed the soot off it, painted it gold, packed it up and freighted it to my mother who was, by then, living in a beautiful old house on the Monterey peninsula. I thought she could make it into something she could put flowers in.

Medical school was more demanding than Peter had anticipated. He had to be at the hospital most of the time. When he came home, he was often exhausted, yet had hours of study to do each night before going to bed. We saw little of him. By contrast, Stanley often came to see me in New York: not only when the band was playing there and when it played nearby, but if he had a day or two off in distant cities he would sometimes take a plane and show up unexpectedly to spend a day or evening. He developed a fascination with Branton and kept insisting that he 'looks so much like me he could be my son'. I have to say I never saw the resemblance. Branton looked more like Peter than anyone else.

Meanwhile, in need of a confidante, Ann would periodically call me to talk. 'Stanley's home for Christmas,' she said during one call. 'I don't like being in the same house with him. He starts drinking at five o'clock and doesn't stop. Then he gets that "lizard" look.' I knew what she was talking about. The 'lizard' showed up whenever Stanley stepped out of his body and his life. When it was present he would take in nothing you said to him nor remember anything he, himself, said or did. When the 'lizard' surfaced my father would be at his coldest, most dissociated and most fearful. He wouldn't remember what had happened even an hour before. People became objects to him – fodder for personal gratification or nothing more than a source of applause and approval.

Ann and Stanley were spending little time together. He was on the road; she was doing two to three week stints singing in various clubs in Las Vegas and other places. By her own admission, Ann did this to further her career but also to get away from the marriage. Her sense of self-esteem, never great at the best of times, seemed to have hit bottom in 1961. Instead of speaking to her on the phone, Stanley had begun to send her telegrams with strangely abstract messages such as, 'Stan Kenton asked me to tell his wife he wishes her the very best for her opening night and that he loves her very much.'

Ann said that she found being with Stanley 'so draining I feel like there is nothing left of me. He is so *needy*.' During another phone call she told me, 'I think I'm bored with him. He tells me his drinking is *my* problem. He treats me like a little girl. I think maybe I married him because I was attracted to his misery – all that crying and thrashing about.' By then the two of them had been living a sad life for five years, each trying to get what they wanted from the other and failing badly.

In the summer of 1961 Ann told Stanley she didn't love him any more and that she wanted a divorce. He agreed but insisted that he keep the children. She was stunned. 'You are not a reliable mother,' he said. 'Everybody knows that. They're better off with me.'

Soon after that she called me in tears. 'What should I do?' she cried.

I told her I thought Stanley was probably right – that the children would be better off on North Alta Drive. After all, that was their home and Margaret, the live-in maid, was a good woman who loved them both. Apart from spending a small fortune taking the kids to dinner on Stanley's American Express card, she was a responsible woman. 'Besides,' I added, 'that will give you a chance to live your own life.' This was what Ann had always insisted she wanted, more than anything else, to do.

In August she filed for divorce. Stanley had put a private detective on her tail to gather evidence of her infidelities, which he hoped would demonstrate to the court that she was an unfit mother. In the end, he paid her $50,000 and they agreed to joint custody of the children, while the court awarded him 'care and control'.

That same year the band won the Best Big Band Playboy Jazz Poll Award for the fourth time – a mark of my father's influence on jazz. Sadly, awards didn't improve business or fatten his bank balance, so he made the decision that he would have to be on the road almost all the time now while the children remained in Beverly Hills with Margaret.

The divorce triggered my father's rage. His hopes for a new life, a good family, a home where he could write, had been shattered. That autumn he gave a journalist at the *New York Herald Tribune* a bizarre interview. It reflected the irrational state he was in, and expressed the bitterness he had come to feel for women, including the most domineering one, Stella. She had still not given up trying to run his life. He told the reporter: 'I'm sick and tired of those sugary jazzmen, those effeminate players with their watered-down sounds. And you know what's causing it? Mothers. More and more they're dominating their sons so that virility is missing in so many young men. How did this ever get started in jazz, anyway?'

Every time Stanley came to New York, he would take Peter aside, quiz him about my behaviour, then give him more advice on how to handle me. To me, as always, he spoke about his work, his worries, how he hated being away from home, his having written nothing since Hollyridge and his fear that he would never write again.

One evening in New York, Stanley picked me up at the apartment. We took a cab to Times Square where we had planned to see a movie. When I got out of the cab he started yelling at me. In the middle of the street, with all the traffic swishing around us, shouted at me about the shoes I was wearing. 'What the hell do you think you're doing?' he bellowed. 'You can't wear those things!' The shoes in question were light green sneakers, hand-dyed to match my green sweatshirt – a fad among college kids at the time. His objection to my shoes seemed to revolve around a belief that sneakers, green or otherwise, were 'lower class'. I stood in the middle of Times Square for five minutes while he screamed at me. 'How can you do this to me?' he yelled. Hurt and furious, I turned on my heel and literally ran all the way from 42nd and Broadway back to East 88th.

Another time, Branton, Gretchen and I were in the park on East End Avenue playing together when Stanley arrived. It was late summer and I was barefoot, sitting on the edge of the sand box watching them play. Again, he attacked me verbally. Like a wounded animal, he raged at me, accusing me of being a 'loose woman' because I was barefoot.

*

When Branton turned one year old, I found a warm, loving woman who could look after him while I went out to find work. The last thing I wanted was a proper job, one that would take me away from him five days a week, so I opted for modelling.

I found out that the top agency in New York was Ford's, so I looked up the address and turned up at their office one morning. There I came face to face with Eileen Ford. She looked at me and said, 'There are only two words that matter: bones and body, body and bones. If you're going to be a model you have to be a beautiful woman – a woman who knows herself inside and out – her face, and her body – and you have to learn to make the most of everything you've got.' Her words scared me. How would I ever come to feel this way about myself? Then she said, 'Lose twenty pounds, then come back and see.'

I lost the weight within a month. I don't know how. I must have stopped eating. I didn't even realise it was happening until, one day, standing in front of a full-length mirror in the apartment I realised that none of my clothes fitted me. I pulled off the knit black dress I had been wearing, looked at my body and felt sure I was seeing someone else. I am five foot nine. The first time I went to see Eileen I weighed 145 pounds. When I looked in the mirror that day my weight was down to below 125. I had never been so thin.

I went to see her a second time. 'Now we have to get you some pictures,' she said, and arranged for me to have test shots taken. Photographs in hand, I returned to Eileen. 'You've come a long way from St Louis,' she observed, quoting the jazz song. I was glad she was pleased with the results. I felt ambivalent about the way I looked. The woman who stared back at me from the photographs didn't seem to be me. I remember one of my modelling clients saying, 'You have an innocence about you – like a milkmaid who just stepped off the boat from Sweden.' His description was so far away from the dark inner world from which I took my sense of self that it scared me. I felt a terrible fraud. It seemed like my physical presence belied what a bad person I really was. To use Eileen's phrase, my 'bones and body' may have looked the way they were supposed to, but I felt like nothing but an empty vessel.

In the end, photographic sessions wore me out. I disliked the way photographers kept looking at me as a 'thing': a body and a face to be used instead of a human being. If I were to survive in modelling, I knew I'd have to fill my life with something that felt real. Remembering how much I had loved studying Russian history and literature at Stanford, I signed up to study Russian at Hunter College at the City University of New York.

That particular summer it was hot and sticky as hell. On the way to Hunter College the subway would be packed with smelly, sweating people. Instead of finding this revolting, I looked forward to taking the train each morning. There was something about being packed into a train with people I didn't know and would never see again that made me feel less alone. I was them and they were me. I felt I belonged to humanity – all of it. The course was tough but I loved every minute of it, even when I had to steal away for a few hours to attend a go-see or a photo shoot. Going there created a sense of context for me.

My loneliness had been made worse by my having started to model and being away from my son for several hours most days. Being so lonely, I was very pleased when Dan Smith, the journalist I'd first met with my father in Worcester, Massachusetts, moved to New York. During my first year at Stanford, Dan had written me scores of letters. Almost every day, a new one arrived. To begin with, I'd answered none of them, except to send him a card at Christmas. He had also sent me books he thought I should read. He had become a kind of mentor, wanting to share with me the things he loved most. Dan was one of very few people who sensed that beneath the cheerful, bold personality hid a confused, frightened young woman. I believe he wanted to help me in any way he could. Peter liked Dan, who was a real ally to me. We'd take walks together and talk about books, movies, the ballet and life.

*

During one of Stanley's visits to New York, he invited Peter and me to hear Duke Ellington at Basin Street East. Peter had an exam the next morning and he had to leave the club early to study. Stanley promised he would bring me home later. We spent time talking with Ellington afterwards, so it was quite late by the time we caught a cab to go back to the apartment. As usual, my father had drunk a lot of Scotch.

We were sitting next to each other in the back seat of the taxi when all at once he reached over, took hold of my shoulders, pulled me towards him and began to kiss me passionately. I didn't know what to do. I reacted with stunned silence, pushing him away. 'Is it wrong?' he kept saying. 'Is it wrong to feel this way about your daughter. Is it wrong?'

His behaviour truly terrified me. I did my best to take things in hand, treating him as you would any drunk on a fantasy trip where there is a threat that if you cross him he could become violent.

'No, no,' I told him. 'Don't worry,' I said, patting him on the chest and keeping him as far away from me as possible in the back seat of the cab. 'It's fine,' I said. 'No problem . . . don't worry.' I tried to keep talking until I could get away.

When we pulled up outside my building, he got out of the cab and started kissing me again. I forced a smile and pulled myself away, making sure the driver knew what hotel to take him to. I eased him back into the cab, trying my best to behave as though nothing unusual had occurred.

I went inside. Peter was asleep. I lay awake for a couple of hours, trying to figure out what had been happening. Had I in some way provoked my father's behaviour? I was pretty sure I had not. But then why? I never told Peter or my friend Dan about what had happened. I guess, when you've been sworn to secrecy, you don't think to reveal things you can't make sense of yourself, especially when, somewhere deep inside, you have become accustomed to blaming yourself for everything that happens.

*

At the end of his second year at New York Medical School, homesick for California, Peter decided he wanted to return there to finish his medical studies. Unfortunately, I came down with one of my high fevers. It turned into an infection that refused to yield to treatment. So when term finished, Peter took Branton and returned to his mother's home in California, while I stayed in New York until I was well enough to join them. The doctor who looked after me was an obstetrician and gynaecologist named Irving Saxe, who had offices on Central Park West. Dr Saxe told me I had to stop work, rest a lot and come to see him once a week.

He monitored my progress – which was slow – while I attempted to fill my time. I took walks along the East River from Carl Schurz Park to Roosevelt Island. I spent time with Dan. I started up a relationship with a good-natured bass player whose name I no longer remember. None of it helped.

I hated the few months spent away from Branton. I would go to bookstores and buy books that I thought he would like, and stuffed animals and cards. I wrapped each separately, then sent them off one by one every two or three days. I missed him terribly. My love for him had formed a foundation for my life. It felt like his absence was taking it away. Being away from me had not been good for Branton either. He had talked early and had turned into quite a chatterbox by the time he was eighteen months old. The moment he left me to go to California with Peter, he stopped talking. It would not be until a few months after I joined them that he would begin speaking again.

The time away from Peter while my body was healing made it clear to me that our marriage was not going to work. I wasn't ready for marriage to anybody. When I joined them in California I told Peter I wanted a divorce. He didn't understand. How could he when all he had known of me was the part I showed to the world – the tip of the proverbial iceberg? He had little idea that the submerged part even existed. How could he ever have guessed the power it exerted over the rest of me and my life?

*

I took Branton and went to spent a week at my mother's house in Carmel before leaving for the East. That was late September 1962.

Stanley had asked me to come and see him in Beverly Hills on my way back to New York. He had been recording at Capitol but he had some days and his evenings free. As usual, we ended up in the rumpus room sitting at the bar drinking Scotch on the rocks. Branton and I were to take the plane to New York around midnight so I had put him to bed in the house until I would have to wake him to go to the airport.

Stanley asked about Peter and why I wanted a divorce. I tried to answer him as completely as I could, but all I could say was that I knew it was wrong for me to be his wife. Stanley's response was surprising. Despite the man-to-man talks he had always had with Peter, and despite what I believed to be his relief at having got rid of me to marriage, he seemed pleased that the marriage was over. Maybe this was because his own marriage had finished – a question of misery loving company. Maybe he felt that I would now be more emotionally available to him.

Around eight o'clock that evening there was a knock at the door. It was Barry Comden, a man I had dated from time to time since I was fourteen but whom I had not seen for five years and with whom I had never had a physical relationship. One of Barry's friends had seen me and told him I was in town, so he had come to visit. The three of us sat and drank together. It was growing late. I decided Branton and I would spend that night at North Alta Drive then fly out in the morning. Barry had been flirting with me and Stanley had been behaving like a jealous lover; in a huff, he left the two of us sitting there and went off to bed. That night, I made love to Barry on a sofa in the rumpus room and I conceived my second child. Again, I knew immediately that I was pregnant.

Dan was waiting for me when I got back to New York. I told him I was pregnant – something Dr Saxe could confirm a few weeks later.

Dan wanted me to stay with him. He said he would look after me and my children, but I wanted to go back to California until the baby was born.

I rang my mother and told her I was going to have another baby. She was wonderful. She invited us to come and stay throughout my pregnancy, for the birth of the baby and whatever time it took for me to recover afterwards. Having left home at thirteen, I was infinitely grateful for her kindness.

I had very little money. United Airlines were offering a special fare of $99 from New York to Los Angeles. I rang and asked if that included free passage for my son who was still very small. The woman said she thought it did. I showed up at the airport in early December, with Branton, Gretchen in an aluminium kennel and over 150 pounds of excess baggage. (I also had a pet rat called George stowed away in my hand luggage.) The man who checked me in laughed out loud when he saw all the stuff I wanted to take with me on my $99 flight. With thinly concealed delight he wrote out my ticket, waived all charges, checked our luggage, including Gretchen, and told us to 'have a great flight'. We flew to Los Angeles where we were supposed to stay overnight with Stanley before carrying on to Carmel the next day by car.

We arrived at North Alta Drive in the afternoon. Stanley himself had only returned a couple of days earlier after finishing another tour. We met in the garden. As soon as we got there I could see he'd been drinking heavily. This was an unusual occurrence since, when he was not working, his self-imposed rule had always been no alcohol until five in the afternoon.

I let Gretchen out of her kennel and she ran off to play with Branton. Stanley came up to me, put his arms around me and held me so tight I could hardly breathe. He had tears in his eyes. Then, suddenly, his face changed and his voice. He pushed me away and began to shout.

'You're a two-time loser!' he yelled. 'I don't want you anywhere near

Lance and Dana. You will never amount to anything. You're poisonous.' Then came that old phrase of his: 'Put that in your pipe and smoke it.'

I had already been feeling desperately ashamed of myself and my second pregnancy. Every word he screamed was like a nail driven into the coffin of what little self-respect remained in me. Once and for all I was being condemned by my father as a pariah, a hideous, less-than-human outcast. Who, but me, could have sex just once with a man I'd known for years and get pregnant?

I was familiar with Stanley's rages. I could see he was way out of control. I feared he might harm my son, so I took Branton in my arms and gathered Gretchen into her kennel. Without saying a word, I walked out.

Thus began a long period of estrangement between us. That day was also the beginning of a physically destructive process in my father which exacted a heavy toll on his health and undermined his vitality more than anything in his life had ever done. Only three years later did he finally tell me what had happened.

The day after I left his house, Stanley had to fly to San Francisco to do an interview and arrange for some work. That evening, after his appointments were over, he went to his favourite steak house in the city to have dinner. While waiting for his steak to arrive he noticed that his mouth was filling up with liquid. Taking his napkin and pressing it against his lips, he realised the liquid was blood and there was a lot of it.

He got up and raced to the men's room. Leaning over the sink, he kept spitting blood into the basin. The restroom attendant standing by went to hand him a towel, saw what was going on and panicked. 'No! No!' he shouted. 'You can't die in here, Mister – you just can't!'

Stanley ran from the restaurant, caught a cab and raced to the airport. 'I knew I had to get back to Los Angeles as quick as I could to see my doctor,' he told me much later. 'They did all sorts of tests then told me that my anger had broken open lots of blood vessels in my head. He told me I had been bleeding from my brain.'

That event triggered one medical condition after another, leading to multiple aneurisms which, together with damage resulting from a lot of medical mismanagement of his other ailments, would continue until his death.

35

LOVE AFFAIR WITH MICHELANGELO

Branton, Gretchen, George and I became guests in my mother's house during my pregnancy and for a few weeks after the birth. Despite my apparent defiance, I had been devastated by Stanley's fury. The viciousness of the encounter brought up a myriad other accusations he had levelled at me in the years before. The curse – that I was a two-time loser who'd never amount to anything, and his professed shame at being saddled with me as a daughter – continued to haunt me, accompanied by fear, guilt and the intense vulnerability a pregnant woman can feel when her body has been taken over by the task of growing a baby.

I think my mother genuinely loved our staying with her. We spent a lot of time together during those months – time that has always been precious to me. There is something both challenging and wonderful about the relationship between mother and daughter. The closer we became, the more I sensed that, like Stanley, she too felt she was missing out on her own life.

In her late forties, she was still beautiful and healthy. She and Branton, then two and a half, would go out into the garden as it was growing dark and dance together in the moonlight. I could see that my mother had become a different woman than she'd been during the fifteen years she was married to my father. Some of her radiance and much of her original fire had gone, smothered beneath a blanket of conventionality. Even her politics had changed. Both she and Stanley had always been flaming liberals – ready to fight with passion for the rights of human beings of any race, class, creed or colour to live the life they wanted to live. Now all that was gone.

After nine months I had still not gone into labour and I was worried. I knew the date I had become pregnant. I had left Peter exactly a week before that. Provided the baby was born at the right time I would be able to get away with letting Peter and his family believe that the child was his. That would be a terrible lie, of course – yet a lie I would tell with absolute deliberation, fostered by my protective instincts as a mother. I was afraid if Peter knew that this baby was another man's he would try to prove to a court that I was an unfit mother and take Branton away from me.

My having been away from Branton for many weeks while I was sick had affected him deeply. I was certain, in my gut, that Branton needed me while he was such a young child. I determined to make sure that he would not be taken from me and that he would never get caught up in the tug-of-war situations I had seen with divorced parents.

Finally, on 17 June 1963, unable to wait a day longer for the baby to arrive, I swallowed a bottle of castor oil and waited for something to happen. Two hours later I started to have mild contractions. My mother panicked. She kept trying to get me into the hospital. I resisted. I've never liked hospitals and saw no reason to spend more time in one than necessary. At about three in the afternoon I gave in. But I made her promise we could stop on the way to get a hamburger. We arrived at the Community Hospital at about 4.30.

They put me in a small room dedicated to labour. I was still ravenous. At six o'clock Jimmy arrived with a pile of sandwiches and a thermos full of frozen martinis. My mother drank the martinis while I devoured the sandwiches, ignoring all warnings about not eating in case somebody had to give me an anaesthetic. My contractions were still mild and I was lamenting having agreed to come to the hospital so early since there wasn't anything to do except try to calm my mother.

When Dr Manor, my obstetrician, arrived at quarter to seven, he examined me and said, 'It'll be hours yet. I'm going home to have dinner then I'll be back.'

'No, it won't,' I said. 'It's going to come very fast. I'm sure of it.'

He left the hospital. Within fifteen minutes my contractions had become intense. They moved me to the delivery room and tried to give me the usual drugs but by then birth was upon me. Dr Manor walked into the room just as the baby appeared – a girl. I named her Susannah.

Susannah wasted no time making her needs heard. Like her brother before her, she had been tucked away in a sound-proofed nursery but she screamed so loud that the whole hospital heard her. It became obvious that there was no point in trying to keep her in the nursery, so in an attempt to bring peace to all the hospital patients, the staff let me keep her in my room. When a woman gives birth to her first child and gets to know him, she believes that whatever he's like, all babies must be like. I certainly did – that is until my second child came along. By the time my third arrived, I would realise that each baby, from the moment it takes its first breath, is completely different from any other.

Three weeks after her birth, I returned to Dr Manor's office for an examination. He discovered that, during my pregnancy, a large tumour had grown near my right ovary. It had been hidden behind the baby so that only now could it be felt. He was shocked. He said he had never seen anything like it in a woman so young. 'What could have caused it?' I asked. He had no answer.

This mystery would begin to be solved only years later. Just as, when I first went away to boarding-school, I developed severe pains in my abdomen and could not walk because my body was crying out for

someone to know all that had happened to me, this tumour is likely
to have been yet another physical manifestation of the traumas I had
lived through but didn't remember. It's said such things happen quite
often in dissociated people with memory loss. I believe the tumour
was another physical manifestation of the trauma I had been carrying
inside me. Whatever its origin, there was one thing on which everyone
agreed: it had to be surgically removed as soon as possible.

I had no money and no place to go. I felt I could no longer accept
my mother's hospitality so I rang Dr Saxe in New York. He told me
he would do the surgery as soon as I returned. Dan Smith, ever my
loyal protector, said he would take care of us all if I wanted to come
back and live with him. Dr Manor sent my medical records on ahead
of me. Within three days we had left Carmel – dog, two children, pet
rat and me.

True to his word, Dr Saxe changed his holiday plans and cancelled
patients to fit me in. He also pulled strings to get me a bed in the
hospital so he could carry out the operation as quickly as possible. At
that time the removal of a growth of this type and size necessitated
major abdominal surgery. Afterwards the patient would have to stay
in hospital for at least a week. Dr Saxe knew I could not afford that.
He also knew I did not want to be away from my children. He believed
I was strong and would recover rapidly so he only made me stay there
for two nights.

The surgery went well. He made an incision in my abdomen in a
way that left almost no scar. 'I was careful to keep it below the hair line
so you could still wear a bikini,' he told me proudly afterwards.

Irving Saxe never sent me a bill. When I would remind him that I
had not yet received one, which I did at regular intervals, he always
said the same thing: 'Oh, that secretary of mine! She is so forgetful.'

While all this was happening to me, Stanley's life had been coming
apart. I would learn this only three years later, when we next met. He
was then alone with two young children. By the skin of his teeth he

had been able to convince the judge in the divorce court that Ann was 'unfit' and that the children should live with him. For a time afterwards the children remained in the Beverly Hills home with the maid, while he was on the road.

After two years of travelling with his Mellophonium Orchestra, he had headed abroad for a sixteen-day tour of England. He had been assured by Capitol that everything was set up for the tour and that advance publicity had been extensive. This wasn't true. He arrived to find that none of his records had been released during the previous five years. The weather was terrible, the transportation abysmal. With no promotion, date after date had to be cancelled. Any *esprit de corps* left in his musicians drained away completely. Stanley's worst fears had finally materialised: 'Stan Kenton and his Orchestra,' the signs said. But no one came to listen.

My father had arrived at a place in his life where performing was the only thing left to him that could give it meaning. Now, even that was ebbing away. Then came the final blow. During a concert in Birmingham in England, his bus driver Eric announced in the middle of the job that President Kennedy had been shot. It knocked him for a loop. 'My life and my career had ended in that moment,' he said.

When he arrived back at North Alta Drive he retreated into a dark solitude which was to last for almost a year. He saw no one. Margaret continued to take care of the children while he nursed his pain and drowned his grief in alcohol. 'I was overcome with shame,' he confessed to me, many years later. 'A bad father, a failed husband, I couldn't even write a bar of music.' His 'guilts' haunted him day and night. He could find no escape from his demons.

One night, Dana, who was six years old by then, called Ann. 'I think Daddy's crazy,' she cried. 'I'm gonna run away from home.'

Ann rushed to the house to find Stanley with a cigarette in one hand and a glass of Scotch in the other, sitting in the front room gazing into space. 'He had the "lizard" look,' she said. Ann took Dana to stay with her in her own house for a few days. She left Lance, then four, with the maid. 'He was so young I figured all this would wash over him,' she explained.

During this period of Stanley's isolation, Lee Gillette from Capitol Records tried to reach him again and again by phone. 'I want to talk about making some new records,' Gillette said when he finally got through.

Stanley was adamant in his refusal. 'It's all over. I never want to record another record for Capitol. I've had enough of your bullshit,' he said. He hung up.

From then on my father answered no phones. Nor did he open his mail for months at a time. During most of 1964, he just sat in the house and drank. For a quarter of a century he had been living the life of a respected leader, the focus of admiration and attention and the centre of many people's lives – his musicians, his fans, and others who never really knew him but thought they did, projecting on to him their own fantasies so they could bathe in what they believed to be his glory.

Stanley had been father-confessor, teacher, guide, psychiatrist, inspirer. The lives and careers of arrangers and composers who worked with him were almost always changed for the better under his guidance. What few of these people realised was that he needed them as much as, if not more than, they did him.

Back in New York, Dan was seeing me through the surgery and helping me get back on my feet afterwards, caring for Susannah and Branton as if they were his own children. We lived in a house on West 19th Street, in Chelsea. He worked for McGraw-Hill as a journalist. I looked after my children, cleaned house, shopped for food, cooked and tried to make ends meet.

I wanted to leave America. My reason for this was twofold: I loved Europe and thought it would be interesting to live there. And in Europe no court would be able to take Branton from me. When Dan was offered a job in Paris as a foreign correspondent we jumped at the chance to go.

We moved into a new high-rise building – still in the process of being built – in Boulogne-sur-Seine, a communist suburb of Paris. At first, living with a young child and a baby in a foreign country, where I knew nobody and couldn't speak the language, wasn't easy. I had to wash all the laundry, including diapers, sheets and towels, in the bath on my hands and knees. I shopped in street markets where nobody spoke a word of English.

I learned enough of the language within six weeks – from the fishmonger and the vegetable stall owners – to get us fed. In another six months I spoke it well and by the end of a year I was dreaming in French instead of English and could play word games in the language. The experience taught me something about myself: for me, the power of a language lies not in the written word but in the spoken one. I learn from the sound of words. Until this day, I have to read a poem out loud for it to sink in.

On 29 July 1964, Dan and I were married. We moved across the river into a three-storey house with a lovely garden in Meudon-Bellevue, close to an excellent school for Branton. Soon after we settled there, Mom came to stay.

With Dan's enthusiasm for French cuisine and Mom's expertise, I became determined to learn to cook properly. I bought a copy of a classic French cookbook, opened it to 'Canard à l'Orange' and began to read: 'Take one young duck and wring its neck. Then quickly pluck all feathers from the breast so blood runs to this area.' Having plucked dozens of chickens in Mom's kitchen when I was little, I remained undaunted by the instructions. Not only did I learn to cook great duck, I became an expert in just about every kind of soufflé you could imagine, and some other dishes. This pleased Dan. I wanted to please Dan. I was trying to be as good a wife to him as I could be. To me this meant doing the outer things well like cooking and taking care of our home. At least I had the capacity to do this.

Although I loved almost everything about living in Paris, I was still wrestling with my own ghosts, just as Stanley was. I still got unexplainable high fevers. I still awakened in the night with terrifying dreams. Despair continued to come in like the tide. It manifested in terrible loneliness and sometimes as a deep, unexplainable fatigue. I was a strong young woman with no reason to be experiencing bouts of exhaustion so severe that I would find it hard to get out of bed some days. Yet there was nothing I could do to change anything.

I loved Dan, but, again, I loved him as a friend or a brother. This was not the way he wanted, needed or deserved to be loved. I was continually chastising myself for this. 'If only I can love him more, everything will be all right,' I kept saying to myself.

That summer the five of us – Dan, Mom, Susannah, Branton and I – piled into a tiny Renault 4 and headed for Spain on holiday. There, in a villa on the coast of the Mediterranean, my third child was conceived. Being pregnant again at the age of twenty-three was a blessing. I was determined that, no matter what, he or she would not be born in a hospital. I wanted a truly natural birth with no drugs. I objected to all the palaver that surrounded childbirth, treating it more like a disease than a natural process.

I had read about the work of Dr Fernand Lamaze, the French obstetrician who had gone to Russia, studied their natural childbirth techniques, then brought them to France. His methods were quickly embraced by French women who looked upon drugs as dangerous and unnecessary. Needless to say, his methods had been totally rejected by most American doctors. I found out that the expert in the field at that time was Dr Pierre Vellay, author of *L'Accouchement sans douleur* (Childbirth without Pain), who had been Lamaze's assistant. Vellay booked me into the *clinique d'accouchement* where he delivered babies with the aplomb of a French chef delivering a gorgeous dessert – a place where women went only to give birth. There, I gave birth in four hours on 12 June, 1965, to my third child, a boy we named Jesse. Afterwards, I lay in bed wondering if Vellay's respectful and natural birth would influence Jesse's view of the world while he was growing up and the way he'd choose to live his life.

Apart from my children, what cushioned me from the darkness inside me was my fascination with French art, movies, design, painting and sculpture; above all, the sculpture of Michelangelo.

In Meudon-Bellevue we had a nanny. This meant that I was able to attend the Alliance Française to improve my written French. For a few weeks I went religiously five times a week. But it bored me. I began to cut classes so I could go to museums, galleries and movies. I felt far more guilty about this than I probably should have. I think at that point in my life, the facsimile Leslie, who since ECT had been trying so hard to 'do the right thing', 'be responsible', 'behave like a normal human being', had been taken over by a deeper part of me which – despite guilt and fear of punishment – refused to be ignored any longer. This more fundamental and truer part ached to be fed. It was desperate to connect with something of real value to me.

The loneliness, which had played such a large part in my life since the summer of 1954, was replaced by a passion to find what was beautiful. To me, the beautiful has nothing to do with the decorative or the pretty. It is much richer – vibrant with light and darkness – an expression of whatever is most undeniably *real*. The need I felt to explore this became an obsession I could no longer deny. Like an animal seeking prey, I prowled the streets of Paris in search of the kind of beauty that could make me feel more alive. Meanwhile Dan went on believing that I was being a 'good girl', attending French classes every afternoon and cooking soufflés.

While wandering through museums, even as a kid, I felt intimidated by the hushed reverence I saw people adopt. I would hear comments on paintings such as 'Can't you just *taste* those apples?' or 'Isn't she charming?' and could never figure out what they were talking about. The paintings and sculpture I was drawn to all grabbed me by the throat and wouldn't let me go until I surrendered to whatever they were demanding of me. A figure or a drawing would call to me from across the room, engendering a craving to get close to it which I could not ignore. At first it would be a feeling of attraction. Sometimes this attraction would create a desire to open my whole being to it and draw it inside me. Occasionally a piece of art seemed to take me over so completely that, for a time, I'd almost become it. Nowhere was all this passion stronger or more compelling than when I was standing face to face with a magnificent sculpture.

I marvelled at Dalou's sculpture – his lions and his children on the corners of Pont d'Alexandre III. I went to the Petit Palais where I came upon his miniatures of women sewing and mothers with their children. There too I discovered the sculpture of Carpeaux and Carriès. Across the Seine, Rodin's theatrical statues fascinated me. But I never took to his work the way I did to the others. I made friends with an eighty-year-old Russian woman I met at the Louvre. Elizabeth Falz-Fein was a sculptor and painter who introduced me to the work of Bourdelle.

I learned from Elizabeth that Rodin's apprentice, Antoine Bourdelle, had done some of Rodin's best work. In Bourdelle's diaries he writes of the frustration he faced while working on *Balzac*. Rodin would return to his atelier after several days away and undermine the work Bourdelle had done on it, completely unbalancing the statue so Bourdelle would have to start over.

With Elizabeth, I visited the Bourdelle museum and was astounded to find a quality of work which in many ways surpasses Rodin's in skill and power – Bourdelle's massive bronze of Adam after the fall, his many heads and busts of Beethoven, his brutal Hercules in the midst of battle.

This happened with a film as well. If I went to see a movie that resonated with me I would end up 'living' it for days afterwards. I told no one about my responses. Because the intensity of them frightened me, I wondered if I were insane. But, by then, my need to *live* had grown so strong I had to follow where these encounters might take me, no matter what price I might have to pay. Nowhere was all this stronger or more compelling than when I was standing face to face with a Michelangelo sculpture.

The Louvre became one of my favourite places to hang out on my stolen afternoons. I would stand for hours in front of Michelangelo's *Slaves*, nourished by their power, beauty and life, longing to fathom the will of the man who had carved them. So often in the previous ten years I'd felt an emptiness that nothing had adequately filled, not even my children. Michelangelo's work filled this hollow space inside me. It also energised me. Like a starving woman, I gorged myself on his *Dying Slave* and his *Rebellious Slave* – my favourite work.

At that time the two statues were badly displayed in a small space in the basement of the museum. A little man, a veteran from World War Two, guarded this space. I went there so often and spent so much time in their presence that, one day, he asked me as politely as he could manage, 'Ma'am, are you crazy or something?'

One afternoon, I was coming out of the Louvre as Dan was driving up the rue de Rivoli. He spotted me. I became paralysed with fear and guilt. It felt exactly as though my husband had caught me in bed with another man. The secret inner world, which had kept me alive and about which I had spoken to no one, had been breached. To this day I don't know if Dan thought that I had been with another man. I suppose it doesn't matter. In a sense he would have been right. The man was Michelangelo. The body was made of marble.

In the spring of 1966, Dan was offered a job in England. We were to join him a month later, when he had found a house for us and settled into his new job.

A few days after Dan's departure, the phone rang. It was Stanley. 'I'm in Europe, in Denmark,' he said. 'Can I come to Paris to see you?'

My father had played no part in my life or the lives of my children since damning me as a two-time loser four years earlier, so I was more than a little surprised by his call. 'Of course,' I said.

'I'll get there tomorrow about three o'clock,' he told me.

He arrived at our house in Meudon-Bellevue laden with gifts for the children – oversized teddy bears, a stuffed dolphin, a huge giraffe.

'This is your grandfather,' I said. Susannah, almost three, looked up at him with great seriousness as though she were examining a skyscraper. Stroking the giraffe he had given her, she began to sing. Stanley stood perfectly still, then he said, 'You know, I think she has perfect pitch.' He held out his hand to her, which she took. Then she turned away and began to climb a small tree in the garden.

My father's movements were awkward. He obviously felt shy, both with the children and with me, and he spoke little.

'Do you know how to play checkers?' Branton asked him.

'No, I don't think so,' Stanley replied.

We spent the rest of the afternoon in the garden with the children, drinking fresh lemonade and basking in the warmth of a spring sun which made us drowsy.

An hour or two after he arrived Stanley said, 'Can we have dinner together tonight?'

'Dinner?'

'Is there a place you specially like?' he persisted.

I told him there was – a small, family-owned restaurant called Le Petit Navire, on rue Fosses Saint-Bernard in the fifth *arrondissement*. Their fish soup was the best I'd ever tasted.

'Is it quiet so we can talk?' he asked. I told him it was, then went inside to call and make a reservation. When I came back I found him lying on his belly on the grass. He had taken off his shoes and socks. He reminded me of the man I had spent so many days with all those years ago on the beach at Catalina, Balboa and Cape Cod. He looked up at me and smiled.

I took Jesse inside and put him to bed for a nap. When I returned to the garden, Branton and Susannah were lost in their own games and Stanley had fallen asleep. I sat looking at him. He seemed so different from the man who had screamed at me four years earlier –

someone I thought would never want to see me again. I wondered why he'd come to Paris. What did he want from me? Would I ever be able to relate to him again in a way that felt safe?

My father slept for a couple of hours that afternoon. By the time he awoke I was getting the children ready for bed, leaving them in the care of their nanny. We said goodbye to the children and got into the car. All the way to the restaurant he talked to me about what he had been through in the previous four years. His words made me sad. Here I was with three children whom I adored, living in a beautiful house in Paris where I had discovered so much that fed and excited me. Although I was still very troubled in so many ways, somehow it felt wrong to me that he should still be struggling so terribly with his life while mine continued, year by year, to get richer.

I see us now as we arrive at the restaurant. The man seats us at a small table at the back. Stanley orders a bottle of their best champagne which we tackle with enthusiasm. He tells me about the Neophonic Orchestra which he put together a year earlier. He says he feels it is his last chance to commission composers and to conduct a symphony orchestra playing music that marries modern classical with jazz.

I know he's wanted to do this as far back as I can remember – probably the whole of his life. I remember endless days and nights when he spoke with such passion about how afraid he was that it would never happen. There were nights when he would wake up from a bad dream covered in sweat, and tell me, 'My music doesn't amount to a hill of beans.' Here, now, in this tiny restaurant in Paris, my father pours his heart out to me once more.

'Are you writing?' I ask, aware that he has written nothing for many years.

'No,' he says, 'I can't write any more. It's no good.'

The conversation shifts. He reaches across the table and takes my hand. 'Do you have any idea how much I love you, Leslie?' I shake my head. Silence. 'You're so beautiful.'

In an instant, dinner between father and daughter turns into a passionate exchange between man and woman. I am sitting across from a man who, first with hesitation, then with overwhelming passion, proclaims undying love for me.

I think back to the night in the taxi in New York. But this man is my father, I say to myself – the father who when I came home with a report card filled with 'As' barely glanced at it, then told me to 'try harder next time'. This is the man who called me a two-time loser, who has had nothing to do with me for years, who did not even ask if there was anything I needed when he knew that, at the age of twenty-one, I had to undergo major surgery with no money to pay for it and nowhere to turn.

Here Stanley sits, barely two feet away: a man obsessed with the woman sitting across from him – me. When, once or twice before, I had experienced a milder version of such obsession from other men, I always dismissed it. This time I know I can't do that. This time is different.

Time disappears. We are back in that secret world of ours – a world we share with no one else on earth – a world where colours are more intense, laughter is uncontrolled and the chasms of grief into which we fall are so deep it seems impossible to crawl out of them. Once again, in this moment, we are living with a strange, enlivening power freeing us from all rules and regulations, all hesitation and all conformity that control people's lives.

I am excited but I am afraid of what is happening across this table. Are we swimming together into a dangerous sea of confusion and formlessness? Then suddenly we wash up on an island – a place untouched by the rest of the Universe, where nothing but the most ordinary love and trust flows back and forth between us.

He speaks of his dreams as yet unfulfilled. I tell him about Michelangelo and how I stopped breathing when I first saw his *David* in Italy.

He laments his failure as a husband to Violet and Ann, and as a father to Lance and Dana.

I talk of my love for Paris. I tell him about the man who comes to read the electric meter and how he knows every painting Cézanne ever painted so well that he might have painted them himself.

Suddenly my father says, 'I ruin everything I touch.' He has tears in his eyes. 'I'm lost, Leslie. I have Dana and Lance, but I have no life, nothing.' I reach out to touch his moist cheek. 'I can draw the best from other men,' he says, 'but I can't get anything from myself. It's like trying to squeeze blood from a stone.'

I am silent, overflowing with love for him.

Before I have a chance to answer him, my father dips his napkin in my glass of water and starts to wipe my face in the way that he has always done since I was a little girl. I laugh. 'It's OK, Stanley,' I say. 'I'm old enough now to do it myself.'

36

DEEP SEA DIVING

LONDON MADE ME cry. It rained all the time, the food was inedible, and nobody talked about anything but the weather. I was lonely for Paris, the light, the beauty, the art. Apart from my children, it felt as if everything that mattered most to me – everything that enabled me to affirm life – had been lost when we left France.

We rented a beautiful Georgian house in the country to the west of London. I found myself thrown into a circle of landed aristocracy who didn't give a damn what anybody thought of them. They lived out their lives in shabby jackets with patched elbows, dresses that looked as though they had lived through the war, clothes like old friends which, above all, they felt comfortable in. This seemed to me the way we should all live. I soon realised that the British not only tolerated eccentricity, they adored it. So did I.

England began to grow on me. We sent Branton to a tiny but excellent Church of England country school with one teacher, one classroom and children aged from five to eight in it. I went to auctions, bought furniture and did everything I could do to turn our house into a real home for us. Yet, I still longed for Paris, the city which had illuminated my life. I could feel myself sinking into darkness again.

Completely dependent on Dan, I had no life of my own. Motherhood had wiped out my dreams of making my living as an actor. By the time we'd been in England for six months, my energy levels had plummeted. I suffered a lot from fear of the dark. When I needed to go from one room in our house to another I would leave lights on in every room and hallway I had to pass through to get there. It felt as if every corner of the house was filled with threats to my safety.

'I've got to do something with my life,' I said to Dan one night. 'If I don't, it feels like I'm going to die.'

I don't think he understood; for that matter, neither did I. But he heard the cry for help from my heart and he responded. 'What do you want to do?'

'I want to work in the theatre,' I said.

In Britain, with three young children, there was no possibility of my going to drama school full time. But since we had help in the house, I was able to manage part-time classes in dance, speech, improvisation and acting at places such as the City Lit in London. I worked hard on my body, my voice, my characterisations. I loved the classes and the acting. My state of mind began to improve. Yet I had begun to get occasional flashes of horrible scenes – hospitals and dark places full of strange people I didn't know.

I missed my earlier mentor Sam Gilman's fierce guidance but I enjoyed what I was doing. I began to go to auditions. I got the lead in James Costigan's new play, *Little Moon of Alban*, at the Little Theatre Club in St Martin's Lane. Next I played the lead in Charles Marowitz's adaptation of *Flash Gordon and the Angel* at the Open Space Theatre in Tottenham Court Road.

After that I landed my first lead in a TV series. Four days before we were to start shooting, the Home Office rang to say I was not allowed to work since I was an 'alien'. (I was told that, unless you were already a US movie star, you had to have lived in Britain for four years before you could work as an actor.) So, after that, everything I did in the theatre was illegal, unpaid, or both.

The fact that I couldn't work legally crushed my hopes. Despite support from directors, teachers and audiences, I was plagued by feelings of shame and worthlessness. I thought I was ugly. I didn't want anyone to see me. If it had not been for my love for my children, and their love for me, I would have ended up seriously depressed.

*

By then, Branton, Susanah and Jesse had taught me so much I needed to learn about love. Children have a singularly unsentimental attitude and show little patience with the romantic notions of grown-ups. To them love is nothing fancy. It's a tangible experience to be taken seriously. 'If you love somebody, then you help him put his boots on when they get stuck,' one of them said. 'When I grow up,' said another, 'I'm going to love somebody even if his handwriting is messy.'

I once had a real demonstration of what love is all about from Branton, then aged eight and to all appearances totally indifferent to his little sister, Susannah. One autumn evening, after we'd all been playing outside together with our two dogs, Fred and Hubert, Susannah went missing. Through a series of misunderstandings she thought we'd gone off for a walk in the woods and we thought she'd gone back to the house.

By the time I realised she was gone, Branton had a dog under each arm and was firmly ensconced on the sofa watching his favourite television programme with a friend. If one thing was certain in our house, it was that Branton would do absolutely nothing anyone wanted him to do – like set the table or wash his hands – while this particular programme was on. If I were to stand in the middle of the room and scream at the top of my lungs he would not even have heard me.

Once I'd searched every room for Susannah, I began to be frightened. It was dark by then and she was only five years old. There were large expanses of land and woods surrounding the house. She could have been anywhere.

Careful not to betray my anxiety, I said, 'Branton, Susannah is gone.' There was a pause – like a slow-take in a cartoon. Then he turned and looked at me. 'I can't find Susannah,' I repeated. 'She isn't in the house, and I don't know where she is.'

It was as if dynamite had blown him off the sofa. The poor sleepy dogs were shaken from their stupor. 'I'll find her,' he said on his way to the door. He stopped and turned to his friend, still engrossed in the television programme. 'Get up,' he commanded. 'We've got to find Susu. Hurry up!'

I have never seen a human being move faster. Within two minutes he had been all over the acre of land surrounding the house and rung two doorbells to ask if the neighbours knew where his sister was. I'd remembered our talk about going for a walk in the woods and headed towards the thicket. Still running at top speed, Branton caught up with me and overtook me, all the time calling, 'Susannah, Susannah!'

As we headed up the big path into the woods, I heard the faraway sound of a child crying out. It was Susannah. I tried to reassure her we were coming, while attempting to avoid falling in the wet mud. Branton plunged on ahead, afraid of nothing. In another minute he had her in his arms. As I approached, I heard him saying over and over, 'Oh, Susu, Susu, are you all right?' with tears streaming down his cheeks.

At the dinner table, later that night, I told Susannah – who frequently suffered Branton's scorn – that now she knew what Branton *really* felt about her. I suggested she remember this evening next time she became discouraged by his taunts – calling her a drip, for instance. She smiled. 'You're a drip,' said Branton.

There was another day in summer when everything seemed to be going wrong for me. For no particular reason I had awoken in the morning feeling that living was just not worthwhile. By ten o'clock not even the brilliance of the sunshine had cut through the heavy black cloud that surrounded me. I was angry with myself and doing my best to avoid being angry with everyone else.

My two younger children, Jesse and Susannah, kept begging me to take them to Lulworth Cove – a beautiful, shell-shaped beach in Dorset with a massive rock arch from the Jurassic period. I didn't want to go anywhere, especially the beach. I did not want to do anything for anyone. In the worst possible spirit, I finally consented; making sure, of course, that they realised I was doing them a big favour.

The warm sand and the fresh sea air on the surprisingly deserted beach did nothing to improve my mood. It felt to me that life was 'out there', while I was locked away in the depths of some gloomy dungeon and was powerless to break out. The more brightly the sun shone and the more beautiful the day became, the gloomier I felt. Finally I could stand it no longer. Despite the fact that the children were playing in the sand nearby and I didn't want to upset them, I broke down and cried.

Susannah asked what was wrong. 'I don't know, just about everything,' I whined.

'I feel like that sometimes,' Jesse said, offering no sympathy whatsoever. 'I think you must be angry.'

'So what if I am?' I snapped.

'Why don't you hit something?' he suggested.

'There's nothing to hit,' I replied irritably, 'and, anyway, that's stupid.'

'No, it's not,' Susannah chimed in. 'It'll make you feel ever so much better, Mommy. Or maybe you could growl like a dog?'

By then I was willing to try anything. Feeling a complete fool and admonishing myself for behaving so stupidly in front of my own children, I growled and complained. I hated everyone, I said. I hated myself. I was lonely and I felt the whole world was stupid. Then I growled some more while the two of them sat listening attentively. Not once did they try to console me, or tell me I was wrong or protest that the world was really a lovely place to be. Not once did they pass judgement on me or make me feel ashamed or foolish. They just sat and waited.

Gradually I started to feel a little better. Jesse had been right, I thought, but I still had no idea where to go from here. At last I grew quiet. Only then did Susannah say, 'I think maybe I know what's wrong with you.'

'What?' I said, sceptically.

'You're always thinking about such serious things. You're always telling yourself what to do and what not to do. No wonder you're angry. I think you forgot how to have fun.'

She was right. Having fun seemed as far away as the moon at that moment. I realised then that for several months I had saddled myself with my work and my responsibilities as if they were the only things that mattered. I'd hated almost every minute of it but had felt proud of being such a 'responsible adult'. 'Maybe you're right,' I conceded. 'But how does somebody who's forgotten something as important as that remember it again?'

'Come on, let's dig a hole,' was her reply.

Feeling like a half-frozen hippopotamus, I lifted myself off the towel, mechanically moved my body towards the site they'd chosen for the hole and started to dig. Jesse, who often played the clown, began sliding down into it while Susannah grumbled, 'Stop it, you're ruining the shape.' As I looked at the two of them fiercely sneering at each other, and saw myself as I had been an hour before, I started to laugh. So did they.

Before long the three of us had dug a fabulous hole. It was the most beautiful hole you've ever seen – or so it seemed to me. We had a contest to see who was best at leaping over it. We drew pictures in the sand and then ran into the ice-cold water, splashing each other. By the time the first wave struck, like the two of them, I had become part of the sea and the sky. There was no more gloom. I was alive again.

On the final day of a speech class at the City Lit, one of my fellow students – a university lecturer from King's College, London – asked me if I would have lunch with him. David Thompson took me to a pub in Surrey Street near his office. That day I would never have dreamed that standing in a pub next to this soft-spoken Scot would become a point at which my life was poised to make a huge shift. David and I talked endlessly, about anything and everything. I spilled out my heart to him. I told him how I loved my children, about my passion for Beethoven, for acting, for Paris, for music, for sculpture. I spoke about my dreams, my fears, my hopelessness. I said things to him I don't think I'd ever said to another living being. And he listened in a way that no one had ever listened to me before. That day was the beginning of a love and friendship that would span forty years and is still thriving. It would also lead to my becoming involved in some of the research being carried out in London into the therapeutic uses of lysergic acid diethylamide – LSD.

It was the late 1960s. Psychedelic drugs, love-ins and peace protests were blossoming. With three children to raise, my acting studies and theatre work, all of it had passed by me unnoticed. I'd never even smoked marijuana. The closest I'd come to it was when the leader of a pop group I occasionally sang with in London had offered me a teaspoon of tincture of cannabis, prescribed by his doctor as a treatment for 'stress'. He mixed it in a glass of water and I drank it. I hated the way it made me feel. I vowed I'd never get anywhere near it again. Even the smell of grass smoke, when I came upon it once or twice in a room, made me want to vomit.

Yet I had always been fascinated by philosophy, religion and the nature of the human mind. I had read Sufi poetry, then some of the writings of Christian mystics such as St John of the Cross, Julian of Norwich and St Teresa of Avila. I had developed an interest in Tibetan Buddhism. All these people seemed to have experienced a larger, more numinous sense of reality, which I had only tasted until then.

I became enthralled by Aldous Huxley's book, *The Perennial Philosophy*. Then two of Huxley's essays came to hold a particular fascination for me: 'The Doors of Perception' and 'Heaven and Hell'. In them he describes experiences of expanded consciousness brought about through his use of mescaline. He also writes about his concept of 'Mind at Large', by which a greater capacity for perceiving reality can become available to all of us.

He claims that each person is at each moment capable of remembering all that has ever happened to him and of perceiving everything that is happening everywhere in the Universe. The function of the brain and nervous system is to protect us from being overwhelmed and confused by this mass of largely useless and irrelevant knowledge, by shutting out most of what we would otherwise perceive or remember at any moment, and leaving only that very small and special selection which is likely to be practically useful. According to such a theory, each one of us is potentially 'Mind at Large'.

As far back as I could remember, I'd had a strong sense that reality is much larger than the way we usually perceive it: that we live in a Universe of infinite possibilities, which few of us ever tap. I was sure there must be ways of exploring the multidimensional Universe, both in us and around us, if only we could find ways of lifting the veil that separates it from consensus reality.

That summer, Dan was entitled to a lengthy vacation because he had been working abroad as a foreign correspondent for three years. We ordered a new Mercedes, took delivery of it in New York, then drove it across America to visit some of my family in California, where we sold the car.

By then Stanley had sold the big house on North Alta Drive and, with his two children and a housekeeper, moved into a more modest one in Palos Verdes. After all the dramas Dana and Lance had been forced to endure, with a father who could be away for many months at a time, they had become troubled children.

Then, at the beginning of July 1967, Stanley flew to Las Vegas and married a woman he had met a few months before – Jo Ann Hill. Keen for me to meet Jo Ann, he had invited us to come and stay with them for a couple of days in Palo Verdes before we headed back to Britain.

I liked Jo Ann. And I was interested to learn that she had been in psychotherapy with LSD, before it was made illegal in the States. I questioned her about her experience with it, becoming ever more interested in the benefits she felt it brought her. A combination of Jo Ann's experience and Huxley's essays drove me to ring David back in London and ask him to find a doctor there doing research with LSD.

David leapt into action and made an appointment for me with Dr Joyce Martin. By the time I returned, he had already started working with her himself.

Dr Martin was one of a handful of physicians who had been licensed in Britain to carry out research into the therapeutic uses of LSD. Born in India in 1905, Joyce Martin had received her medical degree in London in 1933. Then she trained in psychiatry at the Tavistock Clinic. Along with the famous R. D. Laing and Dr R. A. Sandison, she pioneered the use of lysergic acid in the UK at places such as the Marlborough Day Hospital in London.

In the autumn of 1967 I began to work with her at her rooms in Welbeck Street, London. I had no idea what to expect. I was not even sure what I was doing there. I just had a strong feeling that it was right. The room we worked in was small and bare. It contained nothing but a bed on which I sat or lay and a chair for her. Each session began by her giving me an intramuscular injection of 250 mcg – sometimes more – of lysergic acid. It would take fifteen minutes for the substance to take effect. Then colours and textures became intense and my body would begin to fill up with a powerful energy, rather like the light from a laser, which always made me feel slightly buzzy.

Dr Martin worked in a clear and simple way by becoming aware of whatever the drug brought to the surface, then exploring its meaning. A session might be little more than the kind of beautiful experiences commonly reported with LSD, involving psychedelic visions even when my eyes were closed, and intensified connections with the minutiae of whatever happened to be in the room. Simple objects would become luminous, the way figures in dreams are. My voice or hers, saying something quite ordinary, could take on qualities of resonance and perfection impossible to describe.

Each session lasted for six hours, although the effects of the drug would go on much longer. Once we'd addressed the concerns and experiences brought into awareness by the drug, at around the fifth hour Dr Martin would hand me a set of earphones and turn on classical music for me to listen to while she left the room to make me scrambled eggs or something else. She always insisted I have something to eat before leaving her office so I could make my way home in a grounded state. Because I had such a love for music the opportunity to listen to my favourite composers while this extraordinary substance was still in my body was fascinating. The only experience I'd ever had akin to it was when Stanley and I used to lie for hours in the living room listening to music together. But this was even better. Listening to one of Sibelius's symphonies at Dr Martin's office I marvelled, note by note, at the intricacy with which he had composed it. Then, at one point, I could hear that the effort of composing became subsumed by sound itself. For the next few minutes, Sibelius was no longer making the music happen, he had *become* it, and it him. The experience changed for ever the way I heard music.

It was not until my sixth or seventh session that events from my past started to erupt in the form of 'abreactions'. An abreaction is defined as 'the expression and consequent release of a previously repressed emotion, achieved through reliving the experience that caused it'. If you have never experienced abreactions before, they can be very frightening. Because of all the high fevers I was prone to, abreactions were not totally unknown to me, but now, under LSD, their intensity was magnified. My whole body became the medium through which lost memories returned, piece by piece.

In one session I had severe pain in my pelvis – so strong it doubled my body up. While this was going on I saw images of myself scrubbing white tiles in a bathroom, trying to wipe up spots of blood. I could see each tile with surprising clarity – even the tiny black squares at the corners that held the larger white tiles together. There was nothing dream-like about any of this. It was far too physical, as though events that had happened to my body fifteen years earlier were recurring here and now. Yet, at the same time, a small portion of my consciousness remained separate – as the observer – so I maintained awareness that I was in this small room in Dr Martin's office while all this was taking place.

My memories, and the abreactions that ushered them in, would always return piecemeal – never all at once. Two sessions after the first experience of pain in my pelvis and wiping up blood, the rest of the rape at Lake Compounce came together to form a whole picture. I remember the moment it happened. I was lying flat on the bed with pain in my groin when, all at once, I became terrified. I shouted out, 'No, oh God, no!'

'What's happening now?' Dr Martin asked.

'It can't be!' I cried.

'Who is with you?' she said. I refused to answer. 'Leslie, who is there?' she insisted.

'It's him,' I said. I couldn't speak Stanley's name. When I finally got up the courage to blurt it out, I broke down and could not stop crying.

Dr Martin told me that the events that are most painful for us are often the most repressed. I had been doing everything I could not to admit that it was my father who had been in my body.

During another session I felt a sickening, uncomfortable pressure in my throat, the lining of which had swollen up so much it was hard for me to breathe. This was accompanied by colour changes in my vision – mostly oranges and blues – and by flashes: I saw myself in a hospital bed. There were bright lights and people dressed in white gazing down at me. During the next session I was able to begin putting together the pieces of this puzzle. Once they had coalesced, revealing the experience of having had my stomach pumped after swallowing pills in the bathroom, the swelling in my throat began to subside.

Then came a session when my body became paralysed. I saw myself lying on a hard surface surrounded by men and women in a dark room. I kept feeling the presence of my paternal grandmother, which did not make any sense to me. When I opened my eyes and looked over towards Dr Martin sitting in her chair, I hallucinated. Her face changed into the face of Stella. The paralysis vanished instantly. I recoiled, pulling my back against the corner of the room, trying to get as far away as possible. Aware that I was frightened, Dr Martin got up from her chair, reached out a hand and came towards me in an attempt to reassure me. I screamed 'Get away!' She sat down again.

I was terrified. It was the only time I hallucinated under the drug, but the experience held an important clue to unravelling the mystery of that night fifteen years earlier, when Stella had taken me with her to the strange church-like building by the sea.

Fragment by fragment, the memories resurfaced and joined together to form a perfect whole. Now I can recall how Stella led me into the building that night. It is completely dark except for the light of candles. There are twenty or thirty people waiting for us inside. I don't know who they are. I look around for Stanley. He isn't there. I want to leave. 'It's hot,' I say to Stella. 'I feel sick. I want to go home.'

Despite my drugged state, I am scared. I head for the door, take two or three steps, trip and fall. The floor feels rough and smells of dust. Two men rush to pick me up and drag me to the centre of the room. They lift me on to a high table, so I am sitting with my legs dangling over the side.

'These are my colleagues,' Stella says. 'They're here to help you.'

People come closer to circle the table. One woman holds a cup in her hand. It is made of metal, with bumps on the outside of it. She hands it to Stella with a black rag. Stella wipes the rim and puts it to my lips. 'Drink this,' she says. I turn my head away. 'It'll be easier on you if you do as I say,' she says.

The two men push my arms behind me. Another woman takes the rag from Stella's hand and ties it round my upper arm. Then she dips what looks like an old-fashioned pen nib into a small pot and starts scratching the skin on my arm – like a doctor does when he gives a smallpox vaccination. Blood runs down my arm.

'Drink,' said Stella, putting the cup against my lips. I drink. I close my eyes.

When I open them again I am still lying on the table, without most of my clothes. A man waves a crucible on a chain, the way priests do at mass, spreading smoke all round. I hear his voice saying the same words over again: 'Forget, forget, forget, forgotten.'

With my eyes now open, I become curious, in a detached way, about what is happening. I no longer feel afraid. I don't feel much of anything. When I try to get off the table I find I can't move my arms or legs. I can't even lift my head.

Yet I can see what is happening. I hear a woman say to Stella, 'Does she need more curare?' It will not be until I am in my forties that I will learn curare is made from a combination of toxic South American herbs. Natives use it on their arrowheads to immobilise animals they hunt. In the 1930s and 1940s, American doctors used curare, in one form or another, as part of regular anaesthetic procedures since it effectively immobilises muscles but leaves the patient conscious.

At the height of my fear, I hear words from somewhere inside me: 'No matter what they do to you, you will never be harmed.' In an instant, my fear is gone, replaced by a feeling of deep gratitude that I am still alive.

What went on that night? To this day I don't know. I don't think I even want to know. But here, unearthed at last, was the source of the despair that had so nearly destroyed my life.

It was my work with Joyce Martin that cracked the code to my psyche. What came seeping – then pouring – out, were not only memories of incest but the cult-based ritual orchestrated by Stella in the name of 'healing', followed by strait-jackets and padded cells. How do I know they were memories and not delusions? Because suddenly my childhood began to make sense. My work with Dr Martin ushered in the dawn of understanding, giving me a handle on why I had been living in such fear, why at the age of thirteen I lost all sense of my own identity and why, through an effort of will, I had kept trying to construct what I thought might constitute an 'acceptable' human being. My obliterated memories had been carrying subconscious 'sleeping programs' – programs based on the fear, guilt, shame and self-destruction, which had not only split me into pieces but were still preventing me from living my life wholeheartedly. Later, I was able to verify the authenticity of my memories through careful research and conversations with those who had been connected with that key period in my life.

I would love to be able to say that my sessions with Dr Martin 'fixed' it all for me. That would make a great story, but this is not the way it happens. Some memories of past events, such as the ECT, only appeared in fragments under LSD. They would not return in full force for another fifteen years. Although central to the healing process, it is never enough only to relive and remember. It can sometimes take a lifetime to clear away the false ideas you have about yourself, about the world, about what is and isn't of value to you, what is and isn't possible. Every human being requires time and the development of awareness to come into his own power. The process also demands a lot of courage, love from others and grace from the Universe.

One day, during a session, I suddenly knew, beyond all doubt, that Dr Martin was going to die soon. I could feel death in the room. When I got home that evening I said to Dan, 'Don't tell her I said so but Dr Martin is going to die. I'm sure of it.' By this time Dan had become so interested in my reports of what was taking place that he had begun work with her too.

'Don't worry,' he said. 'I won't tell her.'

His urge to reveal all got the better of him. In his next session with Dr Martin, he told her I'd said she was dying. 'That's just her repressed aggression coming out,' she said. When Dan told me her reply it made me laugh out loud.

Three weeks later I had my last session with her. I could feel the presence of death in the room. I could taste it in the air I was breathing. That day turned out to be the last she would work. Two days later she was dead. I have to confess I felt a certain sense of relief. Had she not died I might have felt compelled to continue working with her and I knew I had had enough.

I have great respect for LSD used in a sacred way to expand consciousness or to help heal the psyche and reprogram someone's sense of self. I will always be infinitely grateful for the healing it brought me, with Joyce Martin's help. But lysergic acid diethylamide is a powerful, unnatural substance – something completely foreign to the human body. When you have been given it dozens of times it takes a toll on your body's energy. It took me two years after Joyce Martin's death to regain my vitality. I never took LSD again.

37

TRAGEDY AND GRACE

Twenty-five years would pass between the summer of 1954 and Stanley's death. I would grow to womanhood, give birth to three of my four children, and make a place for myself in the world. Stanley's marriage to nineteen-year-old Ann Richards would collapse. In time, their troubled daughter, Dana, would be made a ward of court and sent to a drug rehabilitation centre in Badger, California. With no place for her brother, Lance, to live, he joined her there a few months later. Stanley's third marriage would fail. So would his health. Ann was to die from a single bullet in the head. Her body would not be discovered until two weeks later – in a state of decomposition so extreme it could only be identified by dental records. The coroner gave a verdict of suicide.

The trail of destruction from my father's unresolved guilt and dissociation was immense. The fear and guilt, the self-loathing and grief got locked away in the darkness of my father's psyche – buried beneath alcohol and denial. There they festered and fermented, year by year eating away his life while spreading collateral damage, like shrapnel, in the lives of those he loved most. Standing by, helpless, I watched this happen. I could see he was never going to be able to fulfil his two great dreams: writing music that would marry jazz with classical, and creating a happy home and family. He never found a way to look into his own darkness. He never felt safe enough.

Despite his worldly success, my father's life was a tragedy – a hideous waste of enormous potential. This sometimes makes me cry. There seems something grossly unfair in my life gradually getting better while his disintegrated. His struggles foundered beneath self-hatred and addiction. My struggles to face my own darkness and heal my own wounds I came to see as gifts of grace.

The grace I received always came in strange shapes and sizes – from doctors who gave me loving care, even though I had no means of paying them, to people clear-sighted and open-hearted enough to encounter the bold exterior of me and the confused, trembling creature hiding beneath and to bless them equally. Their love and acceptance helped create a place of safety for me that fostered healing.

The strange fevers which began when I was ten years old were another form of grace. 'Give me a fever,' Hippocrates said, 'and I can cure any illness.' What he didn't say, but what I know to be true from my own experience, is that some fevers eliminate not only physical toxins from the body but psychic debris and even false notions about ourselves that cripple us. Each of the fevers visited upon me cleared a little more of the emotional and spiritual detritus which had built up and distorted my view of myself and my experience of life.When my fevers arrived – and they came every few months – nothing could assuage them. They were like bushfire destined to destroy old wood while breaking open the hard-coated seeds and allowing new trees to grow. Every time another fever came, some accretion or other I'd been carrying would be dispelled.

Frightening and debilitating though they were, I don't believe the fevers were precipitated by bacterial infections. They never yielded to standard medical treatment. Each time a fever came, the ecstasy of the fire, the crushing hell-realms it took me into, the chaos and the surrender would become a little less daunting. They seemed to come and go in a spiral. At every turn of the circle my life would become a little more transparent and a little less terrifying. And a little more of me was set free just to live.

The last of these wild fevers led me to make one of the scariest decisions of my life at a time when I had no money, no skills, no belief in my ability to do anything, and three children to support.

I had been married to Dan for several years. The longer I worked with Dr Martin the more clear it became that the marriage would never bring either of us the satisfaction which, at its best, marriage has to offer. Dan felt this too. More than once he'd spoken to me about the possibility of a divorce.

In the winter of 1970, we took the three children to spend two weeks in Norway, skiing. No sooner did we arrive at the wooden cabin where we were to spend our holiday than I came down with a colossal fever. I skied the first day despite it, knowing that I could get away with this before its fire prostrated me. Then it arrived in full force.

When these fevers came I was always worried that they would frighten my children, Dan or anyone else in the vicinity. I needed to be alone. I made a bed from two eiderdowns then covered myself with every extra coat and blanket I could find and lay on the wooden floor of the living room to ride out the fury while the rest of my family skied.

It lasted three days. There was not much of the ecstatic about it this time – just hard wooden floors, chills and throwing off bedclothes for five minutes before pulling back over me anything I could grab, including the cushions of a sofa, in an attempt to get warm again. This fever was different: instead of leaving me helpless as the others had done, I felt, when it was over, like I was emerging from a womb of hopelessness into a world of possibility. Some sense of strength had been given me. *I have a right to live. I will live.* The words played over and over in my mind. From that day onwards, I never had another raging fever.

Through the years there has always been a synchronicity in my life leading me into areas of awareness, experience and knowledge beyond the five senses. I have felt often that I was entering a dark wood without a map. I would go in knowing that I had to find my way through it. Now another dark forest presented itself and I knew my first step into had to be to end my marriage.

I had married Dan at a time when I was frightened not only that I could not earn a living to take care of my children but that I might not survive. That was fair neither to him nor to me. Since then, several times I have asked his forgiveness for having married him under such circumstances and for having been unable to love him in the way he wanted and justly deserved to be loved. His response is always the same: 'I have no regrets,' he says. 'I ended up with a wonderful family out of all of this.'

When we returned from Norway, having decided that we would separate, I sensed I needed to be alone, to think and to work out where I was going next. Knowing of my interest in philosophy and comparative religion, Dan said to me, 'Why don't you go and stay in a monastery for a week or two?'

I had been reading a book by Chögyam Trungpa Rinpoche. Someone told me that not long before he had founded the first Tibetan Buddhist monastery in the West at Eskdalemuir in Scotland: Samye Ling. It was three days before Easter 1970. I rang the abbot, Akong Tarap Rinpoche, asking if I could come. He told me there was no room. Then he said, 'Come along anyway. We'll find a place for you.'

This turned out to be another unexpected gift in many ways. When I arrived I spoke to Akong for an hour, at the end of which he gave me two small round pills which resembled rabbit droppings. They had been made from a special mixture of dried herbs called *dutsi*, then blessed in ceremonies carried out by high lamas. Only very rarely is *dutsi* given to anyone. Said to improve physical and spiritual well-being, *dutsi* did far more than that. It stilled my mind and vastly expanded my awareness so the clarity I had been hoping for arrived.

I swallowed the funny little pills then went out to climb a deserted hill. At the top I took off my clothes and lay in the tall grass underneath a rare Scottish spring sun. I lay there for five or six hours. I remember moving only once or twice to turn over. The mixture of solitude and stillness seemed to take away years of struggling.

Something else curious happened. I heard a boy's voice and laughter, then a man's voice. Judging by the things they were saying, the two of them seemed to be flying a kite. But when I stirred from my near-comatose state and lifted my head to look around me, there was no one there. I wondered if I had been picking up events that had happened in that place during other times.

When I returned to the centre that evening I came face to face with a man named David English. David was twenty-two. I was several years older than him. The connections between us were powerful and immediate. As David said, 'I knew when I met you that I was meeting my most precious friend – part of myself. It made me whole in a way I had not experienced before. You were the someone I'd always been looking for but didn't know it. You just made sense to me.'

Engaged to another woman, David quickly broke the engagement, left his home, quit his job and came to live with my children and me in a small house I was able to buy thanks to $5,000 I had inherited at the age of twelve from Pat, Mom's ex-husband.

The house had three bedrooms. I wanted each child to have his own room so David and I ended up sleeping on the floor in the living room. He set to work building wardrobes and shelves in each of the children's rooms while I painted walls and did everything I could to create a beautiful home for us all.

Branton, Susannah and Jesse adored him. David wrote a song for each of them. He went to work building roads – something which, as an electrical engineer, he had never done before. I started to write. This was the only thing I could think to do that would not take me away from my children.

My first professional article was a 4,000-word piece on the state of the heavy-lifting-gear industry for a business magazine called *Industrial Management*. I typed it on an old typewriter on the stairs since we had no desk. This was just after we moved in and the stairs were still lined with carpet strips from which nails protruded. The nails pierced holes in my fingertips. Although I had convinced the editor I was a journalist, I knew nothing about heavy-lifting gear, of course. I went around asking everyone I met, 'What's heaving-lifting gear?'

David's presence brought even more grace into my life – into all our lives. This was less because of all the good things he did for us than because of who he was. Loving and being loved in the presence of deep trust with David taught me something wonderful. The darkness within – that which we most fear and are most ashamed of in ourselves – has a beauty of its own when we dare to open our hearts to its power. This ability comes from the experience of being able to expose ourselves in all our nakedness to another being who accepts us the way David did me.

David and I lived together for five years. By the time we separated I had established myself in journalism, gained financial independence, begun to work in television and was thinking about writing books. Why did we split up? I think because the love between us had worked its necessary magic. The time had probably arrived for each of us to go off on our own discovering new worlds and learning new things. 'While we were together, I always wanted to heal you by loving you,' David said. 'I thought that, if only I could *love* you completely I could *heal* you completely. But what I understood then as love was nowhere near enough to help you overcome everything. That could only be done on a bigger scale.'

That would only go on happening through grace.

Ever since the day in the autumn of 1962 when Stanley began to cough up blood, following the terrible fight we had, grace seems to have been absent in his own life. In 1965 he was treated for an intestinal aneurism with ascites surrounding his internal organs. Again and again he ended up in hospital, often for weeks at a time, then he would head back on the road again. My father's stamina had always been phenomenal. But by now drinking and heavy smoking were well on the way to destroying his life.

In February of 1972, Stanley came to London. He was there for five days at Ronnie Scott's Jazz Club, taping a 'Sounds for Saturday' for the BBC, and playing a concert at the Odeon in Hammersmith. We'd exchanged letters and phone calls but I had not been with him since just before I began working with Joyce Martin.

I went to see my father at the Mayflower Hotel in London. It was time to confront him with the memories that had come back. I was trembling as I got out of the elevator and headed towards his room. I knocked. He opened the door straight away. As he did, I noticed that his right hand was shaking. He seemed unsettled, as though his nerves were on edge. Did he know, at some deep level, what I was going to say? Surely not. Yet, could such a thing be remotely possible?

He ushered me into the room. He turned to cross towards the window, where two chairs stood on either side of a glass table. But on the way, he stumbled and stubbed his toe against a corner of the bed hard enough to bring tears to his eyes. I reached out to steady him. Then I sat down in one of the chairs, expecting him to take the other one. Instead, he stood in front of the window, staring down at the street below.

'We need to talk about some things,' I said.

Still standing at the window, he turned to face me. He knew about my having worked with Dr Martin. But he had no knowledge of what my time with her had brought to the surface.

I began to tell him some of what had come back to me: Lake Compounce with its blood on white tiles; endless nights in strange hotel rooms when he left me by myself with no idea when he would come back; my taking all the pills I could find in the bathroom and having my stomach pumped; the ECT administered by people I didn't know in a facility I would probably never be able to identify, when he went away that summer – turning me over to Stella to 'make everything OK'.

As all this came spilling out of me, I noticed that my body had stopped trembling. This surprised me. After all, he was my father –

the figure who had always loomed largest in my life. My fear of his wrath, his unpredictability, his verbal and physical attacks on me over so many years must have been encoded in the cells of my body as the memories had been. Yet now the fear of him had gone.

The outburst of rage or denial or blame that I think I was expecting never happened. He stood there like a man mesmerised by a force so much larger than he was that even his own nervousness seemed to have disappeared. Blood drains from his ruddy skin, turning it deathly pale. His body, so straight and rigid when I arrived, crumples, making the suit he wears seem to be all that is left of him. He sits down on the edge of the bed and drops his head into his hands. There he stays without moving, except to look up at me to ask a question. 'Where was it . . . I mean the first time?' he wants to know.

Then: 'The gold watch I gave you, you never wore it, did you?' And: 'Does Violet know? What did she say?' Finally, he says, 'Shortstuff, what did they do to you while I was away that summer?'

I answer everything he asks to the best of my ability, until he cannot ask me any more. He sits still. I breathe. I am so glad. I don't see how I can continue to provide him with calm, reasonable answers.

Now he looks like a lost child in a foreign place with no idea what is happening. I know that part of him. I sit on the floor next to his feet. I put my hands on his knees. Words trail off. The memories no longer need them. They have become things, all these memories flooding the room taking up the space, breathing the air. I wonder in an abstract way if there will be enough air left for us to breathe in their silent presence: I see Catalina . . . how he used to put his head in my lap and tell me his dreams; I see the dog he accidentally killed, which we buried together; the way he shakes me like a rag doll and shoves me against the wall of my room when he doesn't know how to reach me. But I say nothing of this. There is no reason to speak of these things too. He knows them. For endless minutes we sit in silence.

When he begins to speak again, he keeps repeating the same words over and over. 'My mother was such a witch,' he says, still holding his head with his hands and shaking it back and forth. I have never heard him say this before.

I don't know how long the two of us spent together that afternoon at the Mayflower Hotel. An hour perhaps, maybe two. I had to take a train home to my children and he had to gather himself to make ready for the evening job. We agreed to meet again the next morning. I left him still sitting on the edge of his bed and made my way towards Paddington Station on foot. Once I was in the open air I found I could breathe normally again.

When I got to his hotel around noon the next day, Stanley looked haggard but he was standing straight again. 'I've been up all night,' he said, 'thinking about it all. I don't know what to say. I'm sorry, Shortstuff. I'm so sorry. I can only say that during that period of my life I hardly knew myself what was going on.'

I am sure he is telling the truth – the truth of a man caught up in something over which he could not or would not exert any control; a vortex, a power of nature which he could only see as something outside himself, a double helix in which he had been caught – and still was. At least he had begun – just begun – to remember some things. He told me what he felt when he looked into my eyes, when, following Stella's interventions, he returned home from Newport Jazz Festival that summer. 'I was terrified,' he said. 'Seeing you vacant and destroyed . . . it was the worst thing that ever happened to me. I looked everywhere for someone to blame – Stella, your mother, anyone. I must have known the blame lay with me but I couldn't handle it. That's when your body started to haunt me in nightmares. You'd appear and reach out to me, then the shape of you would fade to nothing. When I'd try to take hold of you, your body kept evaporating.'

From that day onwards, my relationship with Stanley changed. There were no more fights, no more playful bantering, no more secrets. It was as though a part or several parts of both of us had themselves evaporated, gone, to be replaced by formality – some unconsciously agreed-upon protocol we began to follow where we wrote letters, talked on the phone now and then, sent photographs and did all the 'right' things fathers and daughters are 'supposed' to do. I came to know that I was no longer responsible for him. This brought me a feeling of lightness. I could go on loving him and know that I was free to make a life of my own without him.

Stanley had been without a home of his own from the early 1970s onwards. When he was not on the road staying in hotels he stayed in his mother's condominium. Stella's brain was rapidly deteriorating with Alzheimer's disease. Stanley's marriage to Jo Ann had ended. Audree Coke had taken on the management of the band for him. They worked closely together. She was much more than a manager to him: she turned out to be the best friend he could ever have imagined.

On 29 August 1975 Audree and Stanley hired a car and headed for San Diego. After a few days off, the band was to play a job at El Cortez Hotel on Saturday night, 30 August. The two of them had left a day early in order to do press interviews, radio shows and TV appearances. When they arrived in San Diego, they discovered that inmates at the local city jail had taken the warden hostage and all the media were busy covering the story. Since there was nobody for Stanley to talk to they decided to drive on to Tijuana in Mexico, spend the day there and return on Saturday evening in time for the performance.

The streets in Tijuana are full of shops where you can get instant divorces, abortions and weddings. While enjoying a Mexican lunch – complete with margaritas for Audree and plenty of Scotch for Stanley – they decided it could be great fun to get married. The idea seemed especially attractive since the restaurant they were in was right across the street from one of the wedding shops. After all, they had known each other for decades and got on well. So why not? They got up, crossed the street and climbed the steps to the shop where they tied the knot – complete with a licence to make sure it was legal.

Afterwards they got into the car to drive back to San Diego in time for him to go to work.

On the way back, the effects of all the alcohol wore off. They looked at each other in horror. 'What the hell have we done?' they said. But married they were and married they remained. Yet they told no one – not even the immediate family.

'It was the stupidest thing I ever did,' Audree told me thirty years later.

On 17 January, 1976, I received the following letter from my father written from another hospital bed.

My dear Leslie

I would like to bring you up to date on all that has been going on in my share of this world.

I'm presently doing a spell at the Methodist hospital here in Houston. I've been here about four weeks and I believe I have about three weeks to go. How did I get here?

If you recall I underwent major surgery about four times in the last four years. Because of this the muscles in my abdomen were cut so many different times and ways that I had no control over my stomach. So as a result it stuck out and was most ugly. Then I gained weight which made the situation worse. You know my ego. I was constantly ashamed.

I was told by a couple of doctors that I could be operated on for this condition and have the muscles pulled back into place thereby repairing the damage done. First it was necessary to go on a strict diet to get rid of the excess fat, which I did and that left me which [sic] of the loose flesh that the muscles could not control.

I underwent the surgery in Buffalo, New York around the middle of December. Why Buffalo? I found this Doctor I liked there and besides I was sick of the Beverly Hills treatment.

I left the hospital after twelve days and returned to California and after two weeks of recuperating I went back to work which lasted one week and an explosion took place and the incision split wide open and I had to be taken to this place for treatment because it actually was an emergency. I once more had some minor surgery on the infected part in which they had to cut away the bad tissue to prepare for the healthy to take its place. The recovery from this is long and tedious but as I said I hope to be out of here in three weeks.

Enough of all this. If I don't get over all this soon, I'm going to wind up broke because all this has cost a huge amount of money in addition to the hospital insurance that I fortunately have.

My mother, who is now going to be eighty-six in March, is not well at all. She is almost totally blind and is quite helpless. In addition to this, her mind is slowly going. She doesn't know where she is most of the time. It is most impossible to carry on a conversation because she can't remember from one moment to the next.

I just reread this and learned two things. This letter sounds like an essay on gloom, which couldn't be further from the truth. I'm very happy and well mentally. The other thing I learned is that my penmanship has deteriorated terribly. You will be doing me a favor if you will overlook it.

Please remember me to the children.

I send my love, Stanley

In August 1976 my father did his last European tour. Audree was with him every moment. He had terrible problems with incontinence and had to conduct while sitting at the piano. The tour was miserable. They were based in London and spent three weeks in Sweden, Denmark and other European countries. The weather was awful – sweltering hot wherever they went. Crowds were terrible. They had to travel long distances by bus. Both food and accommodation were bad. His health continued to deteriorate despite his determination to keep going no matter what.

Still on the road, on the afternoon of 27 May 1977, in Reading,

Pennsylvania, where the band was to play at Stokesay Castle, Stanley sensed that something bad was happening with his body. He stripped down to his boxer shorts and socks, and lay down on the bed to rest until dinner. His hotel room was on the eighth floor. A little later he got up and opened the door to the hall, staggered down the stairs and ended up on the third floor – the level where cars were parked. There, in the garage, somehow he fell. Nobody is sure if he slipped and cracked his head, causing a brain aneurism, or if a brain aneurism caused his fall. A woman found him. They rushed him to Reading hospital.

He had experienced a severe stroke. By all odds he should have died. However, one of the best vascular surgeons in the country, Dr Richard C. Johnson, was working at the hospital. When Dr Johnson opened up Stanley's head, he told us, 'His brain exploded, shooting blood all over the operating theatre. I have never seen anything like it.' When I heard this I thought what a metaphor it is for the intensity of the volcanic forces that drove him.

He remained in hospital in Reading from late May until 4 July. During this time, I arrived from England to be with him. When I walked into his hospital room he did not know who I was. But his eyes shone. 'You're so beautiful,' he kept saying. 'So beautiful, so beautiful, so beautiful . . .'

Audree continued to be so much more than Stanley's manager. It was she who collected him when he was released from Reading hospital. She took him to her own home in Hollywoodland above Beachwood Drive (very close to Hollyridge where we lived when I was a child). She rang me in England to ask if he could come and live with us since he needed constant care. My children and I were still living in the small three-bedroom house. I told her there was no possibility of Stanley coming to live with us unless he could help me buy a bigger house, so Audree opened her heart to him, shared her home with him and cared for him until the day of his death.

After the stroke, my father felt ashamed of what had happened to him. The aphasia prevented him from being able to understand or express speech clearly. He mixed up all his words and this embarrassed him. He had no short-term memory and very little long-term memory. The doctors said he would never be able to work again.

Although he had no command of language when he moved into Audree's house, he still wanted to write music. His grand piano was there. She bought everything needed for him to compose, including chart paper. He would go downstairs to the piano then come back a couple of hours later disheartened. He would write on one piece of chart paper, throw it away and do it all over again on another. What he wrote turned out to be total gibberish.

Audree went to the office every day, leaving him in the care of a nurse. The office itself had disintegrated by then: it had lost 75 per cent of its employees. This left Audree in charge of everything from answering letters to shipping records, with only part-time help from a couple of kids.

Confined to the house, my father slept and watched John Wayne movies on TV. When Audree returned from the office, she would find him drinking alcohol. He would order it by phone from the liquor store at the bottom of the hill and have it delivered to the house. In the evenings she would make dinner while Stanley sat on the terrace and gazed at the mountains.

My father saw nobody but his children, and them only infrequently. He refused to see any of his friends and acquaintances. He would not speak to anyone. Despite his condition, he behaved like a caged animal. He was desperate to go back on the road. He was sure he could do it, despite his slurred speech and his inability to stand up and conduct.

In January 1978, he and Audree took a bus from Long Beach and headed cross-country for the first night of a new tour beginning at the Statler Hilton in Buffalo, New York. Being on the road was not easy for either of them. But Stanley got terrific support from men in the band. They loved him and covered for his fumbling speech and his inadequacies. Medical doctors here and there dealt with emergencies as they arose. And emergencies happened continually. Even the press treated him with kindness and respect. They chose not to write about his inability to lead the band. My father was able to keep going until 20 August 1978. After a concert at Sigmund Stern Grove in San Francisco, he finally admitted defeat.

It was in August of 1979, while Stanley was still living in Audree's home, being waited on hand and foot, that I saw him for the last time. We were alone in the bedroom at Audree's house, where he watched his John Wayne movies. He especially loved *The Wake of the Red Witch*, a story about the moral and psychological struggles of a Jekyll and Hyde character with whom my father had always identified. We had gone to see it together several times.

Stanley was naked except for his boxer shorts. He had a two- or three-day growth of beard. Slumped over, he looked like a tramp on the railroad.

'I love you,' I said to him as I was getting ready to leave.

'Yeah, I love you too,' he replied in that automatic voice he used whenever he'd been drinking, as he had all afternoon.

'No,' I said. 'I don't think you get what I'm saying.' He looked up at me. 'I love you more than anyone in the world,' I said.

The old man is suddenly gone. His china blue eyes clear. He is smiling at me from the face of a child.

I knew he had heard me. 'I guess I always will,' I say.

Only two weeks later, back in Britain, I got the news: 'Your father's dead.' I was sitting in a bathtub when one of my children came to tell me that Audree had rung to speak to me.

'Stanley's dead,' I said to myself out loud. 'He's dead. My father's dead,' I kept repeating, trying to get it through my head.

Three weeks later I received the following letter from Audree. It is dated 8 September 1979.

Dear Leslie,

It has been two weeks now since your father died, and I suppose I'm ready to write. Grief takes odd forms: I have trouble concentrating. I have been absolutely inundated with telephone calls, telegrams, sympathy cards, requests for interviews, flowers and plants, requests for photographs, requests for mementos. And letters of condolence from fans and friends, and people who want favors and people who have something to sell, and people who want to do television shows and radio shows. And people who want to buy all the Kenton records, and people who want to arrange memorial concerts and write magazine articles and books.

As you know, your father died Saturday August 25, at 5:45 in the afternoon. He had left instructions for cremation and no funeral. His body was cremated on Tuesday August 28. At 11 am on Wednesday August 29 we met at the Westwood Village mortuary for a brief committal service. It was a warm, overcast, hazy day – typical of smoggy Los Angeles – and a proper day for a Los Angeles boy's commitment to eternity. We planted a ridiculous red rose tree over your father's ashes. Roses are not at their best in August, and I know Stanley would have laughed at his token tree – a lanky, terribly tall, skinny thing, with out-flung, awkward branches. Somehow it seemed exactly right for a reborn Stan Kenton, and perhaps it will become more handsome as it matures, as he did.

As I told you over the telephone, Stanley's death was quite unexpectedly peaceful. The death certificate, which I sent to you, says 'cerebral thrombosis', as the cause of death, with an underlying cause of 'cerebral arteriosclerosis'. Doctors all over the country had told me for the past few years that Stanley's brain would deteriorate to a point of senility (as Stella's did) as I believe it began to in the last two years. In retrospect, I also think he may have been having light strokes in the week before he had the final stroke at home, but they were not evident enough or disabling enough to be obvious to me. He had the big attack at three am. It was his habit to get out of our bed at night, go to the kitchen for a glass of milk or wine, smoke cigarettes and then come back to bed. He fell at the entrance to our bedroom, striking his head and losing consciousness. I called the emergency paramedics and we took him to the closest emergency hospital, where the doctors immediately diagnosed a stroke.

His week in the intensive care unit was an excruciating one because he was in dreadful, continual, convulsive seizures and he was largely non-responsive until the day of his death. It was ghastly to watch, although he was unaware and not suffering. He was paralyzed on the right side and unable to swallow.

I was with him just before he died, and was struck then by his unusual relaxation. No convulsions, no tremors, just tired, clouded blue eyes focused on me. I held him and talked to him, and there was a kind of total comprehension and communication emanating from him. I know, Leslie, that he was at peace and had accepted what was about to happen. There was complete awareness and recognition in his eyes; he was just tired and resigned and unafraid.

How do I feel? Lonely, I guess. I've run the gamut of grief – the anger (how dare you do this to me?), resentment, nostalgia, sentiment. Your father and I were happy together, as you know, and we were constantly astonished that we were tremendously enjoying our isolated existence, and that we had actually established a day-by-day tranquility on top of our Hollywood hill. We used to congratulate each other: 'Look at us – no hotels, no travel, no fans, no demands, no constant smiling sociability.' We sat intimately on our kitchen stools at the counter and liked it. (Stanley would not even answer the telephone, as he felt it was an intrusion.) We had the house that he loved, and music, and we watched the sun go down and the city lights come up, and we talked incessantly because we had thirty-eight years of shared experience and friends, and we had you children, and we loved each other. We were living a private, secluded life, as Stanley desired it. I am glad you were here with us briefly. You will know what I am saying.

I am not altogether stupidly sentimental about the man. Stanley's public image (and as a public relations agent, I am quite guilty of contributing to it), always amused me. When we were surrounded by the Great Man's worshippers, I used to kick him under the table and say, *sotto voce,* 'If you get any more goddamned humble, I will be sick.' Stanley always said what he thought you wanted to hear. I was often contemptuous of the idolatry lavished on him by his cult. He was a paradox. He was considerate, kind, intelligent, creative, talented, full of charisma, and a master at public relations. He was ruthless, hurtful, self-destructive, alcoholic, underhanded, paranoiac, and destructive of others. And he always justified his behavior. He was also calculating, totally self-centered, and a practitioner of self-gratification at the expense of everyone else. In the guise of humanitarianism, he was the most clever manipulator of people and situations I have ever encountered. He had an innate need to be omnipotent. He was an object of misdirected love from his fans and often from his children and his wives.

I never saw Stanley as a hero, and that gave me a strong advantage in our longtime association. He and I fought violently over the years, trying to hurt each other. That was why, I suppose, we were so surprised when our relationship finally balanced out to one of love and easy, trusting, mature friendship and companionship.

I can't even say, as all the sympathy cards and letters are saying, 'He gave me so much.' He didn't give me that much. I gave him. I understood his work and his genuine contribution to contemporary music, but that was done for his own satisfaction, not mine or anyone else's. I am not in his debt. Therefore I feel no guilt about Stanley. I gave him everything, and Stanley did not really have much to give back to anyone on a personal level, as all his wives and children discovered. He was too life-long guilty (thank you Stella), and too afraid and insecure and indecisive to be able to sustain intimate relationships.

Isn't this a very personal and self-revealing letter.

I am trying to write the last chapter of Dr. William Lee's half-finished biography of Stanley and to assure that it will not read like the foregoing. It will be a proper accolade, suitable for public consumption, and I will let The Legend live on.

I should hate to be deprived of your friendship, Leslie, because your father is dead. If your mother is with you when you receive this letter, please tell her I admire her, treasure her, and want her to be well again. We the living have a lot more happy things to do.

My love to you and the children – Audree

As for me, I never shed a tear over my father's death. It was not until a year later that I understood why. I realised that, by yet another act of grace, I had been given the opportunity to reconnect at the deepest level with my father while he still lived. I had been lucky enough, only two weeks before his death – a death that no one expected – to make sure he got the most important message I had to give him. Despite all of the pain and horror, despite the confusion and guilt and fear and shame we'd both experienced, I had got through to him with my own simple truth: 'I love you, Stanley, more than anyone in the world. I guess I always will.'

I was fortunate enough to have known my father's darkness as well as his light. Over the years I have come to love them equally and to bless them. His darkness and his light are my own darkness and light. Knowing this has taught me that we are all dark and light just like the universe in which we live. I could just as easily have been the perpetrator and he the victim. Realizing this has been the greatest gift I could ever have received from the strange double helix that, once so tightly bound the two of us together.

Quite by accident, one day in the years following Stanley's death, I came across a poem written by the Vietnamese monk and peace activist Thich Nhat Hanh. In it, he speaks with great clarity about all of this. In his introduction to the poem he says, 'I have a poem for you. This poem is about three of us. The first is a twelve-year-old girl, one of the boat people crossing the Gulf of Siam. She was raped by a sea pirate, and after that she threw herself into the sea. The second person is the sea pirate, who was born in a remote village in Thailand. And the third person is me. I was very angry, of course. But I could not take sides against the sea pirate. If I could have, it would have been easier, but I couldn't. I realized that if I had been born in his village and had lived a similar life—economic, educational, and so on—it is likely that I would now be that sea pirate. So it is not easy to take sides. Out of suffering, I wrote this poem. It is called "Please Call Me by My True Names," because I have many names and when you call me by any of them I have to say, "Yes." Here is his poem':

Don't say that I will depart tomorrow – even today I am still arriving.

Look deeply: every second I am arriving to be a bud on a Spring branch, to be a tiny bird, with still-fragile wings, learning to sing in my new nest, to be a caterpillar in the heart of a flower, to be a jewel hiding itself in a stone.

I still arrive, in order to laugh and to cry, to fear and to hope.

The rhythm of my heart is the birth and death of all that is alive.

I am the mayfly metamorphosing on the surface of the river. And I am the bird that swoops down to swallow the mayfly.

I am the frog swimming happily in the clear water of a pond. And I am the grass snake that silently feeds itself on the frog.

I am the child in Uganda, all skin and bones, my legs as thin as bamboo sticks. And I am the arms merchant, selling deadly weapons to Uganda.

I am the twelve-year-old girl, refugee on a small boat, who throws herself into the ocean after being raped by a sea pirate. And I am the pirate, my heart not yet capable of seeing and loving.

I am a member of the politburo, with plenty of power in my hands. And I am the man who has to pay his "debt of blood" to my people dying slowly in a forced-labor camp.

My joy is like Spring, so warm it makes flowers bloom all over the Earth.
My pain is like a river of tears, so vast it fills the four oceans.

Please call me by my true names, so I can hear all my cries and my
laughter at once, so I can see that my joy and pain are one.

Please call me by my true names, so I can wake up, and so the door of
my heart can be left open, the door of compassion.

So ends the story of my love affair with the most gifted, charismatic, warm, cold, creative, tortured, funny, fragmented and chaotic man I have ever known. And he just happened to be my father. In my blood runs his blood. In my psyche his pain is etched and his humour. Yes, our story is now ended. But my own dance with the dark continues. It is not a simple thing to clear the scars of shame, of trauma and fear. Yet it must be done – not only for my sake and for his, but for the sake of the lineage from which both of us came. Somehow I feel it is also for the sake of millions of people who, like the two of us, feel at times they have to find a way to live their lives against all odds and wonder if it can be done. I am sure it can.

But then that's another story.

APPENDIX

AMONG THE WORK of professionals considered experts in the field of incest, I most admire the work of Leonard Shengold, MD. Shengold has researched child incest and other forms of child abuse for decades. In his most recent book on the subject, *Soul Murder Revisited,* he writes with discernment about the scars which perverse acts such as incest carve into body and mind. He uses the term 'soul murder' to describe destructive consequences such as when a father absorbs the life of his child through an incestuous act. Whenever the body of one human being becomes the possession of another, the soul of the one in bondage loses the ability to feel joy and love.

To thrive, each one of us needs adequate gratification and a sense that we are wanted and valued. When a parent looks upon his child as an extension of himself – a thing that exists only to satisfy his needs – a terrible abuse of power is taking place. Because a child cannot escape from this situation, whatever identity she had before the abuse gets lost. This was what happened to me and why I spent so many years in my teens and twenties attempting to manufacture an artificial personality, as well as years after that trying to discover who I really was.

Whenever a parent denies what has happened, he is trying to erase history. To have any sense of identity, we need to know what is real and not real. We have to be able to trust our memories so we can separate them from fantasy. As a result of parental denial, the child learns not to trust herself. And the impotence of the child in the face of her father's omnipotence creates a situation where the father becomes God.

Shengold explains that when the tormentor-seducer is a parent, it is frequently necessary for the child to turn for rescue to the very person who abused her – a mind-splitting operation. I likewise had no one to turn to except my father when I became frightened or confused. My mother had long been out of the question since, in my mind, she was the one responsible for Stanley's pain and sense of loss, which I wanted so much to alleviate. Yet going to him for help became impossible. The natural father–daughter bond had been wiped out by the incest.

Eventually I seemed to have become nothing more than an append-age to him: someone whose only purpose was to feed his will and fulfil his needs. Before the incest, when I turned to my father, I believed him to be a source of strength and safety. Afterwards, my looking to him for help would throw me into a sea of mind-splitting confusion. I did not know what I felt, what I had done or what was happening to me. Stanley had usurped my soul.

Shengold makes clear in his writings that these phenomena occur not only in incest: they also happen between a torturer and the tortured. Wherever human beings are deliberately and systematically forced to endure intolerable physical, emotional or spiritual pain, they eventually come to identify with their torturer. Seeing the torturer comes to be replaced by an experience of being the torturer, so close does the identification become. In the process the victim, like the perpetrator, can come to feel no sympathy, either for himself or other human beings.

Leonard Shengold focuses on another of incest's most insidious consequences – something which most experts in the field tend to ignore: *overstimulation*. The intensity of a sexual encounter with an adult is too much for any child to manage. Her body, her psyche, her nervous system, are not capable of discharging the energy in the way an adult would, through orgasm. In some children an urgent need for discharge shows itself in physical symptoms such as fainting or loss of control of the bladder or bowels.

As a child, all I knew was that something overwhelming was happening to me – something over which I could exercise neither control nor choice. I could never have articulated what it was. My body was in no way capable of handling the intensity of sexual energy being directed into it by Stanley. It had neither the hormonal nor the neurological equipment to handle it. Each time sex took place it felt as if a bolt of lightning had broken open every boundary of safety I thought I could rely on and wiped out all sense of who I was. The energetic charge in my body always continued long after penetration was over. I often felt I'd been hooked up to a power source so intense that it just kept overcharging me.

Shengold points out that the long-term overstimulation from repeated sexual acts forced on a child results in ongoing anxiety and a sense that everything in her life is too much to bear. Before long she comes to accept the state of being traumatised and to crave any kind of experience that can bring an end to the horrific intensity of it.

I tried my best to accept what was happening with Stanley; at least to live with it. Despite my dissociation, the trauma prevented my being conscious of the rage inside me. I sensed that surrender was what he was asking of me. I loved him and I did my best to comply. But I can't describe how hard it was to give in to something so powerful and so terrifying. All this created a curious longing for *annihilation* in me – a wish to merge with my father, to be absorbed by him. This sense of longing is also a feature of incest documented by Shengold.

Although not everyone will experience incest, the majority of us will be subjected to traumatic incidents at some point in our lives, which cause acute pain, as in a car crash or the emotional suffering caused by the death of a loved one. Only when the severity of the trauma is highly intense and repeated again and again, as it was in the lives of Stanley and Stella, does dissociation tend to occur. To *dissociate* is to disconnect from the body, to move into an altered state as a means of creating emotional distance from what is going on. It is a practical means of protecting the body and the psyche when terrible things are happening.

Dissociation is usually temporary. It becomes problematic when it becomes permanent, when the victim stays disconnected and doesn't even realise it. Then memory loss occurs, along with the experience of time distortions. People in this state become out of touch with their bodies and themselves. They become split, and, no longer in touch with their own needs, are often pushed around easily by others – like leaves blown about by the wind. Parts of their mind become virtually autonomous in an attempt to protect themselves from remembering events they have experienced as threatening to their life or safety. Powerful impulses and energies often flow through them which are not only unpredictable but at odds with one another. Their inner world becomes chaotic. So difficult can their lives become that many are drawn to drugs and alcohol in an attempt to make living manageable. In time, the psychic chaos they are forced to live with can wreak havoc, not only in their own lives, but in the lives of those around them.

Psychologists have found that the ability to dissociate tends to run in families. Stanley, Stella and I all experienced a condition now known as dissociative identity (DID) which ran through Stanley's bloodline on his mother's side. During Stella and Stanley's lives DID was hardly known except in the context of what was then called multiple personality disorder. This was a condition that few dared to acknowledge because the very idea that someone's personality could be split in pieces and that the individual could behave as more than one person was too frightening to admit into the realm of possibility.

Since the late 1970s, when thousands of severely traumatised veterans returned from the Vietnam War – blanked out, full of fear, plagued by flashbacks, haunted by time loss and displaying unpredictable behaviour patterns – DID has been much studied and research into the phenomenon has intensified greatly. The symptoms associated with DID are so widespread that they have triggered systematic research into the effects of trauma in other people as well – in rape and assault victims, mentally or physically abused children, communities reeling from natural disasters, police and firefighters in extreme situations, as well as those who have been subjected to ritual abuse or mind control in military and covert government operations such as the CIA's MKULTRA.

Experts in the field of post-traumatic stress – such as Belleruth Naparstek, Peter Levine, Robert Scaer and Bessel van der Kolk – are now able to call on a vast amount of epidemiological research carried out over the past thirty years, to help them identify both the psychological and the physical effects of trauma and the DID that tends to accompany it. Leading-edge imaging technologies, such as MRI and PET scans, as well as scientific measurements of hormonal changes in sufferers, have yielded much information about the physiological, biochemical and energetic changes that take place in the bodies of dissociative people. It seems that parts of the mind become virtually autonomous in an attempt to protect a person from remembering something they have experienced as threatening to their life or safety. Like Humpty Dumpty, such people's psyches become shattered – broken apart.

Derealization is another characteristic of dissociation. This is the sense that what is going on is unreal or otherworldly – another mechanism for emotional detachment that is fed by biochemical alterations affecting the brain in the course of repeated trauma: it can trigger 'the magical arrival of the beneficent rainbow to the abused, trapped child', writes Naparstek in *Invisible Heroes: Survivors of Trauma and How They Heal*.

Amnesia is another common result of experiencing a traumatic event in a dissociated state. As Naparstek continues: 'flashback memories are, in and of themselves, dissociated events that are reprises of the original dissociated event . . . Whatever derealized, vivid, or bizarre perceptions accompanied the state of enhanced arousal during the trauma are what gets replayed. Body sensation is altered during the flashback as well, most often by a vague sense of numbness, vibratory sensation and sometimes a sudden weakness in muscle strength.'

The phenomenon of dissociation can seem frighteningly foreign to people who have never experienced it. *The Oxford Companion to the Mind* describes so well the difficulty the ordinary person has in coping with the DID phenomenon:

> ... dissociation of the personality is a puzzling and, indeed, disturbing phenomenon, since it calls into question a basic assumption we all make about human nature, namely that for every body there is but one person; that each of us, despite the passage of time and changes in mood and activity, remains the same person with a single biography and store of memories. Given the fact that all social relations and contracts presume consistency and unity of personality, it is hardly surprising ...

Dissociation is an adaptive manoeuvre used to survive. At any point when the experience we have is more than we can fit into our idea of 'reality' we have to isolate it. The same thing happens physically in the body: the immune system tries to isolate whatever pathogen comes in, in order to be able to deal with it. It is a similar process to having an abscess or when someone gets shot: the body builds a structure around it to try to contain the abscess or bullet and protect the vital organs. The body often carries whatever it perceives as dangerous to areas such as the knees where it may cause trouble but it is not a threat to life.

Psychological dissociation operates in a similar way. A trauma or experience or something that doesn't fit into what we want to believe is true becomes locked into a pocket that is separated from consciousness. When this happens these psychic pockets take on a life of their own. In some people they take on a separate existence. This is what happens to people who are said to have multiple personalities.

*

Stanley had an eerie ability to remember the faces and names of people he had met only once – even years before. Yet he would often forget what he had said or done an hour earlier. Some of this was the result of the alcohol he drank. The older he got, the worse it became. I believe much of my father's remembering and forgetting came from a genetic tendency to dissociation which runs through Stella's bloodline: like his mother, Stanley had a remarkable capacity for it. At times, this would become so extreme it seemed as if his left hand didn't know what his right hand was doing. The rest of us would be waiting for him to go somewhere or do something he had organised for us to do, and he would suddenly turn around and ask what we were waiting for. Or he would promise to do something, then forget the promise half an hour later. We had to learn to put up with it.

Many people my father worked with have remarked on how 'changeable' he seemed to be. But they, like most of us, knew nothing about DID and had no context in which to place their observations and no way to explain his behaviour. Noel Wedder, who knew Stanley only later on in his life, has recorded on his excellent website an insightful description of the way dramatic changes took place in Stanley without warning. 'The Stan Hardly Anyone Knew' describes this behaviour. But, like all the rest who have spoken about my father's 'mercurial' behaviour, Noel could not begin to make sense of what he was describing:

> Stan was everything and nothing like his audiences imagined him to be. He was the antithesis of his stage persona: brilliant but tortured; generous to a fault yet tightfisted when it involved salaries and expenses. He could also be unfathomably complex at times, but just as quickly transform himself into someone rather naive about the world he lived in and worked in . . . On the road Stan's mercurial personality was a study in contrasts. For weeks, sometimes months, he would be out-going, tolerant of minor missteps both on the bus and the bandstand, generous

to a fault and take great delight in his role as surrogate father to twenty-two wandering minstrels . . . Then, like lightning, his temperament would turn dark, brooding, malevolent. For no apparent reason he would become mean, sarcastic, petty, unforgiving and unreasonable. When this happened everyone gave him a wide berth . . .

The consequences of dissociation resulting from ongoing severe trauma have now been so precisely identified and shown to be highly predictable that the military now use deliberately induced trauma to train Special Forces recruits. They even deliberately select their SF candidates from men who have undergone severe trauma in childhood. For the earlier repeated traumas occur, the more hardened a human being tends to become; therefore the more easily they can be trained to carry out extreme tasks under severe physical stress, face the greatest possible dangers – and still survive.

ACKNOWLEDGEMENTS

Writing *Love Affair* took me on a profound journey into my past, the past of my ancestors and the darkness of my own soul. In the end, it claimed almost four years of my life, during which I withdrew from the world as my every sense of safety and security was stripped away. While all of this was happening, many wise, loving friends and helpers held space for me. Never invading my solitude, each one of them in his or her own way remained present around me. They helped pinpoint dates, sent photographs, letters and movies, and shared with me their recollections, useful in validating my own. Others offered gifts of love, support, and infinite patience. At the top of the list is Audree Coke Kenton – a woman of brilliance, honesty, wit and deep compassion. Audree shared with me endless memories and insights, her time and her clarity, from beginning to end. My half-brother Lance Kenton is another who never faltered in his support and trust of me; nor did my own children Branton, Susannah, Jesse and Aaron. Leo Curran – another who, like Audree, had firsthand knowledge of my relationship with my father – was a wonderful pal through it all. His belief in the importance of telling this story never faltered, even when my own reached a low ebb. Others who helped see me through all of this include my cousin Barton Jordan and his granddaughter Sarah Keaty, a young woman whose study of the Newcomb bloodline was invaluable. Thanks go to Gail Rebuck at Random House, who insisted that I tell my story, to Yvette Brown – 'Fox' – who bullied me into getting started, and to Pat Kavanagh, my agent of twenty-seven years, who was so certain mine was an experience that must be told. David Thompson, a friend of forty years, gave of his time, insights and criticism throughout the project. With patience and wisdom, he also helped me deal with the fears and the tears as they arose. I wish also to thank many friends and colleagues, some of whom I have known since I was a small child, who generously shared facts, insights and their support: Reni Rennie, Annie Gant, Anthony Agostineili, Ed Gabel (Gabe), George Morte ('Georgie'), Gunther Hofititz, Howard Rumsey, Pete Rugolo, Virginia Wicks, Michael Dunaway, Lilian Arganian, Carol Easton, Judi Fitzpatrick, Jean Baxter – Aunt Beulah, Kenton Cooper, Rae LaForce, Dick Givens, David English, Graham Jones, John Sturgess, Seiko Tamura, J C Hickman, Janis Jenkins, Judy Fitzpatrick, Ellen Lacter and Melchia Crowne. I am grateful to them all.